Rivals beyond Trade

Rivals beyond Trade

AMERICA VERSUS JAPAN
IN GLOBAL COMPETITION

Dennis J. Encarnation

Cornell University Press

Ithaca and London

First published 1992 by Cornell University Press.
First printing, Cornell Paperbacks, 1993.

This book is a volume in the series
Cornell Studies in Political Economy,
edited by Peter J. Katzenstein.

Library of Congress Cataloging-in-Publication Data

Encarnation, Dennis J.
  Rivals beyond trade : America versus Japan in global competition /
Dennis J. Encarnation
    p. cm. — (Cornell studies in political economy)
  Includes bibliographical references and index.
  ISBN 0-8014-2733-9 (cloth : alk. paper)
  ISBN 0-8014-8122-8 (pbk.: alk. paper)
  1. Investments, American—Japan.   2. Investments, Japanese—United States.
3. Investments, American—Government policy—Japan.   4. Investments, Japanese—
Government policy—United States.   5. United States—Commerce—Japan.   6. Japan—
Commerce—United States.   I. Title.   II. Series.
HG5772.E53   1992
332.6'7352073—dc20   91-57900

To Jody

Contents

Figures

Preface

In RECENT YEARS the United States and Japan have fundamentally
altered their economic relationship. What was once a simple bilateral trade rivalry has been transformed into a global contest dominated by the foreign direct investments (FDI) of multinational
corporations. Indeed, foreign sales generated overseas by FDI in
majority foreign-owned subsidiaries now greatly exceed those sales
resulting from international trade alone; while trade itself has
become so closely associated with FDI that all efforts to isolate the
relative value of either seem inadequate. Simply put, intracompany shipments between multinational parents and their foreign
subsidiaries control international commerce among industrialized
countries, at the same time that offshore production and overseas
distribution by these subsidiaries generate an increasingly independent source of foreign sales. Considered together, such simple
facts support a timely argument: in the practice of measuring the
creation and distribution of wealth among nations, ownership can
and does matter.

By combining trade and investment, the Japanese now sell far
more in the United States than Americans sell in Japan. Explaining
why is the purpose of this book. I begin by examining several of the
"standard" explanations for Japan's relative success. Briefly, that
success does not arise because of America's declining competitiveness, for example, or because of Americans' ignorance of Japan;
nor can it be traced to U.S. exchange rates, or to Japanese trade
policies and practices. Rather, the American failure to outdo Japan

is produced by specific differences in what I term the "strategic investment policies" pursued by business and government in the two countries. Over time, these differences have allowed the Japanese first to trade and then to invest in the United States with much greater freedom than Americans have ever enjoyed in Japan. Outside Japan, surprisingly, the Americans and the Japanese are more alike than different; multinational corporations based in both nations combine foreign investment and related trade in a drive to dominate world markets. To me, these similarities are especially apparent in East Asia, where the Americans and the Japanese actively pursue their competitive rivalry. Back in Japan, however, such symmetries in strategy break down. National government policies and local business practices work together to deny Americans the market access that the Japanese enjoy in the United States. As my answer to this book's central question unfolds, then, some attention to critical conditions in all three settings—the United States, Japan, and East Asia—will be required to complete the account.

My reinterpretation of the U.S.-Japan rivalry recognizes certain fundamental changes that have occurred in the international political economy. In Chapter 1, I examine the trade and investment strategies of corporations and of governments alike. For multinational corporations, offshore production and overseas distribution by majority subsidiaries have dramatically increased, until they now both dominate cross-border exports and represent the most important single weapon in global competition. For national governments, this critical fact creates strong incentives to invoke public regulations and private restrictions—the essential ingredients of strategic investment policies—that inevitably pit business enterprises and government agencies against their counterparts in other countries. Just such a competition is particularly pronounced in the economic rivalry between the United States and Japan.

Japan's strategic investment policies have severely limited the application of those investment and related trade strategies which have proved so successful for multinational corporations elsewhere in the industrialized world. This limitation, documented in Chapter 2, has survived as Japan's strategic investment policy has evolved through stages characterized by different mixtures of government regulations and private restrictions. While the general direction of policy change has favored economic liberalization, government regulations have slowly given way to officially sanctioned private restrictions on foreign investment and related trade. Meanwhile, Americans have been left with only marginal improvements in market access.

By contrast, market access has proved much easier to secure in the United States. The Japanese have managed to implement nearly every foreign-investment and related trade strategy that has been denied to Americans in Japan. Before the Japanese could do so, however, the strategic investment policies of both the United States and Japan had to undergo a symbiotic, two-stage evolution, analyzed in Chapter 3. As the United States tilted away from liberal trade, toward selective protectionism, Japan began to lean in the opposite direction, toward trade and capital liberalization. Both sets of policy changes have unleashed newly powerful competitive forces, moving Japanese business strategy beyond the limits of simple trade to include direct investments, first in U.S. wholesaling and later in U.S. production.

These same competitive forces have also driven the Japanese—as well as the Americans—to invest elsewhere in East Asia, but only after national governments across the region began actively to promote export-oriented investments. For the Americans, I show in Chapter 4, such investments became an especially effective response to both a strong dollar and stiff import (especially Japanese) competition back home in the U.S. market. The Japanese followed a very similar path to East Asia, but only after their own government relaxed its tight restrictions on capital outflows—at the very time U.S. protectionism and a strong yen combined (as they already had in the United States) to mandate new sources of overseas supply for export markets. As a result, nearly every East Asian country has experienced local effects of the U.S.-Japan rivalry.

Finally, as foreign direct investment now advances the current rivalry beyond simple bilateral trade, prior explanations of Japan's success in economic competition with the United States must be reassessed. This I do on the way to articulating in Chapter 5 my preferred alternative. Foreign investment, for example, can overcome the debilitating impact of a strong dollar: Offshore production acts to hedge against unfavorable exchange rates, just as intra-company trade among affiliated buyers and suppliers acts to dilute price changes. Using such strategies, U.S.-owned multinationals have worked tenaciously to overcome the many handicaps imposed on them by Japanese trade policies, but only when Japanese capital controls or restrictive business practices have been absent. In the end, then, we must look beyond the standard causes and cures, to examine the critical role currently played by private institutions—both American multinationals and Japanese oligopolists—in shaping the U.S.-Japan rivalry.

My own search for an answer to the question why the Japanese sell more in the United States than the Americans sell in Japan began in earnest during my year-long stay (during 1988–89) in the Research Institute of Japan's Ministry of International Trade and Industry (MITI). With beneficial guidance from Komiya Ryutaro and logistical support from Takahashi Harumi, I enjoyed liberal access to MITI's unrivaled collection of quantitative data, as well as to a cadre of skilled government managers (past and present). My year in MITI was generously funded by the *Asahi* newspaper, where Murukami Yoshio and Shimomura Mitsuko deserve particular thanks for their help and encouragement. Special thanks also go to the cooperative staff of the International House of Japan, led by Kato Mikio. Additional support came from countless Japanese scholars, most notably Sakarai Makoto and Yoshihara Hideki; as well as from a number of foreign colleagues in Japan, especially Kenneth Courtis, Richard Rabinowitz, and Robert Uriu. My completed story also came to depend on numerous interviews with business managers in the many American and Japanese corporations and industry associations cited by name throughout this book. Many of the managers, as well as those in business, government, and elsewhere will remain nameless, however; I guaranteed them anonymity in exchange for their cooperation.

As my study of the U.S.-Japan relationship became increasingly multilateral, the search took me to several East Asian countries. These I refer to as the Four NIEs (the newly industrializing economies of South Korea, Taiwan, Hong Kong, and Singapore), the

ASEAN Four (Thailand, Malaysia, Indonesia, and the Philippines, all members of the Association of Southeast Asian Nations), and the Big Two (China and India). My several visits—generously financed by the World Bank, the United Nations Center for Transnational Corporations, the Development Centre of the Organization for Economic Cooperation and Development, and the Research Division of the Harvard Business School—brought me into close contact with managers in both business and government. They all helped me to understand just how complex the original bilateral competition has now become in Asia.

Back in the United States, my search for the underlying causes of imbalances in trade and investment led me through the doors of each corporation and subsidiary named in this book. At the U.S. Department of Commerce, David Belli and the professional staff of the Bureau of Economic Analysis proved unstintingly generous in trying to answer my seemingly endless requests for both data and documentation. Julie Herendeen turned mountains of information from the United States and Japan into elegant graphic illustrations designed to assist my readers. Mark Mason served as my enterprising research assistant on both sides of the Pacific; and now on the Yale faculty, he remains a source of inspiration and insight.

Without the unswerving support of my colleagues at the Graduate School of Business Administration, Harvard University, none of my intellectual and physical journeys would have been possible. Thomas McCraw was an early backer while Louis Wells became my sternest critic and most enthusiastic supporter. Across the Charles River, at Harvard's Center for International Affairs, Susan Pharr encouraged me to apply for the *Asahi* Fellowship and then invited me to join the weekly seminars of the U.S.-Japan Program. At MIT, Richard Samuels constantly encouraged me (an outsider) to enter current debates over the causes of Japan's economic success. Helping me to keep my focus on the international political economy were Peter Katzenstein and Roger Haydon, who together warmly nurtured this, my second publication in Cornell Studies in Political Economy. As with my first book, Earl Harbert provided helpful editorial assistance. Finally, Kathryn Graven, a reporter and former Tokyo correspondent for the *Wall Street Journal*, proved an enthusiastic supporter of my ideas and a warm partner while adjusting to the rigors of life back in the United States.

In the end, of course, any errors of fact and interpretation remain my own. This explicit disclaimer will, I hope, free my generous sponsors in America, Japan, and elsewhere in East Asia from any responsibility for the interpretations I offer.

Dennis J. Encarnation

Boston, Massachusetts

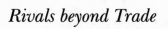

Rivals beyond Trade

CHAPTER ONE

Trade and Investment

Why do the Japanese sell more in the United States than Americans sell in Japan? To answer this question, vocal critics in both countries typically concentrate on bilateral trade in goods and services—often to the exclusion of other causes. In this prominent view, trade balances serve as preeminent indicators of relative success and failure in international competition. Trade, in short, is used to keep score in a bilateral contest, and in that game America and Japan have exchanged the leadership as net exporters. The Japanese appear to be the current winner. On the sidelines, meanwhile, other industrialized countries have also improved their national standing in comparison with America's. Even so, Japan's miraculous success makes it seem unique. Most popular explanations of Japanese success continue to fuel vitriolic debate over both the causes and the cures of persistent imbalances in bilateral trade. But too much remains unresolved.

The single-minded concentration on bilateral trade has already assumed the proportions of national myth, and it has seriously misled observers in both countries. For, in reality, even the best analyses of international trade can provide only partial answers to the pervasive question of Japanese superiority. Trade alone is not enough. Those foreign investments which mix equity ownership with managerial control also need to be considered. At present, such investments in offshore manufacturing and overseas distribution are too important to be ignored. As a result of them, both U.S. subsidiaries in Japan and Japanese subsidiaries in the United

States now report foreign sales that greatly exceed the total value of bilateral trade shipped between these two advanced economies. And much of that same trade actually flows between foreign subsidiaries and their parents back home, where investing to trade has become central to international competition. In accounting for this competition between the United States and Japan, we need an improved method of keeping score. This once simple trade rivalry has now been fundamentally transformed into a modern economic contest—a global game increasingly waged through foreign direct investment rather than through international trade.

Nor can this modern contest properly be viewed as bilateral; instead, it has become multilateral, as foreign investment and related trade increasingly draw other geographic areas into the fray. Most notably in the varied nations and markets of East Asia, giant multinational corporations have introduced additional economic tensions. As the Americans invest in—and export from—East Asia, strategically responding to competitive pressures felt back in the United States, so too the Japanese have begun to employ strikingly similar trade and investment strategies. East Asia represents, in short, a new arena for America and Japan to play out their rivalry. Already, multinational corporations have emerged as large and growing contributors to U.S. trade imbalances with the Asians. Here again, the evidence documents the same conclusion: foreign investment has fundamentally transformed the U.S.-Japan rivalry into a trans-Pacific contest, one that must be far more carefully assessed if we are to determine why the Japanese sell more in the United States than the Americans sell in Japan.

Economic relations between America and Japan do not, of course, exist in isolation. Similar transformations have drastically altered U.S. relations with other industrialized countries as well. In Europe, for example, changes are especially pronounced, in part because they began to occur earlier and in part because they exist on a grand scale. Indeed, across the Atlantic, offshore production and overseas distribution already surpass every measure of simple trade (which itself has become dominated by intracompany shipments among affiliates operating across several national boundaries). Here, American corporations have proved quite adept at combining direct investment and related trade. In fact, their consistent success seems to have guaranteed dominance over their foreign rivals: U.S.-owned exporters and subsidiaries sell nearly $1 billion *more* around the world than *all* foreigners sell in the United States.[1] Yet this American superiority is not based on international trade—a truth amply demonstrated by persistent U.S. trade deficits. Rather, America's continuing domination derives from the huge value of U.S. direct investments in overseas subsidiaries, which generate far more sales than do the multitude of foreign exporters and overseas investors active in America.

Except, it seems, when those exporters and investors come from Japan. The Japanese every week sell well over $1 billion *more* in the United States than the Americans sell in Japan.[2] Surely Japan's trade surpluses with the United States contribute greatly to this sales imbalance, and so do the small but growing intracompany shipments between related Japanese subsidiaries operating in both East Asia and America. Yet, in addition to the legendary Japanese trading prowess, another factor increasingly dominates: foreign direct investment. Indeed, when U.S. sales by Japanese-owned warehouses, assembly plants, and factories in America are added together, they total *twice* the combined value of all Japanese exports to America. By contrast, moreover, this total dwarfs the cumulative sales of all U.S.-owned subsidiaries operating in Japan. So when these new and vital indicators are compared cross-nationally, the U.S.-Japan rivalry provides a unique exception to the otherwise persistent pattern of American dominance through foreign investment. Naturally, this important exception merits closer examination. I shall provide it in the pages that follow.

Seeking to explain why the Japanese sell more in the United States than the Americans sell in Japan, I join an already well-publicized and highly polarized debate. In both countries, for example, bilateral imbalances associated with cross-border trade have long been cited as symptoms of a more crippling national disease—a decline in the overall competitiveness of U.S. corporations.[3] For critics in the two countries, then, the larger decline

[1]Calculated from data reported in Figure 5-2.
[2]Calculated from data reported in Figure 5-3.
[3]That decline became explicitly central to public debate during the early 1980s; see, for example, Bruce R. Scott and George C. Lodge, eds., *U.S. Competitiveness in*

should not be considered solely in terms of bilateral U.S. competition with Japan. Instead, it should be viewed as indicating some more general pattern, the accepted determinants of which also include foreign-exchange rates. Thus, a strong dollar erodes America's industrial base,[4] whereas a weak dollar sells that base on the cheap to greedy foreign investors.[5] From these perspectives, Japan is not a unique case; instead, it emerges as a prominent example of extreme national success.

In Japan, however, critics of the United States frequently cite a very different explanation—one that does appear to be unique to the Japanese. For such critics, the principal cause of bilateral imbalances is entirely *outside* foreign-exchange markets and *inside* the minds of American managers who, their critics insist, remain stubbornly ignorant about how Japan works and indifferent to the great business opportunities that exist there.[6] In response, Japan's critics in the United States retort that such allegations of ignorance and indifference actually point to a prudent American response to the inscrutable business practices and unfair trade policies found in Japan.[7] In their view, once again, that Pacific nation emerges as unique. Finally, by endorsing this joint belief in Japanese unique-

---

the World Economy (Boston: Harvard Business School Press, 1984); William J. Abernathy et al., *Industrial Renaissance: Producing a Competitive Future for America* (New York: Basic Books, 1983).

[4]See, for example, Dennis M. Bushe et al., "Prices, Activity, and Machinery Exports: An Analysis Based on New Price Data," *Review of Economic and Statistics* 68 (May 1986): 248–255; Robert E. Lipsey and Irving B. Kravis, "The Competitiveness and Comparative Advantage of U.S. Multinationals, 1957–1983," NBER Working Paper No. 2051, October 1986; Irving B. Kravis and Robert E. Lipsey, "Prices and Market Shares in the International Machinery Trade," *Review of Economics and Statistics* 64 (Feb. 1982): 110–116.

[5]Felix Rohatyn, "America's Economic Dependence," *Foreign Affairs* 68 (Jan. 1989): 53–65; Norman J. Glickman and Douglas P. Woodward, *The New Competitors: How Foreign Investors are Changing the U.S. Economy* (New York: Basic Books, 1989), pp. 105–111.

[6]James Abegglen and George Stalk, Jr., *Kaisha, The Japanese Corporation* (New York: Basic Books, 1985), esp. p. 217; Ozawa Terutomo, "Japanese Policy toward Foreign Multinationals: Implications for Trade and Competitiveness," in Thomas Pugel, ed., *Fragile Interdependence* (Lexington, Mass.: D.C. Heath, 1986), esp. p. 147.

[7]For a recent rendering of this argument, see Edward J. Lincoln, *Japan's Unequal Trade* (Washington, D.C.: Brookings Institution, 1990); for the most forceful rendering, see Clyde V. Prestowitz, Jr., *Trading Places: How We Allowed Japan to Take the Lead* (New York: Basic Books, 1988).

ness, otherwise competing critics of both countries prove they share a common perspective on the U.S.-Japan rivalry.

Each of these standard explanations, is plausible in part, of course, since each can be supported by voluminous evidence. Yet none of the existing arguments adequately addresses the complexity of current realities. Specifically, they all fail to comprehend two fundamental changes in the international political economy. First, foreign direct investment (FDI) has now driven global competition well beyond the narrower limits of international trade. Foreign production presently accounts for far greater overseas sales than do cross-border transactions. And second (but no less important), FDI has moved national competition beyond simple bilateral rivalries to encompass multilateral contests among the far-flung (but closely linked) subsidiaries of multinational corporations. Today, these transformations must be acknowledged and regarded as fundamental; in their wake, old standards of international trade and bilateral relations have been rendered insufficient as fair measures of national success in economic rivalries among industrialized countries.[8] Yet just such an enlarged understanding has eluded critics in both the United States and Japan.

Each of the grand solutions proposed to remedy the current bilateral imbalance is, I believe, woefully inadequate. Consider, for example, the repeated calls in the United States and Japan to reduce both the foreign-exchange value of the U.S. dollar and the overall level of Japanese trade restrictions. Yet multinationals often invest abroad precisely to sidestep such import barriers in overseas markets, as well as to overcome a costly appreciation in their home-country currencies. Indeed, in recent years, a strong Japanese yen and growing U.S. trade barriers have *together* helped to account for the growth of Japanese investment in the United States. At an earlier time, however, *neither* a strong U.S. dollar nor high Japanese trade barriers did much to improve investment prospects for American multinationals in Japan. The same cannot be said about the situation in other parts of the world, where strong national

[8]This is the central theme of a small but growing body of research; see, for example, DeAnne Julius, *Global Companies and Public Policy: The Growing Challenge of Foreign Direct Investment* (London: Royal Institute of International Affairs, 1990).

currencies and high trade barriers still operate to encourage both American and Japanese multinationals to pursue strikingly similar foreign-investment strategies.

Those common strategies elude American multinationals in Japan, but *not* because U.S. managers remain ignorant of investment opportunities there. Instead, U.S. investments in Japan have been limited for quite different reasons. In fact, if we do not credit the continuing presence of foreign acumen and tenacity, we cannot explain why Japan should have been so eager—for so long—to keep foreign exporters and overseas investors out of the Japanese homeland. Certainly the Japanese must have felt some threat from outside, but *not* a threat generated through cross-border trade, where U.S.-based exporters now experience serious shortfalls. Rather, the Japanese fear foreign investments because U.S.-owned subsidiaries have long posed a real competitive challenge through offshore production and overseas distribution. In response to this tangible threat, the Japanese have made the control of American multinationals a central tenet of both national government policies and private business practices. Had these restrictive policies and practices been matched in the United States, of course, they would have biased market access against the Japanese. To the present time, however, they have not been matched in more liberal America. Instead, persistent asymmetries between the two countries actually operate to prevent American multinationals from pursuing in Japan the foreign-investment strategies that have proved so successful for the Japanese in the United States.

To explain why the Japanese sell more in the United States than the Americans sell in Japan, I turn first to the persistent differences in government policies and industrial structures that characterize the histories of both countries. Long before the Second World War, Japan began to impose government restrictions on both trade and capital inflows, as well as on investment outflows. These restraints have no recent parallel in the United States, resulting in significant asymmetries between the two nations. Historically, such asymmetries in government policy did not begin to diminish until America tilted away from liberal trade and toward selective protectionism— just at the time when Japan began to lean in the opposite direction, toward trade and capital liberalization. In fact, most of the credit for initiating overall Japanese liberalization belongs to American multinationals. By contrast, not much credit goes to Japan's much-vaunted Ministry of International Trade and Industry (MITI), so often acclaimed for initiating policy change in Japan;[9] nor to the U.S. government, frequently identified as the chief source of foreign pressure on Japan.[10]

Even as American and Japanese strategies have begun to converge, however, sharp policy differences between the two countries remain in place. Japanese liberalization, in particular, has left untouched many structural legacies from earlier national policies—policies that encouraged a tight organization of most Japanese industries around a few oligopolistic competitors. These powerful oligopolists, in fact, have continued to control both the timing and the substance of liberalization by aggressively mediating between foreign demands and government responses.[11] From an initial position of unrivaled strength, Japanese oligopolists have moved to replace government regulations with private restrictions on business relationships among shareholders, buyers, suppliers, and

[9]For a forceful presentation of this argument, see Chalmers Johnson, *MITI and the Japanese Miracle: The Growth of Japanese Industrial Policy, 1925–1975* (Stanford: Stanford University Press, 1982), esp. pp. 24, 278–279. Among specialists on Japan, also see T. J. Pempel, *Policy and Politics in Japan: Creative Conservatism* (Philadelphia: Temple University Press, 1982), esp. chap. 2; and Ezra Vogel, "Guided Free Enterprise in Japan," *Harvard Business Review* 56 (May–June 1978): 161–170. For cross-national comparisons of MITI's power, see Peter J. Katzenstein, *Small States in World Markets: Industrial Policy in Europe* (Ithaca: Cornell University Press, 1985), esp. pp. 20–23; John Zysman, *Governments, Markets, and Growth: Financial Systems and the Politics of Industrial Change* (Ithaca: Cornell University Press, 1983), esp. p. 233; Stephen D. Krasner, *Defending the National Interest: Raw Materials Investment and U.S. Foreign Policy* (Princeton: Princeton University Press, 1978), esp. p. 58.

[10]Among Americans strongly advocating this view, see Kent E. Calder, "Japanese Foreign Economic Policy Formation: Explaining the Reactive State," *World Politics* 40 (July, 1988): 518–519; also see his *Crisis and Compensation: Public Policy and Political Stability in Japan, 1949–1986* (Princeton: Princeton University Press, 1989), esp. p. 450. Among the Japanese, this view has actually become a staple conviction; see Kosaka Masataka, "The International Economic Policy of Japan," in Robert Scalapino, ed., *The Foreign Policy of Modern Japan* (Berkeley: University of California Press, 1977), esp. pp. 211, 214; Komiya Ryutaro, "Direct Foreign Investment in Postwar Japan," in Peter Drysdale, ed., *Direct Foreign Investment in Asia and the Pacific* (Canberra: ANU Press, 1972), esp. p. 152.

[11]For an early test of this hypothesis, see Dennis J. Encarnation and Mark Mason, "Neither MITI nor America: The Political Economy of Capital Liberalization in Japan," *International Organization* 44 (Winter 1990): 25–54.

other "stakeholders." In effect, such private restrictions work to deny foreigners access to the Japanese market long after all formal government controls are abolished.

Unimpeded by foreign competition at home, Japanese oligopolists moved on to the United States, where they have been able first to trade and then to invest, doing both with much greater freedom than Americans have ever enjoyed in Japan. In the U.S. market, with the Japanese taking advantage of unequal access, the Americans have faced the discouraging prospect of being driven out of producing at home. Yet even when the Americans moved their production to East Asia and other low-cost export platforms (a move often encouraged by official U.S. policy), their early offshore advantages were later matched, and eventually eroded, by comparable Japanese investments. Meanwhile, back home, the Americans realized that dollar devaluations have done little to improve their country's prospects, even though devaluation has become an integral part of U.S. policy. In practice, such devaluations exercise only limited influence on intracompany shipments between Japanese parents and their overseas subsidiaries, shipments that dominate *both* U.S. imports from Japan *and* U.S. exports to Japan. At the same time, devaluations do act to accelerate imbalances in investment. An investment gap—like the persistent trade gap—results from bilateral asymmetries in both government policies and industrial structures, which combine to form what I later define as the "strategic investment policies" of the United States and Japan. Simply put, these nations treat corporate ownership differently.[12]

By remaining asymmetrical, these two sets of "strategic investment policies" have allowed the Japanese to implement in the United States nearly every trade and investment strategy still denied in Japan to American multinationals—but successfully implemented by the Americans elsewhere in the world. Indeed, outside Japan, American multinationals and Japanese oligopolists pursue markedly similar strategies—and this similarity effectively refutes the widely-held belief in Japanese uniqueness.[13] Business enter-

---

[12]For the relationship between corporate ownership and national strategy, esp. in the U.S., see Robert B. Reich, "Who Is Us?" *Harvard Business Review* 68 (Jan.–Feb. 1990), pp. 53–64, and "Who Is They," ibid. 69 (Mar.–Apr. 1991), pp. 77–88.

[13]Japanese scholars have even identified a unique "Japanese type" multinational, distinct from an "American type"; here, see the ongoing and pioneering work of

prises from both nations invest in majority-owned subsidiaries, generally eschewing minority shareholdings whenever they can. Through these subsidiaries, both report foreign (and especially local) sales far in excess of what their home countries export. And both nations' exports, in turn, have already begun to trail the values of foreign production by subsidiaries based abroad. These majority subsidiaries also trade extensively with their parents and with other overseas affiliates, to create new intracompany markets for foreign sales. To be sure, some differences in strategy persist. The Japanese, for example, engage in intracompany trade far more frequently than do the well-established Americans, just as the Americans engage more actively in offshore production than do the newly-emergent Japanese. Such differences, while noteworthy, have nevertheless diminished significantly over time, as Japanese and American multinationals increasingly confront similar political and economic environments.

AMERICAN AND JAPANESE MULTINATIONALS

The modern multinational corporation defies easy explanation. This simple conclusion arises naturally from the list of diverse institutions that scholars have already identified as functional multinationals. For purposes of discussion, I equate multinationals with FDI; and I make use of familiar definitions provided by the U.S. Commerce Department and Japan's Ministry of International Trade and Industry to identify FDI inflows and outflows.[14] Gener-

---

Kojima Kiyoshi: (with Ozawa Terutomo) "Japanese-Style Direct Foreign Investment," *Japanese Economic Studies* 14 (Spring 1986): 52–82; "Japanese and American Direct Investment in Asia: A Comparative Analysis," *Hitotsubashi Journal of Economics* 26 (June 1985): 1–35; *Japan's Foreign Direct Investment [Nihon no kaigai chokusetsu toushi]* (Tokyo: Bunshindo, 1985), esp. pp. 6–14; *Foreign Direct Investment [Kaigai chokusetsu toushi ron]* (Tokyo: Daiyamondo-sha, 1979); *Direct Foreign Investment: A Japanese Model of Multinational Business Operations* (London: Croom Helm, 1978); "Transfer of Technology to Developing Countries—Japanese Type Versus American Type," *Hitotsubashi Journal of Economics* 17 (Feb. 1977): 1–14; "A Macroeconomic Approach to Foreign Direct Investment," *Hitotsubashi Journal of Economics* 14 (June 1973): 1–21.

[14]For a cross-national comparison of the definitions adopted by various governments to define foreign direct investment, see Stephen Thomsen, "Appendix: FDI Data Sources and Uses," in Julius, *Global Companies and Public Policy*, pp. 109–113.

ally speaking, then, multinationals hold at least the minimum proportion of shareholdings (by today's standards, roughly 10 percent) deemed necessary to exercise some degree of managerial
control over their direct investments abroad. Typically, these foreign investments enter some combination of extractive, manufacturing, and service operations, including the overseas sales and
purchasing offices of those multinationals we often label either
trading companies (such as Mitsui among the Japanese, Cargil
among the Americans) or traditional manufacturers (such as GM
and Toyota). For each of these multinationals, managerial control
varies with the overall level of foreign ownership. This, in turn,
influences an interrelated series of strategic trade-offs affecting
foreign production and international trade.

Majority Subsidiaries vs. Minority Affiliates

Multinationals, regardless of their national origins, create and
sustain competitive advantage through the skillful management of
tangible and intangible assets in technology, marketing, and organization.[15] Such assets are specific to each individual corporation
and are often best exploited when that multinational corporation
owns a majority of the equity shareholdings in its overseas subsidiary. For the foreign parent of this subsidiary, majority shareholdings often bring managerial control over far-flung operations employing precious firm-specific assets. Even if that control remains
less well integrated and coordinated than the multinational's management might prefer, majority ownership still provides a greater
degree of control than minority shareholdings can offer.[16] Managerial control, in turn, helps to reduce the high costs that plague
cross-national transactions between existing suppliers of firm-
specific assets and unaffiliated buyers overseas.[17] So, instead of

[15]For a survey of these assets, see Richard E. Caves, *Multinational Enterprise and
Economic Analysis* (Cambridge: Cambridge University Press, 1982), esp. pp. 1–30,
195–211.

[16]For the organizational challenges posed by both the coordination and integration of international business operations, see Christopher A. Bartlett and Sumantra
Goshal, *Managing across Borders: The Transnational Solution* (Boston: Harvard Business School Press, 1989), esp. pp. 59–94, 157–175.

[17]For the now-classic description of the infirmities afflicting the efficient allocation of intangible assets through conventional markets, see Oliver E. Williamson,

using these "arm's-length" transactions, existing suppliers transfer their tangible and intangible assets internally—directly to their majority subsidiaries abroad. Typically that transfer entails intra-company trade of goods and services, initially from multinational parents to their foreign subsidiaries. Later, that trade may reverse, as these foreign subsidiaries also begin to transfer goods and ser-vices back to their multinational parent (as well as to other related affiliates overseas). Thus, the total pool of technological, market-ing, and organizational assets available to both the multinational parent and its majority subsidiaries is enhanced through intracom-pany transactions. In these transactions, then, ownership matters.

Since the Second World War, American multinationals have con-sistently preferred to invest in majority U.S.-owned subsidiaries rather than in minority affiliates. So strong is this preference, in fact, that IBM and several of the other U.S. corporations discussed in later chapters aggressively pursue 100 percent equity ownership in their foreign subsidiaries. More generally, as early as 1957, American multinationals reported to the Commerce Department (in its first postwar census of the foreign operations of U.S. com-panies) that they owned upwards of three-quarters of the equity invested in their subsidiaries abroad.[18] Similar proportions ex-isted over the next three decades,[19] as fresh outflows of U.S. FDI reached their peak (from the late 1960s to the early 1970s) and subsequently fell off, to be replaced by reinvested earnings.[20] As a

"Markets and Hierarchies: Some Elementary Considerations," *American Economic Review* 63 (May 1973): 316–325.

[18]U.S. Commerce Department, Office of Business Economics, *U.S. Business In-vestments in Foreign Countries: A Supplement to the Survey of Current Business* (Wash-ington, D.C.: USGPO, 1960), table 20, p. 108 (hereafter cited as Commerce Depart-ment, *1957 Survey*).

[19]For example, during 1977, American multinationals reported to the Com-merce Department that over 80 percent of their "owners' equity" resided in major-ity U.S.-owned subsidiaries; see U.S. Commerce Department, Bureau of Economic Analysis, *U.S. Direct Investment Abroad, 1977* (Washington, D.C.: USGPO, 1981), table II.A.18, p. 123 and table III.A.18, p. 242; hereafter cited as Commerce Department, *1977 Benchmark*.

[20]For the evolution of these U.S. flows, see Robert E. Lipsey, "Changing Patterns of International Investment in and by the United States," in Martin Feldstein, ed., *The United States in the World Economy* (Chicago: University of Chicago Press for the National Bureau of Economic Research, 1988), pp. 488–492; David J. Golds-brough, "Investment Trends and Prospects: The Link with Bank Lending," in Theodore H. Moran, ed., *Investing in Development: New Roles for Private Capital?* (Washington, D.C.: Overseas Development Council, 1986).

result of this investment, American multinationals consistently reported between 1966 (in the Commerce Department's first "benchmark" survey of U.S. FDI)[21] and 1988 (in the most recent annual
survey, summarized in Figure 1-1) that their majority-owned subsidiaries contributed upwards of three-quarters of total foreign
sales recorded by all U.S. affiliates abroad. The remaining one-
quarter was dispersed between either equal-partnership joint ventures or minority U.S.-owned affiliates. These include the Japanese affiliates of Ford (Mazda), GM (Isuzu and Suzuki), and
Chrysler (Mitsubishi Motors). With such notable exceptions, however, majority ownership of foreign subsidiaries remains a prominent characteristic of the foreign-investment strategies of American multinationals.

Similarly, majority ownership has become central to the investment strategies of Japanese multinationals, as the histories of trading companies like C. Itoh and of traditional manufacturers like
Matsushita well illustrate. By 1988 (again, the most recent year for
which data are available), these Japanese multinationals reported
to Japan's Ministry of International Trade and Industry that
majority-owned subsidiaries contributed over 85 percent of their
foreign sales. That share—larger, in fact, than comparable sales
reported by the majority subsidiaries of American multinationals—may possibly be of recent origin. Indeed, a long-standing
consensus among Japanese scholars (all reporting data gathered
during the mid-1970s) contends that C. Itoh, Matsushita, and
other Japanese investors have been more likely than the Americans to establish abroad minority-owned and equal-partnership
joint ventures, occasionally with multiple Japanese partners.[22]

[21]U.S. Commerce Department, Bureau of Economic Analysis, *U.S. Direct Investment Abroad, 1966: Final Data* (Washington, D.C.: USGPO, 1975), esp. table J-4,
p. 167, and table L-1, p. 197 (hereafter cited as Commerce Department, *1966
Benchmark*).

[22]This conclusion permeates both the English and the Japanese literature on
Japanese multinationals. In addition to the work of Kojima Kiyoshi cited above
(note 13), these include: Wakasugi Ryuhei, *International Trade, Foreign Direct Investment, and Japanese Industrial Organization, [Boueki-Chokusetsu toushi to nihon no sangyo
soshiki]* (Tokyo: Toyo Keizai Shimposha, 1989), esp. pp. 119–127; Komiya Ryutaro,
The Contemporary Japanese Economy [Gendai nihon keizai], (Tokyo: University of Tokyo
Press, 1988), esp. pp. 221–295; Sekiguchi Sueo, *New Developments in Foreign Investment [Kaigai toushi no shintenkai]* (Tokyo: Nihon Keizai Shinbun-sha, 1979); Ozawa

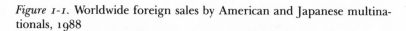

Figure 1-1. Worldwide foreign sales by American and Japanese multinationals, 1988

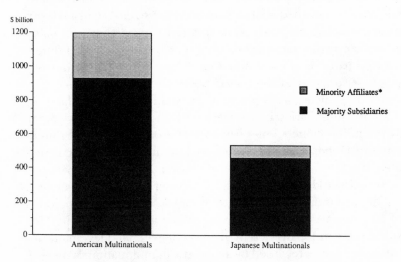

$ billion

- Minority Affiliates*
- Majority Subsidiaries

American Multinationals   Japanese Multinationals

Sources: U.S. Commerce Department, Bureau of Economic Analysis, *U.S. Direct Investment Abroad: Operations of U.S. Parent Companies and their Foreign Affiliates, Preliminary 1988 Estimates* (Washington, D.C.: USGPO, July 1990), tables 6 and 29, n.p.; Japan, Ministry of International Trade and Industry, Industrial Policy Bureau, International Business Affairs Division, *The 19th Survey of the Overseas Business Activities of Japanese Enterprises [Dai jyukyu-kai wagakuni kigyo no kaigai jigyo katsudou]* (Tokyo: Ministry of Finance Printing Bureau, 1990), table 6, p. 10.
*Includes both minority foreign-owned and equal-partnership joint ventures.

These earlier findings, however, may well represent a simple artifact of the specific indicator that scholars examined: the actual number of joint ventures and majority subsidiaries established by Japanese multinationals. Such a measure overestimates the relative importance of small investments in a large number of minority-owned and equal-partnership joint ventures. By this

Terutomo, *Multinationalism, Japanese Style: The Political Economy of Outward Dependency* (Princeton: Princeton University Press, 1979), esp. pp. 227–228; Michael Yoshino, *Japan's Multinational Enterprises* (Cambridge: Harvard University Press, 1976), esp. chap. 5; Yoshihara Tsurumi, *The Japanese Are Coming: A Multinational Spread of Japanese Firms* (Cambridge: Ballinger, 1976); Sekiguchi Sueo and Matsuba Mitsuji, *Japan's Direct Investment [Nihon no chokusetsu toushi]* (Tokyo: Nihon Keizai Shinbun-sha, 1974).

measure, American multinationals during 1977 (a year also cited in many of the Japanese studies) proved as likely to establish minority U.S.-owned affiliates as they did to invest in majority subsidiaries.[23] It therefore seems accurate to claim that—probably by the late 1970s, and surely during the 1980s—the earlier differences in patterns of ownership that distinguished American from Japanese subsidiaries abroad had withered away.

Yet no similar convergence of ownership patterns in favor of majority subsidiaries is apparent in bilateral investment flows. While in the United States, the majority Japanese-owned subsidiaries of Honda, Sony, and other such multinationals have generated the same proportion of sales (over 85 percent) that they recorded worldwide,[24] in Japan the Americans have never seen majority subsidiaries generate their global share (over 75 percent) of foreign sales. To the contrary, as late as 1988, majority U.S. subsidiaries in Japan—led by IBM—still generated less than two-fifths of the sales recorded by all American multinationals there.[25] Here, Mazda and other minority U.S. affiliates accounted for the remainder, the bulk of multinational sales in Japan, even though their relative position had declined over the previous decade. By this measure, Japan actually has as much in common with developing India, where the dislodging of multinationals represents the national strategy, as with industrialized Germany.[26] For in no other *advanced* economy do majority U.S. subsidiaries continue to occupy such a lowly position as they do in Japan. By contrast, in

[23]In fact, during 1977, American multinationals reported direct investments in 11.9 thousand majority U.S.-owned subsidiaries and 11.8 thousand minority U.S.-owned affiliates; see Commerce Department, *1977 Benchmark*, table D, p. 20.

[24]Japan, Ministry of International Trade and Industry, Industrial Policy Bureau, International Business Affairs Division, *The 19th Survey of the Overseas Business Activities of Japanese Enterprises [Dai jyukyu-kai wagakuni kigyo no kaigai jigyo katsudou]* (Tokyo: Ministry of Finance Printing Bureau, 1990), tables 5 and 6, p. 10 (hereafter cited as MITI, *19th Overseas Survey*).

[25]Commerce Department, *U.S. FDI: 1988 Annual Survey*, tables 6 and 29, n.p.

[26]For cross-national comparisons, see ibid. In India, majority U.S.-owned subsidiaries accounted for just 13 percent of all foreign sales by American multinationals; while in West Germany, these subsidiaries accounted for over 75 percent of all sales by American multinationals. To account for this wide difference, see Dennis J. Encarnation, *Dislodging Multinationals: India's Strategy in Comparative Perspective* (Ithaca: Cornell University Press, 1989).

Germany, American multinationals own and control some of that country's largest manufacturers, such as GM's Opel subsidiary. In Germany, moreover, as well as in Canada, the United Kingdom, and France—each with an economy less than one-half Japan's size—Opel and other majority U.S. subsidiaries recorded larger dollar sales than they did in Japan. Thus, the lower incidence of majority subsidiaries in Japan worked to deny American multinationals the same market access they otherwise exploited in other industrialized countries.

Foreign Sales vs. International Trade

After securing majority ownership and managerial control, multinationals typically use their overseas subsidiaries to sell in foreign markets far more than nationally based exporters ship to these same markets. In general, foreign sales come from three sources: the host-country market of the overseas subsidiary, the home-country market of that subsidiary's parent, and third-county markets that are typically in close geographic proximity to the host country. To generate these sales, multinationals may decide to invest directly in foreign production (see below) in export markets protected by both public and private barriers, ranging from import restrictions to local competition; or conversely, they may decide to exploit foreign factors of production by exporting from their overseas subsidiaries to open markets both back home and in third countries. Thus, each source of foreign sales by multinational corporations suggests a different foreign-investment strategy.

For the Americans, the predominance of foreign sales over international trade is not new, although some analysts have only recently discovered it.[27] Indeed, as early as 1957, the overseas (largely majority U.S.-owned) subsidiaries of American multinationals, led by Ford and GM, reported foreign sales at twice the

[27]For example, Susan Strange asserts that in the "evolution of international business . . . the mid-1980s were a milestone as the volume of international production for the *first time* exceeded the volume of international trade" (emphasis added). See her "The Name of the Game," in Nicholas X. Rizopoulos, ed., *Sea-Changes: American Foreign Policy in a World Transformed* (New York: Council on Foreign Relations Press, 1991), p. 242.

Figure 1-2. The ratio of foreign sales by majority subsidiaries to national exports: United States vs. Japan, 1988

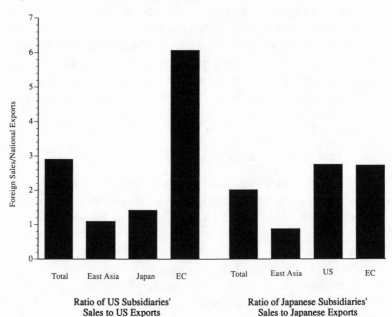

Sources: U.S. Commerce Department, Bureau of Economic Analysis, *U.S. Direct Investment Abroad: Operations of U.S. Parent Companies and their Foreign Affiliates, Preliminary 1988 Estimates* (Washington, D.C.: USGPO, July 1990), table 29, n.p.; International Trade Administration, Office of Trade and Investment Analysis, *U.S. Foreign Trade Highlights: 1989* (Washington, D.C.: USGPO, Sept. 1990), pp. 31–33; Japan, Ministry of International Trade and Industry, Industrial Policy Bureau, International Business Affairs Division, *The 19th Survey of the Overseas Business Activities of Japanese Enterprises [Dai jyukyu-kai wagakuni kigyo no kaigai jigyo katsudou]* (Tokyo: Ministry of Finance Printing Bureau, 1990), pp. 72–83; International Monetary Fund, *Direction of Trade Statistics Yearbook* (Washington, D.C.: IMF, 1990), pp. 244–245.

value of U.S. exports.[28] A decade later, by 1966, the foreign sales of majority U.S.-owned subsidiaries had risen to represent three times the value of all U.S. exports.[29] Since then, that 3:1 ratio of

[28]For sales data, see Commerce Department, *1957 Survey*, table 22, p. 110; for trade data, see U.S. Commerce Department, Bureau of International Commerce, "United States Trade with Major World Areas, 1955 and 1956," *Overseas Business Reports* (May 1957): 2, 8.

[29]For sales data, see Commerce Department, *1966 Benchmark*, table L-1, p. 197; for trade data, see U.S. Commerce Department, Bureau of International Com-

foreign sales to international trade has remained largely unaltered, as several relative newcomers (such as Texas Instruments and Motorola) added their names to the list of emergent multinationals. In fact, during 1988, American multinationals again sold nearly three times as much overseas through their majority subsidiaries as the United States exported to the world (see Figure 1-2)—further testimony to the fact that U.S. FDI continues to carry international competition well beyond cross-border trade.

By comparison, the ratio of foreign sales to national exports has remained smaller for the Japanese, reflecting their prolonged status as traders rather than investors. In fact, during 1988, Japanese subsidiaries (most of which were majority Japanese-owned) reported foreign sales twice as large as all Japanese exports worldwide—the same ratio of foreign sales to national exports last reported for Americans in 1957, over thirty years earlier. For the Japanese, however, the ascendance of foreign sales over national exports represents a more recent occurrence; it has resulted from an especially rapid growth of Japanese FDI abroad during the 1980s, especially in automobiles and electronics. In fact, as late as 1977, Japanese subsidiaries reported foreign sales to be roughly equivalent to Japanese exports worldwide.[30] Moreover, much of this recent growth of Japanese FDI occurred in the United States, where Honda, Sony, and other Japanese multinationals actually seem to be imitating the worldwide performance of American multinationals. Indeed, during 1988, Japanese-owned subsidiaries reported that they sold nearly three times more in the United States than did Japan-based exporters (see Figure 1-2). By contrast, back in Japan, majority U.S. subsidiaries reported 1988 sales that barely exceeded U.S. exports to Japan. Such a modest figure suggests once again that Motorola and other American multina-

---

merce, "United States Trade with Major World Areas, 1965 and 1966," *Overseas Business Reports* (May 1967): 3, 12.

[30]During 1977, when Japanese exports to the world totaled $85 billion, Japanese affiliates abroad reported foreign sales of roughly $85 billion (or ¥22.8 trillion). For sales data, see Japan, Ministry of International Trade and Industry, Industrial Policy Bureau, *The 8th Survey of the Overseas Business Activities of Japanese Enterprises [Dai hachi-kai wagakuni kigyou no kaigai jigyou katsudou]* (Tokyo: MITI, 1979), table 51, p. 54 (hereafter cited as MITI, *8th Overseas Survey*). For trade data, see International Monetary Fund, *International Trade Statistics Yearbook: 1980* (Washington, D.C.: IMF, 1981), p. 243.

tionals have failed to achieve the same performance levels (this time measured in terms of foreign sales relative to international trade) which have long characterized their operations outside of Japan—levels which have become increasingly characteristic of Japanese subsidiaries in the United States.

For both American and Japanese multinationals, the local market hosting foreign investment has typically consumed most of their overseas sales. What has changed over time, however, is the relative importance of that local market. As early as 1957 (in the first postwar survey of American multinationals), and continuing for at least another decade, GM, IBM, and other American multinationals reported that local markets in host countries accounted for three-quarters of all foreign sales generated by majority U.S. subsidiaries.[31] Beginning by the late 1970s and continuing through the 1980s, however, the contribution of host markets to the worldwide revenues of majority U.S. subsidiaries shows a yearly decline, until it reaches two-thirds of total foreign sales.[32] Japanese subsidiaries evidenced a similar reduction between the early 1970s (when local markets also contributed three-quarters of total foreign sales) and the 1980s (when that sales share again dropped to two-thirds).[33] Some of this decrease in the relative importance of host-country sales can be explained by the growth of exports destined for markets back home. Indeed, over the postwar period, exports back home have doubled (for the Americans) and tripled (for the Japanese) their relative contribution to total sales by foreign subsidiaries.[34] Larger still are exports to third countries: From a nearly identical share (one-fifth) early on, the sales contribution of such exports has remained (in 1988) roughly constant for

[31]Commerce Department, *1957 Survey*, table 22, p. 110; Commerce Department, *1966 Benchmark*, table L-1, p. 197.

[32]Commerce Department, *1977 Benchmark*, table II.H.1, p. 318; Commerce Department, *U.S. FDI: 1988 Annual Survey*, table 34, n.p.

[33]For 1971, see Japan, Ministry of International Trade and Industry, Industrial Policy Bureau, *Overseas Business Activities of Japanese Enterprises: Current Situation and Problems [Wagakuni kigyou no kaigai jigyou katsudou: sono gendai to mondaiten]* (Tokyo: MITI, 1973), table 4-2-2, pp. 86–87. For 1988, see MITI, *19th Overseas Survey*, pp. 82–83.

[34]For the Americans, see notes 31 and 32 above for references; for the Japanese, see note 33.

the Japanese, while it has increased moderately (to nearly one-quarter of total sales) for the Americans. Thus, American and Japanese multinationals can again be seen to have pursued similar international strategies, measured this time by the final destination of foreign sales.

Regional differences in these general patterns do persist, of course, but the clear fact remains that American and Japanese multinationals typically have adopted common strategies. Yet this simple conclusion contradicts the popular argument advanced by at least one important school of Japanese scholars, who have long argued that Japanese multinationals—led by Mitsui but also including Toyota and other manufacturers—pursue investment strategies that are far more trade-enhancing than those favored by GM and other American multinationals.[35] For relevant data, these scholars often turn to East Asia (as we shall do in Chapter 4), the only region where both American and Japanese multinationals can claim long histories of direct investment. Yet in that region, at least during the 1980s, the combined exports (back home and to third countries) of American and Japanese multinationals were roughly identical, while both totals continued to exceed local sales.[36] And even when operating in each other's home market, where local sales become far more important, the Americans and the Japanese can be shown to adopt similar export strategies: majority subsidiaries owned by the Americans in Japan and by the Japanese in America export small and roughly identical proportions (one-tenth) of their total sales.[37] What emerges, then, is a general truth: when confronted with common political and economic environments (as in East Asia), or with local markets that prove quite demanding of their attention (as in the United States and Japan), American and Japanese multinationals respond in similar fashion.

Despite such similarities, however, the direct investment pat-

[35]This school of thought owes its origins to the work of Kojima Kiyoshi; see note 13 above. For his most recent rendering of this argument, see "Japanese Direct Investment Abroad," Monograph Series 1, Social Science Research Institute, International Christian University, Tokyo, 1990.

[36]See MITI, *19th Overseas Survey*, pp. 74–75; Commerce Department, *1988 Annual Survey*, table 34, n.p.

[37]See both references in note 36.

terns of multinationals based in these two powerful nations still exhibit three important differences, each with major implications for bilateral competition: First, from the United States, the Japanese (especially the affiliates of Mitsui and other Japanese trading companies) export mostly agricultural products and raw materials back home, principally to their multinational parents; while from Japan, the majority U.S.-owned subsidiaries of IBM, TI, and other American multinationals export manufactured goods both back home and to third countries, typically elsewhere in East Asia.[38] Just such differences in the composition of trade become significant in the present environment, since commodities presumably respond more readily to exchange-rate changes than do differentiated manufactured goods. Second, unlike the Japanese, who invest almost exclusively in majority subsidiaries, American multinationals like GM and Ford rely more heavily on their minority U.S. affiliates for exports from Japan. Indeed, these same affiliates—led by Mazda—export back to the United States three times more than do majority U.S. subsidiaries in Japan.[39] These differences in market orientation also suggest the separate origins of majority subsidiaries and minority affiliates in Japan: majority subsidiaries serve the local Japanese market almost exclusively; minority affiliates often serve as offshore sources of Japanese supplies for American multinationals. Third, when all this bilateral trade is finally tallied, the Japanese in America export more back home—in fact, during 1988, two-and-a-half times more—than do Americans in Japan.[40] Such trade amounts to barely one-tenth of Japan's burgeoning exports to the United States, but it contributes over one-third of America's smaller exports to Japan. This export contribution makes Japanese-owned subsidiaries the largest U.S.-based exporters to Japan, and it effectively guarantees Japanese multinationals uncontested control over bilateral trade.

[38]For the Japanese, see Commerce Department, *Foreign FDI in the U.S.: 1988 Survey*, tables E-3, G-2, n.p.; for the Americans, see Commerce Department, *U.S. FDI: 1988 Annual Survey*, tables 34–38, n.p.

[39]Commerce Department, *U.S. FDI: 1988 Annual Survey*, tables 16 and 52, n.p.

[40]For the Americans, see ibid.; for the Japanese, see Commerce Department, *Foreign FDI in the U.S.: 1988 Survey*, table G-2, n.p.; for trade data, Commerce Department, *U.S. Foreign Trade Highlights: 1989*, pp. 31, 36.

Offshore Production vs. Overseas Distribution

To generate foreign sales, multinationals often invest in majority subsidiaries that produce, in host-country markets, many of the goods and services that their parents otherwise would export to these same overseas markets. As a practical matter, the pressures for offshore production actually increase when *any* of three conditions arise: when national governments severely constrain, or credibly threaten to limit, imports; when foreign competitors derive significant advantage from their location; or when indigenous buyers demand closer relations with their suppliers.[41] Such pressures seem especially pronounced in the sale of manufactured goods. At least as early as 1957, and continuing beyond the next three decades, majority U.S. subsidiaries engaging in overseas manufacturing reported foreign sales to be double the value of U.S. manufactured exports (for 1988, see Figure 1-3).[42] Led by GM and IBM, the Americans concentrated most of this foreign production in industrialized countries. In developing economies, by contrast, international trade continued to exceed offshore production: as recently as 1988, for example, the manufacturing subsidiaries of these American multinationals recorded foreign sales with half the value of U.S. manufactured exports.[43] In short, then, across developing countries, the ratio of foreign production to international

[41]For an early analysis of the relationship between trade policies and foreign direct investment, see Grant L. Reuber et al., *Foreign Private Investment in Development* (Oxford: Oxford University Press for the Organization of Economic Cooperation and Development, 1973), esp. pp. 120–132; for a more recent analysis, see Stephen E. Guisinger et al., *Investment Incentives and Performance Requirements: Patterns of International Trade, Production, and Investment* (New York: Praeger, 1985), esp. pp. 48–54. For a recent study of location-specific advantages, see Michael E. Porter, *The Competitive Advantage of Nations* (New York: The Free Press, 1990), while for the impact of such "buyer power," see his *Competitive Strategy: Techniques for Analyzing Industries and Competitors* (New York: The Free Press, 1980).

[42]For sales data, see the following Commerce Department publications: *1957 Survey*, table 22, p. 110; *1966 Benchmark*, table L-3, p. 199. For trade data, see U.S. Commerce Department, Bureau of International Commerce, "International Business Indicators," *Overseas Business Reports* (January 1973), table 5, p. 14.

[43]For sales data, see Commerce Department, *U.S. FDI: 1988 Annual Survey*, tables 6 and 29, n.p.; for trade data, see Commerce Department, *U.S. Foreign Trade Highlights: 1989*, pp. 51–55.

Figure 1-3. Foreign production, national exports, and overseas distribution: United States vs. Japan, 1988

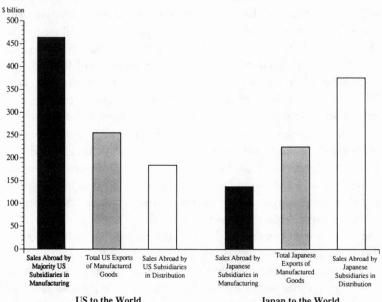

Sources: U.S. Commerce Department, Bureau of Economic Analysis, *U.S. Direct Investment Abroad: Operations of U.S. Parent Companies and their Foreign Affiliates, Preliminary 1988 Estimates* (Washington, D.C.: USGPO, July 1990), table 29, n.p.; U.S. Commerce Department, International Trade Administration, Office of Trade and Investment Analysis, *U.S. Foreign Trade Highlights: 1989* (Washington, D.C.: USGPO, Sept. 1990), p. 29; Japan, Ministry of International Trade and Industry, Industrial Policy Bureau, International Business Affairs Division, *The 19th Survey of the Overseas Business Activities of Japanese Enterprises [Dai jyuukyuu-kai wagakuni kigyou no kaigai jigyou katsudou]* (Tokyo: Ministry of Finance Printing Bureau, 1990), pp. 82–83; Organization for Economic Cooperation and Development, *Statistics of Foreign Trade* (Paris: OECD, 1990), table 32.2, pp. 104–105.

trade actually reversed what was visible in more industrialized economies, where more competitive markets with powerful buyers and stronger states long ago forced American multinationals to move beyond simple cross-border trade.

By comparison, Japanese manufacturers in their worldwide investments more closely paralleled those American multinationals producing locally in developing, rather than industrialized, countries. Like the Americans, Japanese subsidiaries principally engaged in foreign manufacturing during 1988 recorded foreign sales worldwide with barely half the value of all Japanese manufactured exports. For the Japanese, however, this 1:2 ratio of foreign production to international trade actually represented a significant *increase* in offshore manufacturing. Indeed, only a decade earlier (in 1977), Japanese manufacturers had reported exports from home four times larger than their worldwide production abroad.[44] Subsequently, during the 1980s, Honda, Sony, and other Japanese multinationals made a much greater effort to increase foreign production in their principal export markets. In the United States, for example, those Japanese subsidiaries engaged principally in local manufacturing recorded U.S. sales roughly comparable in value to U.S. imports of Japanese manufactured exports.[45] In fact, the ratio of foreign production to international trade recorded by the Japanese in America nearly equalled comparable ratios recorded in Japan by majority U.S. subsidiaries. (Mazda and other such minority U.S. affiliates, by contrast, boasted foreign production with twice the value of U.S. manufactured exports to Japan.) Thus, for both American manufacturers in Japan and Japanese manufacturers in the United States, foreign production competed almost evenly with international trade as a source of overseas sales.

In addition to offshore production, overseas distribution by majority subsidiaries also serves to increase the foreign sales of both American and Japanese multinationals, typically by creating dedicated sales and service networks for shipments from their parents (see Figure 1-3). Such networks become especially important in advanced markets with tightly controlled distribution systems and other high marketing barriers to entry. In Japan, for example, local producers tightly control their distribution channels, and thereby (as we shall see in later chapters) severely constrain the market access of foreigners.[46] To overcome such barriers, American multi-

[44]For sales data, see MITI, *8th Overseas Survey*, table 51, p. 54. For trade data see, International Monetary Fund, *Direction of Trade Statistics Yearbook: 1980*, p. 242.

[45]For U.S. sales by the Japanese, see Commerce Department, *Foreign FDI in U.S.: 1988 Survey*, tables E-3, G-2, n.p.; for trade data, see Commerce Department, *U.S. Foreign Trade Highlights: 1989*, pp. 51–60; for Japanese sales by the Americans, see Commerce Department, *U.S. FDI: 1988 Annual Survey*, table 29, n.p.

[46]For an early survey of these barriers, see Michael Yoshino, *The Japanese Marketing System: Adaptations and Innovations* (Cambridge: MIT Press, 1971); for more

nationals such as Merck have invested aggressively in majority subsidiaries engaged principally in Japanese distribution; in this way, they have pursued an unusual strategy, without parallel for Americans operating elsewhere in the world.[47] Through their sales subsidiaries, American multinationals during 1988 sold one-tenth of all U.S. exports to Japan, twice the contribution of those U.S. subsidiaries manufacturing in Japan. Outside Japan, however, the majority U.S. subsidiaries of Merck and other multinationals engaged principally in foreign manufacturing—and not just marketing—actually serve as more important final markets and intermediary channels for U.S. exports. In fact, during 1988, these manufacturing subsidiaries bought one-fifth of all U.S. exports, three times the global share sold through U.S. sales subsidiaries.

In sharp contrast, the Japanese consistently make far greater use of their sales subsidiaries overseas (see Figure 1-3), which market roughly half of all Japanese exports worldwide.[48] And that contribution is higher still for Japanese exports to the United States, where nearly three-quarters of all such trade enters through Japanese subsidiaries principally engaged in U.S. distribution. Here, we find the sales offices not only of Mitsui and other Japanese

---

recent surveys, see Itoh Motoshige, "The Japanese Distribution System and Access to the Japanese Market," and Ito Takahashi and Maruyama Masayoshi, "Is the Japanese Distribution System Really Inefficient?" in Paul Krugman, ed., *Trade with Japan: Has the Door Opened Wider?* (Cambridge: MIT Press for the National Bureau of Economic Research, 1991); Robert Z. Lawrence, "Efficient or Exclusionist? The Import Behavior of Japanese Corporate Groups," a paper prepared for the Brookings Panel on Economic Activity, April 4–5, 1991; American Chamber of Commerce in Japan, *Trade and Investment in Japan: The Current Environment* (Tokyo: ACCJ, June 1991), esp. pp. 13–27.

[47]For sales data below, see Commerce Department, *U.S. FDI: 1988 Annual Survey*, table 29, n.p.; for trade data, see *U.S. Foreign Trade Highlights: 1989*, p. 31.

[48]For the U.S. trade of Japanese sales subsidiaries, see Dennis J. Encarnation, "Cross-Investment," in Thomas K. McCraw, ed., *America versus Japan* (Boston: Harvard Business School Press, 1986), tables 4-2 and 4-3, pp. 120, 126; for updates of these data, see Commerce Department, *Foreign FDI in U.S.: 1988 Survey*, tables E-3, G-2, n.p.; and Commerce Department, *U.S. Foreign Trade Highlights: 1989*, p. 36. For data on the worldwide trade of Japanese sales subsidiaries, see MITI, *19th Overseas Survey*, 92–93; for total Japanese trade, see IMF, *International Trade Statistics: 1989*.

trading companies but also of such traditional Japanese manufacturers as Toyota and Nissan, Matsushita and Sony, NEC and Fujitsu. For these Japanese, sales subsidiaries become a foreign extension of their own national industrial organization, whereas for the Americans, sales subsidiaries in Japan represent another adaptation to the peculiarities of the local market.

In addition to downstream marketing of home-country exports, foreign subsidiaries engaged in distribution abroad also increase foreign sales, by serving as upstream sources of overseas supplies. Indeed, these subsidiaries often serve as purchasing agents, both for their parents back home and for affiliated subsidiaries in third countries. Of particular significance to American multinationals have been U.S. wholesaling subsidiaries that supplied third-country markets (especially those in Europe, where for GM, IBM, and other multinationals, affiliated subsidiaries were among their major buyers).[49] Otherwise, for the Americans, wholesaling subsidiaries have been of little value as purchasing agents for shipments back home, supplying less than 2 percent of all U.S. imports during 1988.

For the Japanese, however, wholesaling subsidiaries represent much more important sources of shipments back home. These subsidiaries reported in 1988 that they had supplied nearly two-fifths of all Japanese imports worldwide—and the figure was higher still (roughly three-fifths) for Japanese imports from the United States.[50] These imports consisted largely of agricultural products, metals, and other raw materials—all of which remained in short supply in Japan but were plentiful in America. So, in marked contrast to the Americans, the Japanese (especially trading companies) invested in wholesaling subsidiaries in order to insure

[49]For sales data, see Commerce Department, *U.S. FDI: 1988 Annual Survey*, tables 6 and 29, n.p. For intracompany trade within Europe, the most recent data are for 1982; see U.S. Commerce Department, Bureau of Economic Analysis, *U.S. Direct Investment Abroad, 1982* (Washington, D.C.: USGPO, April 1984). For total U.S. trade, see Commerce Department, *U.S. Foreign Trade Highlights: 1989*, p. 36.

[50]For the worldwide trade of these Japanese subsidiaries, see MITI, *19th Overseas Survey*, 82–83, for their U.S. sales, see Commerce Department, *U.S. FDI: 1988 Annual Survey*, table 6 and 29, n.p.; for total U.S. and Japanese trade, see IMF, *International Trade Statistics: 1989*.

the security of imported supplies. Holding this protective position, they exercised unprecedented control over Japan's imports from the United States and from elsewhere in the world.

Intracompany Shipments vs. Arm's-Length Trade

Today, much of the trade conducted by multinationals is shipped intracompany (see Figure 1-4), among and between parents and their subsidiaries, a fact that has important implications for both companies and countries.[51] For corporate parents, intracompany trade insures greater control over both upstream supplies and downstream markets than do more arm's-length transactions among unaffiliated buyers and suppliers. Intracompany trade also substantially lowers the high costs that arm's-length transactions normally would impose on cross-border exchanges of the technological, marketing, and organizational assets necessary to compete successfully through foreign production and overseas distribution. Thus, relationships resulting from equity ownership and managerial control—rather than only those transactions based principally on relative prices—can be expected to determine patterns of intracompany trade (a proposition we shall test in later chapters). By this same logic, intracompany trade may prove far less vulnerable to short-term swings in foreign-exchange rates, thereby blunting national policies designed to alter currency movements. And just such an impact on national policy can be sizable, because intracompany trade has now grown to dominate international trade among industrialized countries.

For both American and Japanese multinationals, intracompany trade is especially crucial to overseas operations—a fact only recently recognized by academic scholars.[52] During 1988, for example, Opel and other majority U.S. subsidiaries purchased nearly all of their U.S. inputs from their American parents who, in turn,

---

[51]For a review of these implications, see Caves, *Multinational Enterprise and Economic Analysis*, pp. 23–24, 75–77, 143–146.

[52]See, for example, Robert Z. Lawrence, "How Open Is Japan?" in Krugman, *The United States and Japan;* Leo Sleuwaegen and Yamawaki Hideki, "Foreign Direct Investment and Intra-Firm Trade: Evidence from Japan," Discussion Paper #9002/G, Institute for Economic Research, Erasmus University (Rotterdam), n.d.

Figure 1-4. U.S. trade with the world: Intracompany vs. arm's-length shipments, 1988

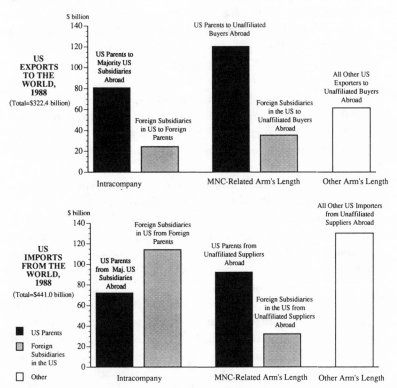

Sources: U.S. Commerce Department, Bureau of Economic Analysis, *U.S. Direct Investment Abroad: Operations of U.S. Parent Companies and their Foreign Affiliates, Preliminary 1988 Estimates* (Washington, D.C.: USGPO, July 1990), tables 50 and 57, n.p.; U.S. Commerce Department, Bureau of Economic Analysis, *Foreign Direct Investment in the United States: Operations of U.S. Affiliates of Foreign Companies, Preliminary 1988 Estimates* (Washington, D.C.: USGPO, Aug. 1990), table G-2, n.p.; U.S. Commerce Department, International Trade Administration, Office of Trade and Investment Analysis, *U.S. Foreign Trade Highlights: 1989* (Washington, D.C.: USGPO, Sept. 1990), p. 29

bought nearly all of their subsidiaries' shipments back to the United States.[53] Similarly, what data exist on Japanese multina-

[53]The share of trade in both directions is roughly 85 percent; see Commerce Department, *U.S. FDI: 1988 Annual Survey*, table 50, n.p.

tionals suggest comparable patterns of intracompany trade between Japanese parents and their overseas affiliates. Specifically, in the United States, Japanese subsidiaries during 1988 purchased over four-fifths of their U.S. imports (principally automobiles and electronics) from their parents back home, and they shipped over three-fifths of their U.S. exports (principally raw materials and agricultural products) back to their Japanese parents.[54] Once again, American and Japanese multinationals have pursued similar strategies; this time the results are measured in terms of the intracompany trade resulting from foreign investment.

Largely because of such intracompany trade, foreign investment exerts an impressive influence on a nation's trade. During 1988 (the most recent year for which data are available, summarized in Figure 1-4), intracompany trade contributed over two-fifths of total U.S. imports, and over one-third of total U.S. exports worldwide. Shipments from U.S. parents to their majority subsidiaries worldwide (e.g., from IBM to its several subsidiaries) contributed much more to these U.S. exports than did shipments from foreign subsidiaries in the United States back to their parents (e.g., from Honda of America to its Japanese parent). By comparison, Honda in Japan and other such foreign parents contributed much more to U.S. imports through shipments to their subsidiaries in the United States than did Ford and other American multinationals engaged in comparable intracompany trade. In addition, the U.S. parents of American multinationals—led by Boeing—provided the greatest source of arm's-length trade involving both unaffiliated buyers and unaffiliated suppliers abroad. This has left all other U.S.-owned enterprises to ship, again through arm's-length trade, less than one-quarter of all U.S. exports worldwide, and less than one-

[54]For intracompany trade data, see Commerce Department, *Foreign FDI in U.S.: 1988 Survey*, table G-2, n.p.; for total U.S. trade data, see Commerce Department, *U.S. Foreign Trade Highlights: 1989*, pp. 31, 36. More generally, worldwide, Japanese affiliates abroad reported in 1980 (the most recent year for which data are available) that they purchased 75 percent of their Japanese inputs from their Japanese parents who, in turn, bought 95 percent of their affiliates' shipments back to Japan; see Japan, Ministry of International Trade and Industry, Industrial Policy Bureau, International Business Affairs Division, *The First Comprehensive Survey of Foreign Investment Statistics [Kaigai toshi tokei soran]* (Tokyo: Ministry of Finance Printing Bureau, 1982), table II-53-8, pp. 340–341 and table II-57-8, pp. 426–427.

third of all U.S. imports. In short, American and foreign multinationals together dominate U.S. trade.

Moreover, that multinational dominance increases when we narrow our attention to international trade in manufactured goods, especially shipments among industrialized countries. Here, while the available data remain sketchy, and are limited to U.S. exports, they are nevertheless suggestive. Since 1957, the parents of American multinationals have consistently shipped roughly 65 percent of all U.S. manufactured exports to the world,[55] with their majority subsidiaries the principal overseas buyers of these U.S. exports. General Electric (GE), for example, has consistently ranked first or second among America's exporters of manufactured goods, thanks in part to intracompany shipments to its several majority U.S. subsidiaries. Most of that manufactured trade by GE and others went to industrialized countries, where U.S. parents shipped during 1988 nearly 70 percent of all intracompany trade with their majority subsidiaries overseas.[56] While comparable data on the Japanese do not exist, a less extensive examination of their shipments to the United States (nearly all manufactured goods) reveals familiar results. Over two-thirds of all U.S. imports from Japan are shipped intracompany, largely from the parents of Japanese multinationals like Toyota and Matsushita to their (principally majority) subsidiaries in the United States (see Figure 1-5). By contrast, intracompany trade contributed barely 50 percent of all U.S. exports to Japan, principally commodities. These are shipped from the United States mainly by Mitsui and other trading-company subsidiaries back to their Japanese parents. For both the Americans and the Japanese, then, intracompany trade is presently the *principal* channel for exporting manufactured goods to other industrialized economies. Here, ownership determines trade.

But for foreign investment to exercise a sizable impact on a nation's exports, majority subsidiaries—rather than minority affiliates—must represent the principal class of buyers abroad. For

[55]Robert E. Lipsey and Irving B. Kravis, "The Competitiveness and Comparative Advantage of U.S. Multinationals, 1957–1983," NBER Working Paper No. 2051, October 1986, Table U1, p. 29.

[56]Commerce Department, *U.S. Foreign Trade Highlights: 1989*, p. 51; Commerce Department, *U.S. FDI: 1988 Survey*, table 50, n.p.

Figure 1-5. U.S. trade with Japan: Intracompany vs. arm's-length shipments, 1988

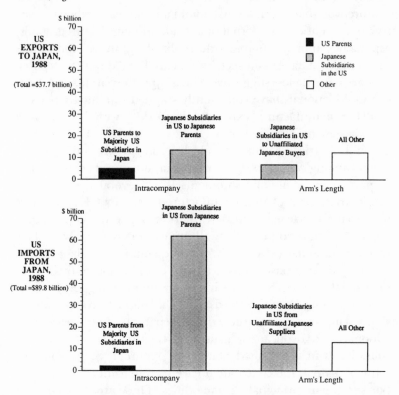

Sources: U.S. Commerce Department, Bureau of Economic Analysis, *U.S. Direct Investment Abroad: Operations of U.S. Parent Companies and their Foreign Affiliates, Preliminary 1988 Estimates* (Washington, D.C.: USGPO, July 1990), table 50, n.p.; U.S. Commerce Department, Bureau of Economic Analysis, *Foreign Direct Investment in the United States: Operations of U.S. Affiliates of Foreign Companies, Preliminary 1988 Estimates* (Washington, D.C.: USGPO, Aug. 1990), table G-2, n.p.; U.S. Commerce Department, Bureau of Economic Analysis, *Foreign Direct Investment in the United States: 1987 Benchmark Survey, Final Results* (Washington, D.C.: USGPO, Aug. 1990), tables G-28 and G-34, pp. 146, 152; U.S. Commerce Department, International Trade Administration, Office of Trade and Investment Analysis, *U.S. Foreign Trade Highlights: 1989* (Washington, D.C.: USGPO, Sept. 1990), pp. 31, 36.

Note: The 1988 survey of U.S. FDI abroad provides data on arm's-length trade by Japanese subsidiaries in America both to unaffiliated foreign buyers and from unaffiliated foreign suppliers. To verify that over nine-tenths of these U.S. imports and nearly three-fifths of these U.S. exports principally entail trade with Japan, see the *1987 Benchmark Survey* of FDI in the United States.

only with majority ownership do multinationals exercise sufficient managerial control to dictate their subsidiaries' decisions to import supplies from their parents. Indeed, Mazda and other minority affiliates typically represent poor markets for U.S. exports, even in those host countries (e.g., Japan) where affiliates' sales are relatively large. Indeed, for 1988, U.S. exports to minority affiliates remained virtually negligible—only 5 percent of all U.S. exports to American multinationals abroad—even though these affiliates contributed just under 25 percent of total multinational sales.[57] (By comparison, U.S. imports from minority affiliates such as Mazda fared slightly better in 1988, contributing one-tenth of all U.S. imports shipped by American multinationals abroad. For trade in that direction, majority ownership is simply not necessary to convince foreign suppliers to sell to their U.S. parents.)

Generally, the relationship between majority ownership and intracompany trade ultimately determines the influence of foreign investment on a nation's exports. More specifically in Japan, the lower incidence of majority U.S. subsidiaries has effectively denied to American multinationals the same access for U.S. exports that they have enjoyed in other industrialized countries. This important truism can be put another way: because Japan has long hosted a disproportionately large share of minority affiliates, and because these affiliates generally refrain from purchasing U.S. exports (while contributing more to U.S. imports), American multinationals in Japan have contributed a relatively small share of this bilateral trade. By contrast, for the Japanese, the higher incidence of majority subsidiaries in the United States actually has granted to Japanese exports far greater access to the U.S. market than the Americans, through their minority affiliates, have been able to secure in Japan. Thus, Japanese sales in the United States continue to grow, just as U.S. sales in Japan continue to lag far behind.

STRATEGIC INVESTMENT POLICY

To explain why the Japanese, through this combination of intracompany trade and foreign production, sell more in the United

---

[57]For U.S. exports to U.S. affiliates abroad, and overall sales data, see Commerce Department, *U.S. FDI: 1988 Survey*, Tables 6, 16, 29, and 50, n.p.; for overall U.S. exports, see Commerce Department, *U.S. Foreign Trade Highlights: 1989*, p. 31.

States than the Americans trade and produce in Japan, I now turn
to consider some recent advances in our understanding of "strategic trade policy." While the literature on this subject remains diverse,[58] one common conclusion does emerge: national policies
that restrict imports and promote exports can increase national
income by raising a country's share of the above-normal profits
that local producers can otherwise earn as a consequence of imper-
fect competition. Even in the absence of government intervention,
market imperfections ultimately can narrow competition to only a
few global competitors, who then earn profits *above* the rate of
return prevailing in purely competitive industries. Here, government policies merely help determine the national location of these
oligopolists and, therefore, the cross-national distribution of their
above-normal profits. To raise national income at foreign expense,
however, these policies must be implemented unilaterally, so that
the resulting asymmetries in policy favor local producers (say, in
Japan) at the expense of their foreign (in this instance, U.S.) rivals.
Unable to compete in the protected national (Japanese) market,
these foreign (U.S.) rivals later face an even more discouraging
prospect: being driven out of producing in their own market and
abroad. One result is a persistent bias in the distribution of gains
(e.g., foreign sales) from bilateral trade between two countries (the
United States and Japan) adopting asymmetric strategic trade policies, a bias that favors oligopolists in the more interventionist
country (namely, Japan).

For strategic trade policies to work, two market imperfections—
large economies of scale and steep learning curves—must exist.[59]
With large-scale economies evident in such industries as auto-

[58]Here, I have been greatly influenced by the work of Paul R. Krugman; see his
Rethinking International Trade (Cambridge: MIT Press, 1990); Elhanan Helpman
and Paul R. Krugman, *Trade Policy and Market Structure* (Cambridge: MIT Press,
1989); Paul R. Krugman, ed., *Strategic Trade Policy and the New International Economics* (Cambridge: MIT Press, 1986). For a recent review of this literature, see
J. David Richardson, "The Political Economy of Strategic Trade Policy," *International Organization* 44 (Winter 1990): 107–135.

[59]Krugman, *Strategic Trade Policy*, chaps. 2 and 4. A third market imperfection
results from sizable research and development (R&D) requirements; see James A.
Brander and Barbara J. Spencer, "International R&D Rivalry and Industrial Strategy," *Review of Economic Studies* 50 (Oct. 1983): 707–722.

mobiles and electronics, sizable initial investments result in high fixed costs, placing producers and distributors under considerable pressure to increase sales volume in order to realize greater returns. Under these circumstances, firms and governments have strong incentives either to protect domestic markets while securing the minimum scale necessary for profitability, or to promote exports when domestic markets are simply not large enough to achieve minimum scale. Both strategies, as we shall see, were pursued in Japan. The success of either strategy, however, depends on the combined reactions of foreign (principally U.S.) competitors and their government, which may also respond with import protection or export promotion. Such reactions thus may deny to foreign (in this instance, Japanese) oligopolists that power in the marketplace necessary to capture the potential gains from strategic trade. That power is especially great in those industries subject to large learning effects (e.g., reduced production costs as manufacturing experience and knowledge multiply over time, as they do in automobiles and electronics). Here, producers overcome steep learning curves when they manage to attain lower costs that cannot be profitably replicated by their competitors—at least not without either major technological innovations or rapidly changing markets, both of which make existing processes and products obsolete.[60] To remain profitable in the face of low-cost competition, producers not enjoying these advantages (e.g., U.S. automakers) could again seek government protection or subsidies—just as competitors (e.g., Japanese automakers) actually enjoying such "first-mover advantages" may have sought to profit from earlier government interventions. Thus, the size and distribution of corporate profits and national incomes are *both* dependent on the strategic interactions between industry oligopolists and government policymakers operating across political boundaries.

While early academic research focused mainly on international trade, recent studies have proposed a parallel interpretation of foreign direct investment.[61] In practice, strategic policies regard-

---

[60]Pankaj Ghemawat, "Sustainable Advantage," *Harvard Business Review* 64 (Sept.–Oct. 1986), pp. 53–58.

[61]Edward M. Graham and Paul R. Krugman, *Foreign Direct Investment in the United States* (Washington, D.C.: Institute for International Economics, 1989), p. 54; also

ing investment actually complement strategic trade policies, especially in Japan and other advanced economies, where most trade is intracompany. However, two additional market imperfections—high transaction costs and large economies of scope—provide both governments and oligopolists with strong incentives to adopt what I call "strategic investment policies." As noted in our discussion of majority ownership, unique technological, marketing, and organizational assets are often difficult for multinationals to transfer abroad at "arm's-length," without foreign investment linking overseas buyers to their parent suppliers. In fact, intracompany transactions of experience, knowledge, and other intangible skills can assist foreign subsidiaries in overcoming the same steep learning curves encountered earlier by their multinational parents. Similarly, large economies of scope can also require foreign investment to overcome the high costs associated with coordinating and integrating the joint distribution and production of multiple products across several markets.[62] Once again, such market imperfections serve to narrow competition to only a few multinational competitors earning above-normal profits, whose geographic location is then greatly influenced by national strategy. That strategy often necessitates government controls on capital inflows as it did in Japan, but it is not limited to public policies alone. In addition, such a strategy may also include private restrictions on foreign investments (e.g., Japanese limitations on corporate acquisitions or on distribution channels), which often owe their origins to government policies, and which have the same practical effect. Yet, for these public and private restrictions to raise (say, Japanese) national income at foreign (in this example, U.S.) expense, they must be implemented unilaterally, without retaliation by either foreign

see Edward M. Graham, "Government Policies towards Inward Foreign Direct Investment: Effects on Producers and Consumers," unpublished paper, March 1991.

[62]For economies of scope, principally in production, see David Teece, "Economies of Scope and the Scope of the Enterprise," *Journal of Economic Behavior and Organization* 1 (Sept. 1980): 223–247; John C. Panzar and Robert D. Willig, "Economies of Scope," *American Economics Review* 71 (May 1981): 268–272. For economies of scope in both production and distribution, see Alfred D. Chandler, Jr. *Scale and Scope: The Dynamics of Industrial Capitalism* (Cambridge: Belknap Press of Harvard University Press, 1990), esp. pp. 17, 21–31.

(U.S.) competitors, or their government, so that the resulting asymmetries favor local (Japanese) oligopolists at the expense of these outsiders. Multinationals (such as GM and Ford), unable now to invest in the protected (Japanese) market, eventually face the discouraging prospect of being driven out of producing and distributing back in their home (U.S.) market. The result is a persistent bias in the distribution of gains (e.g., foreign sales) from foreign direct investment between any two countries (the United States and Japan) adopting asymmetric "strategic investment policies," a bias that once again favors multinationals based in the more interventionist country (again, Japan). Here again, in the application of national strategy, corporate ownership matters.

Finally, in practice, strategic policies regarding investment (and trade) result from fundamental political differences that pit local oligopolists and national governments against their counterparts in other countries. In none of these countries—not even in Japan—do business and government habitually think alike. Similarly, national governments do not act as monoliths—just as local oligopolists differ in the corporate strategies they adopt. Indeed, when local oligopolists begin to trade and then invest outside their national markets, they proliferate and grow until they share the role of other multinationals engaged in foreign production and intracompany trade. By then, newly empowered oligopolists begin to abandon their earlier support for protection from import competition and foreign investment.

As a result of these changes in politics and economics, strategic investment (and trade) policies evolve over time. Yet, in the case of the United States and Japan, that evolution has not eradicated critical differences. And as we shall see in the next two chapters, exactly such persistent asymmetries, which are evident in the "strategic investment policies" of the two countries, have allowed the Japanese to sell more in the United States than Americans sell in Japan.

CHAPTER TWO

Americans in Japan

IN JAPAN, Americans have managed to implement only a few of the same foreign investment and related trade strategies that have proved so successful elsewhere in the world. Elsewhere, but seldom in Japan, American multinationals typically have invested in majority subsidiaries both to produce and to sell more goods locally than the United States exports abroad. These majority subsidiaries, in turn, have created final markets and intermediate channels for their U.S. parents' exports, contributing sizably to America's trade in every industrialized country except Japan. Only in Japan, in fact, do minority U.S. affiliates actually outsell majority U.S. subsidiaries—not simply as local producers and overseas buyers of U.S. exports, but also as offshore suppliers to their U.S. parents. These U.S. imports from Japan are shipped principally by minority affiliates, while U.S. imports from most other advanced economies are shipped by majority subsidiaries that dominate such intracompany trade. Indeed, minority affiliates—so common in Japan—are actually rare elsewhere in the world, where American multinationals strongly prefer unrivaled equity ownership, with its related managerial control. In Japan, that preference for majority subsidiaries is seldom satisfied, leaving American multinationals without the institutional linchpins employed in other advanced economies to hold together a combined strategy of local production and intracompany trade.

To explain why American multinationals have evolved differently in Japan, this chapter analyzes the principal components of

36

Japan's strategic investment policy: government controls on the inflow of both goods and capital, and private restrictions on inter-firm relations. These components are highly interrelated. Without capital controls, trade restrictions could actually serve to attract foreign investment to supply local markets.[1] Without trade restraints, capital controls would not greatly limit foreign exporters, but they could limit profits and other sources of financing available to local producers. Finally, without private restrictions on interfirm relations (affecting intercorporate shareholdings, mergers and acquisitions, and buyer-supplier relations), government controls must be retained in order to continue protecting domestic industries from the direct investments and related trade of American multinationals. As noted in Chapter 1, governments and oligopolists often have strong incentives to invoke both public policies and private restrictions, especially in industries where increasing returns to scale and scope would ultimately narrow competition to a few global competitors. For two such industries—automobiles and electronics, both examined in this chapter—Japan's strategic investment policy has long prevented American multinationals from freely investing and trading in Japan. Unimpeded by foreign competition at home, Japanese oligopolists later moved to exploit their advantages abroad, where (as we shall see in the next chapter) Japanese automakers and electronics producers would eventually account for most of Japan's exports to—and, later, investments in—the United States. But long before that happened, Japan's strategic investment policy evolved in two distinct stages (see Figure 2-1), each differentiated from the other by the relative importance of government regulations and private restrictions.

The first stage of Japan's strategic investment policy actually transcended the Second World War, and it invited comparisons—not with advanced economies but, rather, with countries far less

[1]For the impact of trade restrictions on foreign direct investment, see Grant L. Reuber et al., *Foreign Private Investment in Development* (Oxford: Oxford University Press for the Organization of Economic Cooperation and Development, 1973), esp. pp. 120–132; for a more recent analysis, see Stephen E. Guisinger et al., *Investment Incentives and Performance Requirements: Patterns of International Trade, Production, and Investment* (New York: Praeger, 1985), esp. pp. 48–54.

Figure 2-1. The evolution of "strategic investment policy" and U.S. FDI in Japan, 1929–89

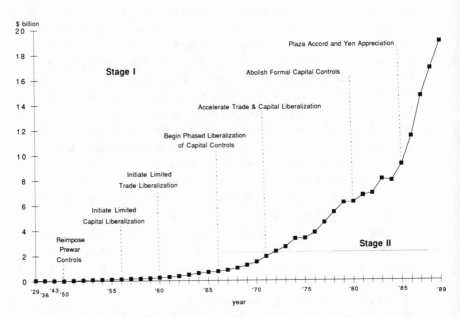

Sources: For the events highlighted, see Chapter 2 below; for data on U.S. FDI, see U.S. Commerce Department, Office of Business Economics, *U.S. Business Investments in Foreign Countries: A Supplement to the Survey of Current Business* (Washington, D.C.: USGPO, 1960), esp. table 4, p. 92; U.S. Department of Commerce, Bureau of Economic Analysis, *Selected Data on U.S. Direct Investment Abroad, 1950–76* (Washington, D.C.: USGPO, Feb. 1982), table 1, pp. 1–27; U.S. Department of Commerce, Bureau of Economic Analysis, *U.S. Direct Investment Abroad: Balance of Payments and Direct Investment Position Estimates, 1977–81* (Washington, D.C.: USGPO, Nov. 1986), table 1, pp. 1–5; U.S. Department of Commerce, Bureau of Economic Analysis, "U.S. Direct Investment Abroad: Detail for Position and Balance of Payments Flows, 1985," *Survey of Current Business* (Aug. 1986), table 44, p. 95; U.S. Department of Commerce, Bureau of Economic Analysis, "U.S. Direct Investment Abroad: Detail for Position and Balance of Payments Flows, 1989," *Survey of Current Business* (Aug. 1990), table 44, p. 95.

economically developed. Like such countries, Japan imposed strict capital controls in an effort to limit foreign investment attracted to growing markets otherwise protected by high import barriers. As a result of these capital controls, securely in place by the 1930s, Japan emerged as one of the least likely hosts for direct investment by American multinationals, whose prospects improved little for at least three decades after the Occupation.[2] By 1950, in fact, U.S.-occupied Japan hosted less American investment than did newly independent India, where dislodging multinationals would become the national strategy.[3] A decade later, Japan still lagged far behind as a host to American multinationals: through 1960, for example, the Philippines continued to boast more U.S. FDI, as did each of the eight largest Latin American economies.[4] Majority U.S.-owned subsidiaries remained especially rare in Japan; in fact, through the mid-1960s, their meager domestic sales failed to exceed otherwise restricted U.S. exports to Japan. That trade, in turn, was further constrained by the absence of majority subsidiaries in Japan that could serve as final markets and intermediary channels for exports from their U.S. parents. By contrast, outside of Japan, in other industrialized countries, local production by the majority subsidiaries of American multinationals not only stimulated much intracompany trade but also greatly exceeded the value of all U.S. exports.

During the late 1960s, and continuing through the next two decades, Japan's strategic investment policy gradually entered a second stage, distinguished first by the phased liberalization and then by the abolition of most trade and capital controls. Liberalization brought a subtle change in process, and yielded modest changes in outcome: officially sanctioned private restrictions on foreign investment and related trade slowly replaced government

[2]For summaries of available data on U.S. FDI stocks, 1929–81, see the following publication of the U.S. Commerce Department: Office of Business Economics, *U.S. Business Investments in Foreign Countries: A Supplement to the Survey of Current Business* (Washington, D.C.: USGPO, 1960), esp. table 4, p. 92 [hereafter referred to as Commerce Department, *1957 Survey*]; Bureau of Economic Analysis, *Selected Data on U.S. Direct Investment Abroad, 1950–76* (Washington, D.C.: USGPO, Feb. 1982), table 1, pp. 1–27; *U.S. Direct Investment Abroad: Balance of Payments and Direct Investment Position Estimates, 1977–81* (Washington, D.C.: USGPO, Nov. 1986), table 1, pp. 1–5.

[3]Commerce Department, *U.S. Direct Investment Abroad, 1950–76*, table 1, p. 1; for India's strategy regarding foreign direct investment, see Dennis J. Encarnation, *Dislodging Multinationals: India's Strategy in Comparative Perspective* (Ithaca: Cornell University Press, 1989), esp. pp. 1–31, 176–225.

[4]These include Argentina, Brazil, Chile, Columbia, Mexico, Panama, Peru, and Venezuela; see Commerce Department, *U.S. Direct Investment Abroad, 1950–76*, table 1, pp. 1–21.

regulations, leaving American multinationals with only marginally improved market access. Early in this stage, Japan continued to invite comparisons with newly industrializing economies. Indeed, three such economies—Brazil, Mexico, and Venezuela—each hosted more American multinationals than did Japan well into the 1970s, a preeminence Brazil retained for another decade.[5] By then, only five industrialized countries—Canada, the United Kingdom, Germany, Switzerland, and the Netherlands—actually hosted more stocks of U.S. FDI than did Japan. In Japan, most of these investments remained tied up in minority affiliates, while in other major economies, majority subsidiaries predominated and received from their American parents a sizable share of U.S. exports. In Japan, however, all such intracompany trade remained severely limited, except for the growing shipments of minority affiliates. Nevertheless, majority subsidiaries in Japan did begin to replicate a strategy pioneered in other industrialized countries, selling locally more goods and services than U.S. exporters shipped to that market. As a result, foreign direct investment slowly began to rival foreign trade as the principal means available to American multinationals seeking access to the Japanese market.

Evolution in Japan's strategic investment policy did not come easily or quickly, nor was it initiated by the Japanese. On the contrary, the principal initiative for change came from American multinationals. Only a few such multinationals (identified in this chapter) greatly influenced the course of Japanese policy, so that each one could easily be singled out by name and eventually heralded by the Japanese as a foreign "success story." Each of these "success stories" achieved competitive advantage in global markets through their skill in managing tangible and intangible assets in technology, marketing, and organization—all of which they successfully exploited in Japan through majority subsidiaries that engaged in

[5]Commerce Department, *U.S. Direct Investment Abroad, 1950–76*, table 1, pp. 1–27; *U.S. Direct Investment Abroad, 1977–81*, table 1, pp. 1–5; U.S. Department of Commerce, Bureau of Economic Analysis, "U.S. Direct Investment Abroad: Detail for Position and Balance of Payments Flows, 1985," *Survey of Current Business* (Aug. 1986), table 44, p. 95; U.S. Department of Commerce, Bureau of Economic Analysis, "U.S. Direct Investment Abroad: Detail for Position and Balance of Payments Flows, 1989," *Survey of Current Business* (Aug. 1990), table 44, p. 95.

both foreign production and intracompany trade. Their success, however, typically followed years of very difficult and often bitter negotiations, involving a complex web of trade restrictions, capital controls, and industrial structures. These negotiations, moreover, unfolded in at least partial view of other potential investors, who typically reacted negatively to both process and outcome. This negative signaling undoubtedly discouraged countless other would-be investors, who concluded that investing in Japan assured high up-front costs, but offered much less certain prospects of future benefits. So, as we shall see, only a very few American multinationals in Japan have achieved success through investments in majority subsidiaries.

To be successful, American multinationals found they had to add political skills to their existing business assets, in order to establish majority subsidiaries in Japan. These multinationals sometimes, but not always, solicited the official assistance of the U.S. government. In fact, foreign official pressures on Japan were often feeble and inept. And even when they were not, a domestic constituency drawn largely from among Japanese oligopolists still was needed to achieve policy change. These oligopolists naturally figured among the principal beneficiaries of Japan's strategic investment policy, so their resistance to change remained great. To overcome their reluctance, the tangible benefits of any change (e.g., improved access to foreign technology or markets) had to exceed its potential costs (e.g., loss of domestic market share or foreign market access). To reduce their risks, Japanese oligopolists gradually moved to replace public regulations with private restrictions, and they learned to manipulate foreign demands to their domestic advantage over both local competitors and the Japanese state, and to their foreign advantage over those who would restrict Japanese export markets and overseas investments. Feeling such pressures, skillfully mediated by local oligopolists, the Japanese state became increasingly responsive, albeit at times reluctantly and incompletely. Thus, as aggressive intermediaries between American multinationals and the Japanese state, Japanese oligopolists managed to control both the timing and the substance of changes in their country's strategic investment policy. In the end, Japanese oligopolists took charge.

STAGE I: CAPITAL CONTROLS AND TRADE RESTRICTIONS

Japanese restrictions on foreign investment and related trade can claim a lengthy history.[6] As far back as 1640, in concert with its other isolationist policies, the Tokugawa government closed Japan to most trade and investment from abroad. What minuscule foreign investment did persist served merely to facilitate the limited foreign trade allowed by the regime. In fact, these government controls endured for more than two hundred years—until Commodore Perry's arrival in the early 1850s and the creation of the so-called Treaty Settlements. In the few ports subsequently opened to foreigners, local authorities did permit some foreign capital flows, principally to facilitate foreign commerce without local production. Foreign direct investment outside these ports would have to await the turn of the century when, in 1899, the Meiji regime explicitly permitted foreigners to invest in joint ventures and wholly owned subsidiaries in the domestic Japanese market.

Prewar Legacies

Even after the Meiji liberalizations, only a few American multinationals invested in Japan. The first was Western Electric, which entered Japan immediately after the 1899 liberalization with a majority U.S.-owned joint venture, Nippon Electric Company (NEC).[7] Over the next two decades, a small but growing number of America's emergent multinationals began to invest in Japan, typically through joint ventures, often with Japanese *zaibatsu* (industrial and trading combines) as partners. By 1929, U.S. FDI in Japan had climbed to $61 million, roughly one-half of total direct investment by all foreigners in Japan.[8] While large for Japan, such

[6]For that history, see Mark Mason, "United States Direct Investment in Japan: Studies in Government Policy and Corporate Strategy" (Ph.D. diss., Harvard University, 1988); and *American Multinationals and Japan: The Political Economy of Japanese Capital Controls, 1899–1980* (Cambridge: Harvard University Press, 1992).

[7]Mark Mason, "With Reservations: Prewar Japan as Host to Western Electric and ITT," in Yuzawa Takeshi and Udagawa Masaru, eds., *Foreign Business in Japan before World War II* (Tokyo: University of Tokyo Press, 1990), pp. 175–192.

[8]For data on U.S. FDI in Japan, see U.S. Commerce Department, Bureau of Foreign and Domestic Commerce, *American Direct Investments in Foreign Countries,*

U.S. investment paled in comparison to the burgeoning operations of American multinationals elsewhere in the world. Even in East Asia, as early as 1929, those multinationals had larger direct investments in China, the Philippines, and the Netherland East Indies (later, Indonesia) than they had in Japan.[9] Moreover, nearly every country in Europe and in Latin America could boast more U.S. FDI than could Japan. When totaled, American multinationals in Japan during 1929 contributed less than one-tenth of one percent of the cumulative value of all U.S. FDI worldwide. Subsequently, through the outbreak of the Second World War, Japan's relative position actually worsened, as American multinationals exploited better opportunities elsewhere in East Asia and around the world.

Early on, among the few Americans who did find Japan attractive, Ford and General Motors combined both trade and investment to dominate the local market—at least initially.[10] Both automakers sought to exploit in Japan the same product and process innovations that had made them dominant in the U.S. market and around the world. In their way stood the Pacific Ocean, as high transportation costs inflated the import prices of fully made cars. Also in the way stood Japan's ever-growing import restrictions, plus "Buy Japan" campaigns and other official efforts designed to nurture infant domestic industries. Still, these government efforts yielded lackluster results, at least initially, and local competition

---

1929 (Washington, D.C.: 1932), pp. 26–28, 38; Cleona Lewis, *America's Stake in International Investments* (Washington, D.C.: Brookings Institution, 1938). For data on all FDI in Japan, see Mark Mason, "Foreign Direct Investment and Japanese Economic Development," *Business and Economic History,* 2d series, 16 (1987): 95. By 1913, stocks of foreign direct investment in Japan totaled $50 million nationwide. Over the next decade, that investment more than doubled, to reach a prewar high of $122 million in 1929. Note, however, that this 1929 figure represents an upper limit, since other estimates range from $57 million in 1931 to between $75 and $100 million in 1934.

[9]Commerce Department, *American Direct Investments in Foreign Countries, 1929,* table IV, p. 26; Commerce Department, *1957 Survey,* table 4, p. 92.

[10]Unless otherwise noted, the following discussion of Ford and GM in prewar Japan comes from the following sources: Mira Wilkins, "American-Japanese Direct Foreign Investment, 1930–1952," *Business History Review* 56 (Winter 1982), esp. pp. 498–504; Mason, *American Multinationals and Japan,* chap. 2, "The Sliding Door: 1930–1940"; also see the limited treatment of Ford and GM in Michael A. Cusumano, *The Japanese Automobile Industry: Technology and Management at Toyota and Nissan* (Cambridge: Harvard University Press, 1985).

languished: during 1930, only 458 automobiles were fully manufactured in Japan by locally owned producers.[11] The Japanese
share amounted to 2.5 percent of the local market; Ford and GM
supplied the remainder through imports, which largely consisted
of complete "knocked-down" kits shipped from the United States
and assembled in Japan using American-made machinery. Even as
late as 1935, Ford alone sold in Japan two-and-a-half times the
number of cars and trucks produced by all Japanese-owned automakers combined. Thus, for Ford, GM, and other American multinationals, foreign direct investment created, and then expanded,
markets for intermediate components and assembly machinery
exported from the United States.

As political tensions between America and Japan heightened on
the eve of the Second World War, U.S. direct investment in Japan
encountered more and more government restrictions. In automobiles, greater local content became central to Japanese policy,
leading Ford to apply during 1936 for a license seeking to manufacture complete automobiles in Japan. By then, however, new legislation restricted such applications to companies at least 50 percent Japanese-owned, with the principal recipients being Nissan
and Toyota—already the country's two largest suppliers of replacement parts to local buyers of Fords and Chevrolets.[12] To
counter, first GM and then (by 1936) Ford sought local joint-
venture partners, but with little success. Despite these setbacks,
however, Ford remained quite profitable. So, in 1937, the Japanese
government blocked Ford's remittances and, the following year,
severely cut back its (and GM's) import permits for "knocked-
down" kits. With foreign direct investment effectively frozen and
related trade sliced, fledgling Japanese producers soon overtook
their American competitors in Japan.

This story of U.S. automakers in prewar Japan is not unique.
Official Japanese hostility soon affected other American multina-

[11]For actual market-share data during the 1930s, see Wilkins, "American-
Japanese Direct Foreign Investment," p. 499.
[12]While Wilkins notes that such licenses went only to Toyota and Nissan, Mason
reports that Isuzu also was a recipient; see Wilkins, "American-Japanese Investment," p. 55; Mason, *American Multinationals and Japan*, chap. 2.

tionals, and for the remainder of the 1930s, already meager U.S. investments plummeted.[13] Between 1929 and 1936, cumulative U.S. FDI in Japan declined by one-quarter, falling to $47 billion. And it declined by another 25 percent between 1936 and 1941 when, at the time of the attack on Pearl Harbor, cumulative U.S. FDI in Japan reached $33 billion. As the Pacific War raged on, the Japanese government expropriated and dispersed what few assets remained under American ownership. For example, assembly plants owned as late as 1941 by Ford and GM were later broken up and parceled out to Nissan, Toyota, and other Japanese-owned motor vehicle manufacturers. While wartime profits from nationalized operations collected in escrow accounts to be dispersed after the war, few of the physical assets survived the Allies' bombing. What the Allies did not destroy, however, was the elaborate system of trade and capital controls steadily erected since the late 1920s; instead the Occupation drew heavily on these prewar antecedents when it constructed a postwar regulatory regime for Japan.

The Occupation

Immediately after the war, numerous prewar investors petitioned the Allied Occupation for the recovery of previously nationalized assets, but nearly all of their petitions were rejected.[14] Initially, the Allies had hoped to break up the same Japanese *zaibatsu* that had been joint-venture partners of foreign multinationals; the Occupation's trust-busting zeal, therefore, extended to such foreign partners. In any case, capital controls were designed to be temporary, to remain in operation only during the initial stage of economic, political, and military reform in Japan. In Germany, by contrast, similar prohibitions appeared in the Soviet-occupied sector alone, while the American, British, and French

[13]For data in this paragraph, see Commerce Department, *1957 Survey*, table 4, p. 92; Wilkins, "American–Japanese Investment," table 2, p. 506, and pp. 510–14; Mason, *American Multinationals and Japan*, chap. 3, "The Closed Door: 1940–1950."

[14]For histories of American multinationals in Japan during the U.S. Occupation, see Mason, *American Multinationals and Japan*, chap. 3; Wilkins, "American-Japanese Investment," pp. 514–518.

sectors encouraged the reentry of foreign multinationals.[15] Of course in the prewar German economy these foreigners had occupied a much more important position than they had in Japan; thus, they figured more prominently in Allied plans for German reconstruction. More generally, the American "New Dealers" who populated the Allied Occupation in Japan viewed large multinationals with a suspicion not evident in Germany.[16] So, in Japan, when rapid economic growth (and not reform) became central to Occupation policy, the Allies proved more willing to drop their plans to break up Japanese *zaibatsu* than to liberalize capital controls. Many Occupation officials feared, however, that before such growth could occur, Japanese assets would remain grossly undervalued as a result of the war's destruction and its chaotic aftermath and therefore vulnerable to foreign takeover. In order to prevent these takeovers, capital controls became more nearly permanent—with the full approval of Japanese business and government.

Specifically, the Allied Occupation constructed the two grand pillars of Japan's postwar regulatory regime: the Foreign Exchange Control Law (FECL), promulgated in 1949, followed in 1950 by the Foreign Investment Law (FIL). The FECL granted the Ministry of Finance (MOF) control over nearly all foreign exchange transactions, while the FIL expressly extended MOF's exchange controls to include foreign enterprises operating in Japan. In addition, the FIL granted the Ministry of International Trade and Industry (MITI) and other government agencies a broad range of ill-defined powers intended to guarantee that proposed investments would contribute to "the development of essential industries or public enterprises" or to "the improvement of the international balance of payments."[17] Even after Japan's chronic

[15]Here, I rely extensively on Simon Reich, *The Fruits of Fascism: Postwar Prosperity in Historical Perspective* (Ithaca: Cornell University Press, 1990), esp. chaps. 1, 4, 7. As a comparison of the relative position of American multinationals in Germany and Japan during the decade after the war, the U.S. Commerce Department estimated that U.S. FDI in Germany was ten times larger than U.S. FDI in Japan; see *1957 Survey*, table 4, p. 92.

[16]Theodore Cohen, *Remaking Japan: The American Occupation as New Deal* (New York: Free Press, 1987), esp. pp. 351–377.

[17]Article 8, the Foreign Investment Law, No. 163 of 1950. Remittance of principal, not permitted during the Occupation, was from 1952 limited to 20 percent per year.

foreign exchange crises had ended in the mid-1960s, deeper fears regarding the loss of Japanese control over its own economic development remained palpable through the 1970s. Thus, the postwar regulatory regime articulated during the Occupation survived largely intact for the next thirty years.[18]

Under Japan's regulatory regime, foreign applications for investment never received automatic government approval—unlike the review procedure common to many other industrialized countries. Instead, in Japan approval required time-consuming negotiations between prospective foreign investors and those government ministries responsible for nurturing Japanese industry. Ostensibly, government approval should have been exercised by a single coordinating body, the Foreign Investment Deliberation Council (FIDC), first organized during the Occupation and reconstituted in 1952. However, MITI and other ministries staffing the FIDC actually decided which foreign investors—if any—would enter an industry, and under what conditions.[19] Ministry decisions were not made in a vacuum; instead, they depended upon close consultation with those Japanese enterprises most directly affected by such decisions. In the regulation of foreign investment, MITI typically insisted that technology licensing be decoupled from foreign equity; or, if the requisite technology could not be secured without equity attached, that minority or, at most, equal-partnership joint ventures be organized, rather than majority foreign-owned subsidiaries (see Figure 2-2). Additional conditions stipulated that these foreign-affiliated ventures could not enter related or new industries, could not augment their capitalization, and could not remit abroad more than a specified amount of currency during a given period. To enforce compliance, responsible ministries also limited the duration of these FIL licenses.

[18]For this thirty-year history, through 1980, see Dennis J. Encarnation and Mark Mason, "Neither MITI nor America: The Political Economy of Capital Liberalization in Japan," *International Organization* 44 (Winter 1990): 25–54.

[19]Ibid., p. 31; so-called automatic approvals under the FIL, which amounted to exemptions from this regulatory machinery, were typically limited to foreign direct investments of insignificant scale. For all other investments, MITI hoped that foreigners would be prepared to license their products and processes as the only way to share in the market, since foreign firms could neither export manufactured goods to Japan nor make direct investments there.

Figure 2-2. FIL-approved projects, 1956–64

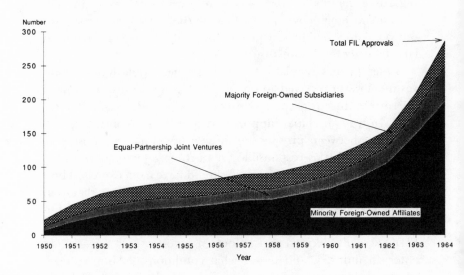

Sources: Recalculated from MITI data reported in Mark Mason, *American Multinationals and Japan: The Political Economy of Japanese Capital Controls, 1899–1980* (Cambridge: Harvard University Press, 1992), p. 193.

Thus, throughout their operations, foreign multinationals had to secure multiple, time-consuming permissions from government ministries—and, by extension, from industry oligopolists—that together controlled the conduct of business in Japan.

Imports of machinery, raw materials, and (especially) final goods became the specific targets of government oversight, as Japan sought to conserve precious foreign exchange while also protecting domestic industries from international competition. As with the inflow of foreign capital, so too with the inflow of foreign goods: Japan required prospective importers of either to seek government approval for all transactions. And once again, MITI—operating with the active participation of Japanese oligopolists—stood at the center of this regulatory regime. Prior to granting final permission, MITI and other government agencies categorized imports in terms ranging from "most desirable" (food and raw materials) to "least desirable" (targeted products and consumer goods). MITI then imposed quantitative restrictions (quotas) on the least desirable, while it granted automatic approval to only a few of the most desirable imports. Next, upon receiving applications for import licenses, MITI and other agencies required that prospective importers pay collateral, based on the value of the proposed import, and then forfeit that collateral should an approved import not be forthcoming. Despite such elaborate regulations, with an exchange rate fixed at ¥360 to the dollar, Japan continued to run persistent deficits in merchandise trade—and on its current account—well into the 1960s. Burgeoning imports of raw materials outpaced languishing exports of manufactured goods even as Japanese trade restrictions denied market access to foreigners.

In other countries, such trade restrictions have proved to be powerful determinants of foreign direct investments designed to service local, as distinct from export, markets.[20] But they have not done so in Japan, where capital controls continued to hold multinationals at bay, even in those industries dominated by foreigners before the war.[21] Consequently, immediately after the war, only a limited number of new investors ventured into Japan, especially given the sorry state of the economy relative to opportunities elsewhere. In fact, during the Occupation and continuing through 1952, only ninety foreign-affiliated (mostly American) projects, totaling roughly $20 million, were approved under the FIL.[22] This equaled one-tenth of one percent of all U.S. foreign direct invest-

[20]Reuber, *Foreign Private Investment in Development* esp. pp. 120–132; Guisinger, *Investment Incentives and Performance Requirements,* esp. pp. 48–54.

[21]In a sensational case of the late 1950s, Singer Sewing Machines, the prewar market leader, sought to overcome MITI's objections to its expansion by proposing the merging of its own repossessed assets into a joint venture with a leading Japanese company (Pine). MITI, intent on fostering a domestic sewing-machine industry, feared that the proposed joint venture would do little to stop Singer from recapturing its old market position, so it imposed severe production quotas before approving the venture. See Chalmers Johnson, *MITI and the Japanese Miracle: The Growth of Japanese Industrial Policy, 1925–1975* (Stanford: Stanford University Press, 1982), p. 246.

[22]Calculated using data from Foreign Capital Research Society, Bank of Japan, *Statistical Data and List of Principal Cases of Foreign Capital Investment in Japan as of the End of 1952* (Tokyo), p. 21. The U.S. Commerce Department reports that total U.S. FDI in Japan during 1950 stood at $18.6 million out of total U.S. FDI worldwide of $11.8 billion; see "Foreign Investments of the United States," *Survey of Current Business* (Supplement 1953), p. 48. Following the Americans, British investment, nearly one-eighth the total, continued to rank second as it had before the war.

ment worldwide—making Japan the least likely destination among industrialized countries to attract American multinationals. Indeed, by 1950, U.S.-occupied Japan hosted less American investment than did newly independent India. And for at least a decade following the Occupation, prospects for foreigners barely improved (see Figure 2-2). In fact, during the 1950s only 101 new investment permits—totaling no more than $59.7 million— were approved under the FIL.[23] As a result, by 1960 the Philippines continued to boast more U.S. FDI, as did each of the eight largest Latin American economies.[24] The paucity of U.S. FDI in Japan continued to invite comparisons with economies far less industrialized than was Japan's.

Early Hints of Capital Liberalization

Prospects for investment in Japan did improve whenever a foreign investor sidestepped provisions of the FIL, to participate instead as a "yen-based company."[25] During the Occupation, prewar investors became the first to benefit from such exemptions, provided that they agreed to resume earlier operations and that they did not later seek foreign exchange for the repatriation of profits and fees. Beginning in 1950, a total of twenty-four prewar investors satisfied these conditions and received government permission to reenter Japan through the reinvestment of domestically acquired yen in existing businesses (see Figure 2-2). For these investors, however, any deviation from a narrow definition of

[23]Ministry of International Trade and Industry, *Annual Report on Foreign Capital Investment in Japan [Gaishi donyu nenkan]* (Tokyo: Shoko kaikan, 1969), p. 15, as reported in Ozawa, "Japanese Policy toward Foreign Multinationals," p. 148.

[24]These include Argentina, Brazil, Chile, Columbia, Mexico, Panama, Peru, and Venezuela; see Commerce Department, *U.S. Direct Investment Abroad, 1950–76*, table 1, p. 1–27.

[25]In addition, almost any foreign company could establish a branch office in Japan from 1949, for the FIL did not regulate such business entities. In practice, however, this mode of entry proved unpopular because the FECL empowered the Ministry of Finance (MOF), at its discretion, to block both the outflow of remittances from those branches and the inflow of investments to them. MOF typically rejected such inflows when the branch attempted to engage in manufacturing as distinct from sales. See Robert S. Ozaki, *The Control of Imports and Foreign Capital in Japan* (New York: Praeger, 1972), p. 111.

their original businesses or any application for foreign-exchange remittances brought them under FIL control, at least until 1956. Late that year, and continuing through mid-1963, the Japanese government designated a second class of yen-based companies by according "national treatment" to American (and later British) enterprises exempted from other regulations as a result of their country's bilateral commercial treaty with Japan.[26] Japan extended these exemptions reluctantly: nearly three years elapsed after the signing of the U.S.-Japan treaty (in April 1953) before any U.S. multinational became eligible to receive national treatment (in October 1956). Over the next seven years (until June 1963),[27] in exchange for national treatment, foreign investors could remit dividends or principal only after securing foreign-exchange licenses under the FECL—a task that, in practice, proved virtually impossible. But when foreign investors remained willing to reinvest their yen profits in Japan, rather than remitting capital abroad, this regulatory loophole created new opportunities otherwise unknown to them in Japan (see Figure 2-3).

Compared with the FIL approval process, this new and more liberal regime permitted a greater number of multinationals to establish a larger share of majority foreign-owned affiliates more evenly spread across industries. Admittedly, initial investments remained quite small: through 1963, foreign multinationals had invested just $85.7 million in 289 yen-based companies; this compares to $235 million invested in 209 projects operating under the FIL without benefit of national treatment.[28] Most of this

---

[26]The "national basis" commitment was explicitly contained in the "most-favored-nation" clauses of the U.S.-Japan Treaty of Friendship, Commerce, and Navigation (FCN) of April 1953, and was later (after April 1960) extended to Great Britain through the most-favored-nation clauses contained in its own bilateral FCN treaty with Japan. For the provisions of these treaties, see Dan Fenno Henderson, *Foreign Enterprise in Japan* (Tokyo: Charles E. Tuttle, 1975), p. 270.

[27]From July 1, 1963, all "yen-based" entries were subjected to a control scheme virtually identical in practice to the FIL regulation system.

[28]Data on yen-based companies from MITI and reported in Mason, *American Multinationals and Japan,* chap. 4, "The Screen Door: 1950–1970." Note that this sum of $85.7 million (¥0.8 billion) differs dramatically from earlier estimates (valued at $500 million) derived from assorted OECD documents, and reported in Encarnation and Mason, "Neither MITI nor America," pp. 37–38. Data on the dollar value of FIL-approved investments from Organization for Economic Coop-

Figure 2-3. FIL-approved vs. yen-based companies in Japan, 1950–63

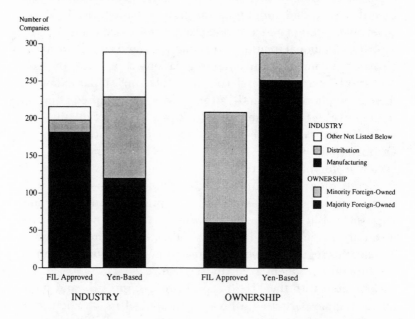

Sources: MITI data reported in Mark Mason, *American Multinationals and Japan: The Political Economy of Japanese Capital Controls, 1899–1980* (Cambridge: Harvard University Press, 1992), pp. 150–198.

larger, FIL-approved investment entered minority foreign-owned or equal-partnership joint ventures. By contrast, very few yen-based companies had to settle for something less than majority foreign ownership. Combined through 1963, these yen-based companies actually accounted for two-thirds of all majority subsid-

eration and Development, *Liberalisation of International Capital Movements: Japan* (Paris: OECD, 1968), p. 25; the sum $235 million is probably for 1965. Data on the actual number of FIL-approved investments from Fig. 2-2, where totals through 1965 (209 projects) differ drastically from the totals (150 FIL-approved projects) estimated by Komiya Ryutaro, "Direct Foreign Investment in Postwar Japan," in Peter Drysdale, ed., *Direct Foreign Investment in Asia and the Pacific* (Canberra: ANU Press, 1972), p. 151. In fact, according to Figure 2-2, through 1964, the number of projects approved under the FIL reached 286 (three short of the number approved under the yen-based regime just eighteen months earlier).

iaries operating in Japan. For majority subsidiaries established as yen-based companies, 95 percent foreign ownership proved common, thus assuring multinationals of unrivaled managerial control.[29] Such foreign control eluded most projects approved under the FIL, as did entry into Japanese wholesaling, where U.S. exports were largely denied markets. Again in contrast to FIL-approved investments, most of which had entered Japanese manufacturing, yen-based companies became more widely dispersed across industries, with Japanese wholesaling and Japanese manufacturing attracting roughly comparable attention (see Figure 2-3). Reviewing this period, Itoh Motoshige and Kiyono Kazuharu conclude: "The major multinationals functioning in Japan today [that is, by the late 1980s] used the partial relaxation of foreign capital inflows under the 'system of free purchase of yen-denominated stock' . . . to make inroads into the Japanese economy."[30] Thus, when permitted to choose between majority foreign ownership and the repatriation of yen profits, most multinationals preferred larger shareholdings; and wholesaling, in particular, attracted almost as much attention as did manufacturing.

Foremost among these foreign multinationals was IBM, whose reentry negotiations transformed a wholly U.S.-owned wholesaler of American-made products into an import-substituting (and eventually export-oriented) manufacturer that remained 99 percent foreign-owned.[31] Before the war, IBM conducted a modest business in Japan, one that leased, distributed, and serviced imports from America. After the war, the Japanese government threatened that wholesaling business, placing tight restrictions on foreign exchange to limit imports and to promote domestic production. So, during the late 1950s, after reclaiming its pre-

[29]MITI, *Annual Report on Foreign Capital Investment*, p. 18.

[30]Itoh Motoshige and Kiyono Kazuharu, "Foreign Trade and Direct Investment," in Komiya Ryutaro et al., eds., *Industrial Policy of Japan* (Tokyo: Academic Press, 1988), p. 166.

[31]For a more limited rendering of this story, see Marie Anchordoguy, *Computers Inc.: Japan's Challenge to IBM* (Cambridge: Harvard University Press, 1989); compare this to Mason, *American Multinationals and Japan*, chaps. 2–4. Also see International Business Machines, *IBM Japan: A Chronological Survey, 1925–74*. Nihon IBM, *A Fifty-Year History of IBM Japan [Nihon ai bi emu gojyuunen shi]* (Tokyo: unpublished manuscript), esp. chap. 3.

war properties, IBM sought MITI's permission to expand beyond wholesaling by becoming Japan's first local producer of computers.[32] MITI's permission, however, proved difficult to secure: negotiations dragged on for more than three years, with IBM controlling access to computer technology and MITI controlling access to the Japanese market. In exchange for granting IBM limited market access, MITI sought to license that multinational's basic computer patents, which otherwise threatened to block development of the entire Japanese computer industry. Indeed, MITI's chief negotiator made no bones about his objectives: "We will take every measure possible to obstruct the success of your business unless you license IBM patents to Japanese firms and charge them no more than a 5 percent royalty." Even in the absence of such a deal, MITI's negotiator continued, "we only need time and money to compete effectively."[33] Fearing this alternative, "IBM ultimately had to come to terms," in the words of Chalmers Johnson.[34] In exchange for manufacturing in Japan, IBM licensed its computer patents to potential Japanese competitors; it accepted MITI's restrictions on IBM's local production and market share; and it agreed to export a proportion of that Japanese production to help pay for necessary imports. Subsequently, such linking of direct investment with both technology licensing and foreign trade became standard conditions in most negotiations with the Japanese government.

At the same time, MITI—prodded by Japanese oligopolists— also had to come to terms with America's twenty-seventh largest (in 1960) industrial corporation.[35] In fact, IBM succeeded in securing exemptions that were, until then, unprecedented in the postwar

[32]Although the Japanese government did provide FIL validation for certain IBM–Japan activities, authorities did not provide any foreign-exchange guarantees necessary for IBM to repatriate abroad its yen-denominated profits. As a result, IBM–Japan represented an early example of a yen-based company, one formed *before* 1956 and the implementation of national treatment provisions in the U.S.-Japan Treaty of Friendship, Commerce, and Navigation. Coca-Cola, on the other hand, set up a yen-based company to supply the civilian Japanese market *after* 1956; see Encarnation and Mason, "Neither MITI nor America," pp. 34–35.

[33]Statement attributed to Sahashi Sigeru, then-deputy director of MITI's Heavy Industries Bureau, and quoted in Johnson, *MITI and the Japanese Miracle*, p. 245.

[34]Ibid.

[35]*Fortune*, "The 500 Largest Industrial Corporations: 1961."

history of Japan: notably, government validation of IBM's 99 percent equity ownership in a local production facility and marketing network, as well as government guarantees not to restrict foreign remittances to the home office for five years.[36] These concessions also allowed IBM to retain its premier share of the Japanese computer market well into the 1970s, and thereafter, to continue to rank among the top two or three suppliers in that market. And even after the erosion of IBM's market share, few other foreign multinationals could boast of having a comparable penetration into Japan. For IBM's eventual Japanese competitors, of course, local production by a foreign multinational represented merely a small price to pay for access to that multinational's technology. Indeed, with each Japanese competitor more eager than the next to gain preferential access to "Big Blue's" patents and knowhow, representatives from Fujitsu, Hitachi, Oki, Matsushita, Mitsubishi, and Toshiba all seemed (at least to IBM's chief negotiator) to be demanding that MITI come to terms with IBM.[37] Finally, MITI relented. Thus, the same proprietary technology that had made IBM the market leader in the world computer industry also forced MITI to grant a dispensation from foreign capital controls, by mobilizing political support for IBM's application among the same Japanese enterprises that MITI had hoped to protect.

Notably absent from this fray was the U.S. government—left outside at IBM's insistence.[38] In fact, IBM's chief negotiator actually feared exciting U.S. antitrust action should he insist that Japanese competitors pay a higher royalty on IBM patents than IBM was charging its domestic U.S. competitors. In any case, the U.S. government itself showed no intention of getting involved. Instead, for at least a decade after the Occupation, the State Department remained preoccupied with the promotion of Japan as a democratic bulwark—if not a base camp—against possible Communist encroachments in the South China Sea and on the Korean

[36]The remaining 1 percent equity in IBM–Japan went to the Japanese directors of that subsidiary. This formula allowed MITI to claim that it had not compromised the FIL by allowing a wholly foreign-owned subsidiary to be established. See Encarnation and Mason, "Neither MITI nor America," p. 36.

[37]Based on interviews with IBM's chief negotiator, and reported in Mason, *American Multinationals and Japan*, pp. 187–191.

[38]Encarnation and Mason, "Neither MITI nor America," p. 37.

peninsula. The promotion of U.S. exports and investments in Japan, by contrast, received merely scant attention at the U.S. embassy in Tokyo. Rather, its staff was busily negotiating a new security treaty (and other military and political matters) with Japan during the late 1950s, just as IBM and several other U.S. multinationals were entering the critical stages in their own negotiations.[39] Even the subsequent arrival of a new American ambassador to Japan did little to alter this situation, which provided sufficient cause to justify a popular complaint by multinationals that the embassy was "not doing enough" for U.S. business.[40] Appearing as he did so close on the heels of the security treaty riots of 1960, Ambassador Edwin Reischauer consciously took note of continued U.S. trade surpluses with Japan and chose to concentrate on non-economic relations. Thus, he pursued a "less rigorous" response to the demands of those American exporters and investors "already complaining about unfair treatment."[41]

Early Steps toward Trade Liberalization

The volume of such complaints diminished somewhat during 1960, when the Japanese government took its first hesitant steps toward trade liberalization.[42] "While not of great significance in the aggregate," according to Lawrence Krause and Sekiguchi

[39]Indeed, according to recently declassified documents from the U.S. National Security Council, those economic initiatives that the U.S. government did take toward Japan aimed at assuring both open overseas markets for Japanese exporters and appropriate conditions for the promotion of economic development and Japanese self-reliance. See, for example, two separate documents, both entitled "U.S. Policy toward Japan" in NSC 5516, dated March 29, 1955, and in NSC 6008, dated May 20, 1960.

[40]Also, looking back on these negotiations, DuPont's chief arbitrator openly complained that the staff of the embassy remained patently unhelpful (if not harmful) to that company's efforts to establish a chemical plant in Japan; see Encarnation and Mason, "Neither MITI nor America," p. 37. For more such complaints, see Mason, *American Multinationals and Japan*, pp. 150–198.

[41]Quoted in Encarnation and Mason, "Neither MITI nor America," p. 37.

[42]For a general discussion of trade liberalization, see Itoh and Kiyono, "Foreign Trade and Direct Investment," p. 166; Komiya Ryutaro and Itoh Motoshige, "Japan's International Trade and Trade Policy, 1955–1984," in Inoguchi Takashi and Daniel I. Okimoto, eds., *The Political Economy of Japan, Volume 2: The Changing International Context* (Stanford: Stanford University Press, 1988), pp. 173–224.

Sueo, these phase-one liberalizations did make new policy tools available to government:[43] tariffs replaced quotas, as price mechanisms replaced quantitative restrictions. Initially, the government abolished quotas on 257 commodities, which together accounted for 44 percent of the value of all Japanese imports in 1960.[44] That share rose to 90 percent by the end of 1963, when the government had completed the abolition of more than 1,837 quotas, leaving fewer than 200 in operation for the rest of the decade.[45] However, according to Krause and Sekiguchi, this "weakening or removal of quota restrictions had little impact on imports," because it "only exposed a tariff barrier that was itself very limiting."[46] Indeed, in place of quotas, Japan imposed high tariffs, which escalated up the value-added chain, from raw materials to intermediate inputs to final goods. For example, iron ore and scrap metals entered Japan duty-free, while rolled steel made from this scrap incurred a 15 percent nominal tariff (or a 35 percent effective rate of protection); and automobiles made from this steel suffered a higher 36 percent nominal tariff (or a 67 percent effective rate of protection), even after liberalization in 1965.[47] The government, fearing drastic increases in imports following liberalization, also devised other restrictions, but no combination seemed effective: in 1961, Japan suffered an unprecedented deficit of $1 billion on its current account, fueled by an equally unexpected deficit in its merchandise trade.[48] That trade deficit, however, reversed dramatically during the following year; and beginning in 1964, a continuing surplus

[43]Lawrence Krause and Sekiguchi Sueo, "Japan and the World Economy," in Hugh Patrick and Henry Rosovsky, eds., *Asia's New Giant: How the Japanese Economy Works* (Washington, D.C.: Brookings Institution, 1982), p. 426.

[44]Ibid., p. 414; these commodities consisted of four-digit items covered by the Brussels Tariff Nomenclature (BTN) system.

[45]Komiya and Itoh, "Japan's International Trade and Trade Policy, 1955–84," p. 182, and table 4, p. 192; Krause and Sekiguchi, "Japan and the World Economy," table 6-12, p. 426.

[46]Krause and Sekiguchi, "Japan and the World Economy," p. 427.

[47]Ibid.; Itoh and Kiyono, "Foreign Trade and Direct Investment," pp. 160–161.

[48]Fearing such a deficit, the Japanese government established a "negative" list of imports requiring explicit government approval, and it abolished the Bank of Japan's preference for projects seeking approved imports over purely domestic projects in competition for finance; see Krause and Sekiguchi, "Japan and the World Economy," pp. 416, 453.

first appeared. To account, at least in part, for such a dramatic reversal, Krause and Sekiguchi declare: "Few further steps toward liberalizing the treatment of imports were taken, while measures to promote exports were still being initiated until late in the decade."[49] Thus, even trade liberalization favored Japanese exporters at the expense of foreign competitors seeking access to the local market.

What little liberalization did occur actually helped Japan to blunt the growing criticism from abroad. Already by 1955 a signatory to the General Agreement on Tariffs and Trade (GATT), Japan in 1963 added the GATT's Article 11 to its earlier commitments— several years after similar commitments were made by other industrialized countries. In such countries, as in Japan, Article 11 forbade any imposition of quantitative restrictions on most imports, although it did permit the negotiation of "residual quotas" during an unspecified period of transition. More than any other industrialized country, Japan invoked these exemptions: residual quotas accounted for 155 of the 192 quantitative restrictions that Japan left in place at the end of 1963.[50] The following year, Japan moved to liberalize comparable restrictions on foreign exchange by adding Article 8 from the charter of the International Monetary Fund (IMF) to its earlier (1952) membership commitments. After 1964, the Japanese government could no longer restrict the conversion and subsequent repatriation of a multinational's principal and local earnings so easily as it had done with yen-based companies. Similar restrictions on financial movements across national borders were also proscribed in the capital liberalization code of the Organization for Economic Cooperation and Development (OECD), which Japan joined in 1964. But before finally agreeing to make the yen a convertible currency, Japan negotiated a larger number of formal reservations than did any of the other sixteen OECD member-countries except Spain and Portugal.[51] Thus, Japan moved slowly and reluctantly toward a foreign model of capital liberalization.

[49]Ibid., p. 426.

[50]Ibid.

[51]Despite these reservations, Japan nevertheless gained several advantages from OECD membership, including greater ease in floating its securities in overseas markets; see Johnson, *MITI and the Japanese Miracle*, p. 276.

A Setback for Capital Liberalization

Meanwhile, Japan actually reversed its own limited experiment with capital liberalization, at just the time when foreign investors were beginning to profit from the new incentives. According to Ozawa Terutomo, "the government suspended the yen-based investment program in 1963 on the pretext that all restrictions would be removed" during the following year, with the liberalization of foreign exchange controls.[52] The timing of that Japanese suspension followed a sudden influx of foreign investors who were seeking to establish yen-based companies, following both Japan's early steps toward trade liberalization and the successful completion of IBM's much-publicized negotiations, all in 1960. Subsequently, Exxon, Kaiser Aluminum, and Scott Paper, among American multinationals, plus Hoechst and Olivetti among European investors—all entered Japan as yen-based companies. In fact, during the eighteen months between January 1961 and June 1963, these multinationals established ninety-five yen-based companies, nearly one-third of the total established to that date. Here, as with other yen-based companies (see Figure 2-3 above), multinationals typically invested in those majority foreign-owned subsidiaries that granted them a level of control beyond the grasp of most FIL-approved joint ventures. And they invested in a broader array of industries, including wholesaling—again, beyond the scope of most FIL projects. "Alarmed," to quote Ozawa, by this large influx of majority subsidiaries in both wholesaling and manufacturing, the government abruptly suspended postwar Japan's first halting experiment with capital liberalization.

The suspension of the yen-based regime forced eager multinationals back to seeking FIL approval as their sole means for securing market access. And their rush continued unabated: in just two years, 1963 and 1964, 132 FIL-approved projects entered Japan (see Figure 2-2 above). This total represented nearly one-half (46 percent) of all projects approved under that law since its inception in 1950. As before, the machinery industry still attracted the greatest overall attention, accounting for fifty-three projects between 1963 and 1964—nearly one-half (46 percent) of all FIL approvals

[52]Ozawa, "Japanese Policy toward Foreign Multinationals," p. 150.

to enter that industry since 1950.[53] But in a sharp break with the past, marketing now enjoyed the largest relative increases, as foreign exporters sought improved market access: after receiving no new FIL approvals since 1952, foreign multinationals invested in four FIL-approved wholesalers during 1963 and in another seventeen during 1964. While these approvals typically granted foreigners only minority ownership in their Japanese affiliates (see Figure 2-2 above), they nevertheless provided multinationals with the sole vehicle for gaining access to a Japanese market that remained resistant both to imports from abroad and to local production by majority foreign-owned subsidiaries.

Still, persistent government regulations made investing in Japan exceedingly difficult, even in an industry (machinery) seemingly favored by FIL approvals—as the continuing saga of Texas instruments (TI) amply illustrates.[54] In 1964, TI petitioned MITI to establish a wholly foreign-owned subsidiary for the local manufacture of semiconductors. These and other products were already being imported in limited quantities through TI's fully owned wholesaler in Japan. The timing of TI's application coincided with IBM's introduction, during the same year, of its first computer (the System 360) to make extensive use of integrated circuits. Earlier, in 1960, just as IBM was concluding its own negotiations over entry into Japan, TI sought patent protection from the Japanese government for its then-revolutionary products and processes. However, the government proved reluctant to grant such protection in the absence of TI's agreement to license its technology. Such licensing—of process (not product) technology from Fairchild—actually did launch NEC's 1963 entry into the semiconductor industry.[55] And while other Japanese competitors expected to follow, their

[53]Industry-level data in this paragraph from the source cited in Figure 2-2.

[54]For further details, see Dennis J. Encarnation, "Cross-Investment: A Second Front of Economic Rivalry," in Thomas K. McCraw, ed., *America versus Japan: A Comparative Study of Business-Government Relations at the Harvard Business School* (Boston: Harvard Business School Press, 1986), pp. 123–124; Encarnation and Mason, "Neither MITI nor America," pp. 44–45; Mason, *American Multinationals and Japan,* chap. 4.

[55]Two years later, in 1965, Hitachi became the second Japanese semiconductor company, followed in 1966 by Toshiba and others; see Encarnation, "Cross-Investment," pp. 129.

progress remained blocked for a time by TI's stranglehold on critical patents, even as their demand for semiconductors grew with the introduction of the electronic calculator. To supply that demand, and to exploit technological barriers to entry, TI in 1963 set up a marketing office in Japan to distribute imports from America. Then, during 1964, TI sought to become IBM's principal semiconductor supplier in Japan, following a strategy already pursued with success back home in America. Unable to export from its home base to a growing market abroad, TI (like IBM before it) viewed high Japanese import barriers and the persistent threat of local competition as powerful incentives to invest directly in Japanese manufacturing—even as capital controls kept the multinational at bay.

Investment and Trade: 1966

While the Japanese government denied TI and other multinationals access to the local market, many Americans nonetheless negotiated entry, under either the FIL or the expanded yen-based regime. Between 1956 and 1966, in fact, U.S. FDI in Japan actually grew fivefold, from $140 million to $731 million (see Figure 2-1)—well above the threefold increase enjoyed by American multinationals in most other industrialized countries.[56] Of course, this rapid Japanese growth came on top of a very small base: Japan by 1966 accounted for only 2 percent of the cumulative stock of U.S. FDI in industrialized countries, admittedly twice its share a decade earlier. Germany, by comparison, accounted for nearly 8 percent of such stock invested in industrialized countries that same year, after growing over the previous decade at a rate greater than that in Japan. Perhaps the better comparisons were not with Germany and other industrialized countries, but rather with the resource-rich economies of Latin America. Indeed, Japan in 1966 hosted roughly the same cumulative levels of U.S. FDI found in Argentina, Chile, Panama, or Peru—but well below levels in Brazil, and

[56]For the cross-national comparisons in this paragraph, see Commerce Department, *U.S. Direct Investment Abroad, 1950–76*, table 1, pp. 7–17. By 1966, U.S. FDI in all industrialized countries had reached $35.3 billion, up from $12.4 billion in 1956. More specifically, in Germany, U.S. FDI grew sixfold between 1956 and 1966, from $450 million to $2.8 billion.

less than one-half the total value of all U.S. FDI in Mexico and Venezuela. Thus, in 1966, U.S. FDI in Japan still invited comparisons not with investments in other industrialized countries but with levels found in developing and newly-industrializing countries.

Much of this investment entered minority U.S.-owned joint ventures rather than majority subsidiaries, again following a pattern found in developing countries. Here, the data remain incomplete, since the U.S. Commerce Department through 1973 ignored all foreign joint ventures with U.S. equity of less than 25 percent. Nevertheless, the data that do exist suggest that Japan had more in common with developing India than with industrialized Germany. In Germany, as in most advanced economies, over 90 percent of all U.S. FDI entered majority subsidiaries.[57] But in India, as in Japan, that share fell closer to 70 percent—lower still if we add the large number of minority subsidiaries that, because of capital controls operative in the two countries, attracted less than 25 percent foreign equity. To avoid these controls, nearly all majority subsidiaries that entered Japan before 1964 did so as yen-based companies, accounting for 252 of the 342 majority subsidiaries permitted to enter through 1964 (see Figure 2-3). As noted above, these companies typically attracted much smaller foreign investments than did the minority joint ventures that predominated under the more onerous FIL-approval system—lending further credence to the contention that available statistics underestimate the relative position of minority affiliates. Indeed, through the FIL, over two-thirds (196 of 286) of all successful applicants entered Japan before 1964 as minority affiliates. In fact, before that date, the FIL accounted for nearly all (196 out of 233) minority affiliates that entered Japan. Only in India and a few other developing countries did American multinationals confront a regulatory regime that so strictly limited foreign ownership.[58]

Japan's regulatory regime also channeled U.S. FDI into key

---

[57]U.S. Commerce Department, Bureau of Economic Analysis, *United States Direct Investment Abroad, 1966: Final Data* (Washington, D.C.: USGPO, 1975), esp. tables A-2 and A-16, pp. 30, 44.

[58]For an examination of capital controls in India, see Encarnation, *Dislodging Multinationals*, esp. pp. 14–15, 198–199, 204.

industries, imitating patterns that could be found in both developing and industrialized countries.[59] For example, as in developing countries, the petroleum industry in Japan accounted during 1966 for roughly two-fifths of all U.S. FDI, nearly twice that industry's relative position in industrialized countries. In Japan, American oil companies exploited their oligopolistic control over upstream sources of crude oil, located principally in developing countries, to enter downstream refining and processing (followed distantly by distribution and marketing)—mimicking a pattern reminiscent of petroleum investments in other industrialized economies. Moreover, in such economies—as in Japan—manufacturing attracted one-half of all U.S. FDI, twice that sector's share in developing countries. Yet, even within manufacturing, Japan again stood out: Machinery accounted for nearly two-thirds of all U.S. FDI in Japanese manufacturing—more than twice that industry's relative share in other advanced economies, where chemicals (followed by metals and food products) also attracted a sizable share of manufacturing investments. In Japan, the more liberal yen-based regime did permit multinationals to operate in a broad range of industries. But under the FIL, multinationals in the machinery industry were relatively more successful than other manufacturers in securing government approval: in fact, machinery received one-half of all FIL approvals granted by the Japanese government to foreign manufacturers.[60] Thus, Japan's regulatory regime limited local production by foreign manufacturers to a very few industries—most notably, petroleum and machinery.

Local production by American multinationals remained so constrained, in fact, that majority subsidiaries generated smaller local sales than did U.S. exporters, whose access also remained restricted by Japan's import quotas and high tariffs. During 1966, for example, local sales by majority subsidiaries approached $2.0 billion, well below the $2.4 billion shipped to Japan by U.S. expor-

---

[59]For the cross-national comparisons in this paragraph, see Commerce Department, *U.S. Direct Investment Abroad, 1950–76,* table 1, pp. 17; Commerce Department, *Benchmark Survey: 1966,* p. 42.

[60]In fact, between 1950 and 1964, only 47 foreign machinery manufacturers entered Japan as yen-based companies, compared to 114 approved under the FIL regime; for source, see Figure 2-2 above.

ters.[61] By comparison, across most industrialized countries, majority subsidiaries recorded local sales three times larger than all U.S. exports to these markets. If one looks only at manufacturing, the ratio of local subsidiaries' sales to U.S. exports was over 2:1 in most industrialized countries. But in Japan that ratio actually reversed—meaning that U.S. exporters recorded sales in Japan twice those recorded by majority subsidiaries actually engaged in Japanese manufacturing. Thus, in Japan, capital controls on foreign investment had a more devastating impact on local production by American multinationals than did trade restrictions on U.S. exports.

Capital controls restricted not only local production but also U.S. exports, since American multinationals often relied on majority subsidiaries, especially in manufacturing, to create final markets and intermediary channels for intracompany shipments. In advanced economies, for example, U.S. multinational parents during 1966 shipped to their majority subsidiaries over one-quarter of all U.S. exports.[62] By contrast, in Japan, such intracompany trade contributed less than one-tenth of all U.S. exports ($0.2 billion out of $2.4 billion). American parents shipped three-fifths of that trade to their subsidiaries operating in Japanese wholesaling, where they leveraged $50 million in direct investments to generate $136 million in U.S. exports. Most of these wholesalers originally entered Japan as yen-based companies: indeed, of the 125 wholesalers established by all multinationals prior to the abolition of the yen-based regime in 1963, only sixteen received FIL approval (see Figure 2-3). Most existed expressly to market foreign products in Japan; in fact, for majority U.S.-owned wholesalers, American-made goods generated 80 percent of their total sales in Japan. By contrast, outside Japan, U.S. parents exported most (three-quarters) of their intracompany shipments to majority subsidiaries

[61]For sales data in this paragraph, see Commerce Department, *1966 Benchmark*, table L-2, p. 198; for trade data, see Commerce Department, "United States Trade with Major World Areas, 1965 and 1966," *Overseas Business Reports* (May, 1967), table 1, p. 3.

[62]For data on subsidiaries' trade in this paragraph, see Commerce Department, *1966 Benchmark*, tables E-2, E-5, E-16, and L-3, pp. 83, 86, 97, 199; for overall trade data, see Commerce Department, "United States Trade with Major World Areas, 1965 and 1966," pp. 3, 12; for U.S. FDI data, see Commerce Department, *Direct Investment Abroad, 1950–76*, table 1, p. 17.

manufacturing in advanced economies. But in Japan, majority U.S.-owned manufacturers received less than one-third of the exports shipped by their parents. Thus, by drastically limiting U.S. FDI in Japanese manufacturing, Japanese capital controls also had a devastating effect on intracompany trade, and especially on U.S. exports to Japan.

By 1966, these continued constraints on foreign investment and related trade had incited unprecedented foreign protests which, in turn, provoked extraordinary public debate in Japan.[63] During that year, for example, U.S. Commerce Secretary John Connor publicly characterized MITI's handling of TI's investment application as a transgression of the bilateral commerce treaty; he then called upon Japan to reduce restrictions on the flow of capital across its boundaries.[64] Immediately afterwards (in September) the Federation of Economic Organizations (*Keidanren*), representing Japan's leading enterprises, announced that its members favored only very modest deregulation. These sentiments found additional support in a separate poll of small- and medium-sized businesses, whose managers feared that capital liberalization was "still too early," even if Japan imposed a 50 percent ceiling on foreign ownership. Such ownership restrictions were viewed by the American Chamber of Commerce in Japan (ACCJ) as "the very antithesis of liberalization, the very essence of control," in one of its numerous reports documenting Tokyo's unrelenting opposition to the free flow of capital.[65] Nor was the Chamber alone; its European counterparts joined the critical chorus, as did their govern-

[63]As Johnson notes (*MITI and the Japanese Miracle*, p. 276), these pressures had been building steadily during 1965, as the slowness of Japan's compliance with the OECD's capital liberalization code became apparent to foreigners. For additional evidence, also see Encarnation and Mason, "Neither MITI nor America," pp. 38–42.

[64]His comments came on the heels of unusually heated exchanges over Japan's FDI controls, which marked the annual meeting of the high-level Joint U.S.-Japan Committee on Trade and Economic Affairs. See, for example, Secretary Connor's comments at a joint meeting of the ACCJ and the American–Japan Society, reported in the *Journal of the American Chamber of Commerce in Japan* (Aug. 1966), pp. 25–29. For the subsequent Japanese response, see ibid., Dec. 27, 1966 and ibid., Sept. 13, 1966.

[65]While this quotation comes from *Journal of the ACCJ* (October 1970), p. 10, it aptly reflects the sentiments that ACCJ members expressed in their several publications throughout the entire process of capital liberalization.

ments and the OECD—which reported that Japanese FDI policies remained "excessively restrictive."[66]

By contrast, Japan's leading dailies wondered in print whether their nation was restrictive enough, as their front pages discussed the impending threat of a "foreign capital invasion," the "merits" and "demerits" of "capital liberalization," and the nature of the most appropriate national response to mounting foreign pressures for change.[67] Finally, responsibility for responding fell to the FIDC which had just been reconstituted with the appointment of an unprecedented majority of industry representatives.[68] Now reflecting opinions widely shared among Japanese business leaders, this reorganized FIDC (along with MITI's Industrial Structure Council) announced that "liberalization should not be influenced by 'foreign pressure,' but [instead by] consideration of improvement of industrial structure and stability of the international balance of payments."[69] As a leading Japanese newspaper reported, "the program for decontrol of foreign capital was worked out carefully with the utmost consideration of the views and positions of individual industries."[70] Once again, Japanese oligopolists had acted to mediate their government's response to foreign demands; making use of their key position, they controlled both the timing and substance of the next step in the evolution of their country's strategic investment policy.

STAGE II: CAPITAL AND TRADE LIBERALIZATION

"Our country has been endeavoring to strengthen its ties with the international economic community through such means as the

[66]Iwao Hoshii, "Japan's Liberalization of Direct Investment," *Journal of the ACCJ* (March 1967), p. 12. In particular, the OECD's Business and Industrial Advisory Committee openly condemned Japanese FDI policies, and its Capital Transaction section reported that Japanese FDI policies remained "excessively restrictive." Subsequent meetings of the OECD's Committee on Invisible Transactions and the Joint U.S.-Japan Committee—both scheduled for June, 1967—promised still stronger foreign criticism unless Tokyo liberalized its FDI policies.

[67]At least as early as 1964, the *Nihon Keizai Shimbun* employed bold headlines to announce actual and expected changes in foreign capital controls (see, for example, the issue of Jan. 19, 1964), and to detail visits by prominent foreign industrialists suspected of probing the market for investment prospects. Soon, a full spectrum of Japanese periodicals and newspapers joined in the public debate.

[68]Encarnation and Mason, "Neither MITI nor America," pp. 41–42.

[69]Quoted in *Journal of the ACCJ*, Jan. 1967.

[70]*Japan Economic Journal*, June 6, 1967.

liberalization of international trade and foreign exchange. . . . Now we are prepared to move ahead also with the liberalization of capital movements."[71] With this statement of June 1967, the Japanese government announced the opening of a projected four-phase program of capital liberalization, scheduled to begin operation within thirty days. No longer would case-by-case screening of FIL applications represent the sole procedure available to foreign investors seeking access to the Japanese market. Foreigners could, in addition, receive "automatic approval" for their FIL applications when they proposed to acquire a small equity stake in existing Japanese companies;[72] or when they proposed to establish new companies in those product groups specifically enumerated by the government in either of two "positive" lists. The first list specified products for which majority foreign-owned subsidiaries would receive automatic approval; the second, products for which approval would be extended to minority and equal-partnership joint ventures. Overall, by putting these procedures into place, Japan took what could have been a giant step toward granting foreign multinationals greater access to the Japanese market for their local production and related trade. As it slowly unfolded, however, the truth became something quite different.

The Unraveling of Regulations

To the surprise of few who knew the country well, Japan's march toward capital liberalization proceeded at a snail's pace, with every step introducing new complications. Deciding which product groups to open to foreign investment eventually proved an especially onerous task. Each government ministry resisted including any industry under its jurisdiction; each preferred instead to list

[71]Quoted in *The Japan Times*, June 7, 1967, p. 7.

[72]Under these new rules, no single foreign shareholder could own more than 7 percent in an existing Japanese company; the earlier limit had been 5 percent. Three or more such foreign shareholders could now hold up to 20 percent of the equity in any existing Japanese company that operated in a so-called non-restricted industry, up from 15 percent under earlier rules. Otherwise, if the Japanese company operated in a restricted industry, combined foreign shareholdings could not exceed 15 percent, up from 10 percent earlier. These restricted industries included: several utilities (including water, electricity, gas, and broadcasting), most of the transportation sector (expressly road, rail, and marine), some extractive industries (specifically fishery and mining), and the entire financial sector.

some alternate industry, which inevitably lay outside of its own purview. In addition, MITI already had determined that fully 90 percent of all Japanese industry could not be regarded as "sufficiently competitive" to permit foreign investment inflows.[73] Finally, bureaucratic infighting created a stalemate that could be broken only when the FIDC's chairman appealed directly to the prime minister, who personally ordered the transportation ministry to open shipbuilding to limited foreign investment. Other ministries soon followed suit by making equally modest concessions; MOF, for example, continued to argue that beer remained the only industry under its jurisdiction that could be fully opened to foreign investment in 1967. Yet, in the end, the government did open seventeen products to majority foreign-owned subsidiaries, during the first phase of capital liberalization, and another thirty-three products to minority foreign-owned and equal-partnership joint ventures. At no point in this process, however, did prospects seem optimistic. One Tokyo law firm, for example, after examining the actual list of products enumerated by the government, went ahead to advise its foreign clients: "an unarticulated special condition applicable to 'industries' in the 100% 'automatic validation' category is that there be a strong presumption that the investment, if 'automatically validated,' will not be economically viable."[74] This dim view was shared by Japanese business: the daily press reported that managers responded "calmly" to the government's phase-one announcements.[75] And foreign investors remained calmer still: not one submitted an application for "automatic approval" during the first ten months following the opening of phase one, in September 1967. Subsequently, for the remaining nine months of this phase ending in March 1969, only four such applications were both submitted and approved; the four totaled less than $2.2

[73]Quoted in the *Japan Economic Journal*, Dec. 13, 1966; for subsequent maneuvering by MITI and MOF, see Encarnation and Mason, "Neither MITI nor America," p. 42.

[74]Quoted from a memorandum entitled "The July 1, 1967 Capital Liberalization Program—A Selective Analysis and Evaluation" and included in Richard W. Rabinowitz, ed., *The Law of Foreign Investment in Postwar Japan: Material for a Course in Comparative Law*, Part X (Cambridge: Harvard Law School, 1988), p. 67.

[75]*Japan Economic Journal*, May 2, 1967 and May 14, 1968.

million.[76] Of course such minuscule investments could do little to expand local production and related trade by foreign multinationals.

Outside of listed product groups, prospects for foreigners did not improve, because case-by-case screening was still required for FIL approval. Here again, few investors succeeded in establishing majority foreign-owned subsidiaries in Japan. One of these, Texas Instruments (TI), finally concluded during 1968—after four long years of fighting—its battle for permission to construct a semiconductor plant in Japan.[77] Actually, TI cut a separate deal with MITI midway through the first phase of capital liberalization, but only after several Japanese electronics companies had reversed their earlier opposition to foreign competition at home. That reversal, in turn, followed two key realizations by Japanese companies: first, that Texas Instruments would not license its valuable integrated circuit patents to them until it had gained permission to build and wholly-own a local plant; and second, that TI would never permit products containing patent-infringed semiconductors to enter the U.S. and European markets, from Japan or from elsewhere. These two conditions became crystal clear in 1968, when Japan's total domestic production of semiconductors—after five years of increasingly intensive activity—still amounted to less than 10 percent of TI's total world production. So now with no alternatives in sight, "lots of [Japanese] companies wanted that IC [integrated circuit] technology," as Sony's Chairman Morita Akio later recalled, and these Japanese oligopolists pressured MITI to approve direct investment in Japan by Texas Instruments.[78]

Not before that time did Texas Instruments win its demand for a wholly-owned subsidiary; and then, not without agreeing to grant MITI and TI's Japanese competitors three important concessions: First, TI agreed to establish an equal-partnership joint venture

[76]Allan Pearl, "Liberalization of Capital in Japan—Part II," *Harvard Law Review* 13 (Spring 1972), p. 269.

[77]Unless otherwise specified in this paragraph and the next, for the following account of TI, see Encarnation, "Cross-Investment," p. 123–124; James Abegglen, *Kaisha, the Japanese Corporation* (New York: Basic Books, 1985), pp. 221–222; Mason, *American Multinationals and Japan*, pp. 150–198.

[78]Morita Akio, *Made in Japan* (New York: E.P. Dutton, 1986), p. 193.

with a Japanese electronics company. Here, one candidate, Mitsubishi Electric, was both a major buyer of integrated circuits and a potential competitor; while a second, Sony, emerged as another major buyer but one unlikely to become a potent competitor. In the end, Sony won out. (Indeed, TI and MITI reportedly hammered out their final deal at Sony President Morita's private residence.) Although few knew it at the time, TI's joint venture with Sony originally was scheduled to last only three years—just long enough for MITI to claim that the arrangement represented no new precedent regarding foreign ownership. By 1971, Sony had completed the sale of its equity holdings to TI at a prearranged price. Until that date, as a second concession, TI agreed to "consult" with MITI about local production and market shares attained by TI's Japanese subsidiary. Finally, by agreeing to make its proprietary technology available to Japanese companies for a 3.5 percent licensing fee—well below the percentage demanded elsewhere—TI granted its Japanese competitors an unprecedented concession. Once again, now from the TI agreement, one lesson emerged: Japanese oligopolists could control the timing and substance of a foreign multinational's entry into the home market; and indeed, they had colluded with government to extract from TI a very high price for liberalization.

For its part, Texas Instruments gained market access otherwise denied to foreign competitors, who were kept at bay by tariff barriers, capital controls, technology restrictions, and other such regulations. In fact, aside from TI, IBM became the only foreign semiconductor manufacturer to establish a plant in Japan (a wholly foreign-owned subsidiary for its own internal supply) during the early phases of capital liberalization. All other foreigners were forced to settle for licensing agreements or, at the conclusion of the fourth phase of capital liberalization, for a single equal-partnership joint venture.[79] By comparison, Motorola—soon to

[79]In fact, among TI's foreign competitors, Fairchild was the first to license its semiconductor technology to a Japanese firm (NEC, in 1959), and the second (after TI) to establish an assembly plant (in 1969) in the Japanese archipelago. However, that wholly foreign-owned transistor and diode assembly plant was established in Okinawa, still a U.S. protectorate with preferential access to the Japanese market. Earlier, MITI had refused to allow Fairchild to establish its subsidiary on the

emerge as TI's principal U.S. competitor—was "discouraged" (according to Motorola CEO Robert Galvin) by MITI and Japanese electronics companies from investing in semiconductor manufacturing.[80] So, Motorola settled in 1968 for the right to open a small Japanese sales office and to market a few imports from the United States, while closely monitoring TI's Japanese expansion. That successful expansion, in fact, signalled TI's development of technological prowess, its control of market access overseas, and its skillful bargaining to exploit firm-specific assets. All these things also worked to speed the formation of Japanese political coalitions determined to help craft mutually beneficial agreements with at least a few multinationals.

Just as continued screening of FIL applications held multinationals at bay, so too did the Japanese system of "positive lists" and "automatic approvals," which persisted through the second phase of capital liberalization, beginning March 1969. During this phase, fresh inflows of foreign investment actually declined: from $2.2 million during the nineteen months of phase one, to $1.7 million during the eighteen months of phase two.[81] Such decline vindicated the opinion expressed by the *Nihon Kaizei Shimbun*, Japan's leading business daily: "it is not necessary to make a big fuss over this second phase," given so few substantive changes.[82] Once again, government ministries proved reluctant to offer industries under their jurisdiction as candidates for liberalization. As a result, during phase two the number of product groups finally opened to majority subsidiaries increased by only forty-four, while the number opened to minority and equal-partnership joint ventures grew by a slightly larger figure, sixty. These products included wigs, soy

---

Japanese mainland; so when Okinawa reverted to Japanese control in May 1972, MITI forced Fairchild to merge its plant in a joint venture with a Japanese competitor. By then, National Semiconductor had also established a wholly foreign-owned plant in Okinawa after failing to secure MITI's approval to enter the Japanese mainland. But unlike Fairchild, National refused to reorganize as a joint venture after 1972. For the evolution of foreign investment in the Japanese semiconductor industry, see Encarnation, "Cross-Investment," p. 124.

[80]Quoted in Mason, *American Multinationals and Japan*, pp. 150–198.

[81]Pearl, "Liberalization of Capital in Japan," p. 269.

[82]*Nihon Keizai Shimbun*, Nov. 11, 1968, as quoted in *Journal of the ACCJ* (Feb. 1969), p. 30.

sauce, and oatmeal—among the more unlikely targets for foreign investment—but not automobiles and other so-called strategic industries, for which MITI reportedly argued that liberalization would be too "difficult" to undertake given the consolidation currently underway.[83] MITI itself had initiated that consolidation as one of several countermeasures designed to stifle the unwanted entry of foreign competitors.

But in automobiles, at least, industry consolidation actually accelerated foreign investment, as smaller Japanese automakers sought alternatives to unwanted, MITI-initiated mergers. Their alternative strategy first came to public attention during May 1969, less than three months after the beginning of phase two, when a vice president of Mitsubishi Heavy Industries (head of its then-unprofitable passenger car division) returned to Tokyo from secret meetings in Detroit. At the airport he announced, to MITI's surprise, that Mitsubishi and Chrysler had just signed a letter of understanding to establish a manufacturing joint-venture assembling automobiles, for sale locally and through Chrysler's global dealer network.[84] Termed the "Mitsubishi shock," the pact with Chrysler both scuttled MITI's forced merger of smaller Japanese automakers with either Toyota or Nissan, and defied MITI's ban on foreign investment prior to restructuring. Then, following Mitsubishi's lead, Toyo Kogyo (later renamed Mazda) initiated its own discussions with Ford—as did Isuzu with General Motors. Like Mitsubishi, Isuzu and Mazda were both experiencing financial troubles; so in exchange for cash, design capabilities, and (especially) overseas distribution, both offered U.S. partners reliable sources of supply and limited access to the Japanese market. But these exchanges did not take place until MITI had galvanized substantial domestic opposition, and until all other domestic options had been explored. Only then (in the late 1970s) could U.S.

[83]*Japan Economic Journal*, Jan. 16, 1968 (and other issues).

[84]Johnson, *MITI and the Japanese Miracle*, esp. pp. 172–73; William C. Duncan, *U.S.–Japan Automobile Diplomacy: A Study in Economic Confrontation* (Cambridge, Mass.: Ballinger, 1973), esp. pp. 31–52, 83–95; Nihon Keizai Shimbun Kogyobu, ed., *Where Is Domestic Manufacturing Headed? The Invasion of Foreign Capital and Reorganization [Kokusan wa doko e yuku ka: gaishi jyouriku to saihensei]* (Tokyo, 1969), p. 1; Tadaki Yoshi, *Mitsubishi Motor Company [Mitsubishi jidousha kogyou]* (Tokyo: Asahi Sonorama, 1980), pp. 35–41.

automakers conclude minority-owned joint ventures for local production and export sales.

While MITI did slow the entry of American multinationals into the Japanese auto industry, it could do nothing to reverse that trend while Japan and the United States were embroiled in a bitter textile trade dispute. That dispute officially began during 1968, and by December, according to Krause and Sekiguchi, "a political decision was made really to open the economy to foreign competition"—though admittedly "the change was to take place over a three-year period rather than immediately."[85] Spurred by the Kennedy Round negotiations of the GATT (1963–72), Japan dismantled much of what had remained of its postwar trade regime, and even reversed its earlier efforts at trade liberalization. In particular, by 1970 Japan had effectively (if not legislatively) abolished its decades-old system of import deposits. And by 1972, Japan had cut its import quotas in half: from 161 to 79, where they would remain well into the 1980s.[86] Next, rather than compensate for reduced quotas by raising tariffs, Japan actually slashed tariffs, reducing nominal rates along an escalating value-added chain, from raw materials (2–3 percent nominal tariff) to intermediate products (9–10 percent) on to final goods (11 percent). As a result, by 1972, the average effective rate of protection on consumer goods reached 14 percent, one-half the rate of 1968, and no more than one-fifth the rate in effect a decade earlier, when in 1961 Japan suffered an unprecedented $1 billion current account deficit. Ten years later, Japan enjoyed an equally unprecedented $6 billion surplus on that account. The United States, by contrast, suffered in 1971 its first global trade deficit in seventy-eight years, valued at over $2 billion. The resulting "Nixon shocks" then precipitated a revaluation of the yen—which the Japanese government sought to limit by reducing its current account surpluses. These surpluses, in turn, encouraged further relaxation of trade and capital controls.

Still, even as Japan amassed record-high surpluses on its current

[85]Krause and Sekiguchi, "Japan and the World Economy," pp. 426–427.

[86]For data in this paragraph on quotas, tariffs, and effective rates of protection, see Komiya and Itoh, "Japan's International Trade and Trade Policy," table 4, p. 192.

account, its capital liberalization progressed slowly and unevenly. On paper, the Japanese government during 1970 lengthened its "positive lists" and expanded its "automatic approvals" in still another (the third) phase of capital liberalization. Yet, foreign acquisitions of existing Japanese companies continued to be impossible in practice, since foreign equity purchases greater than 25 percent (with individual foreign holdings in excess of 7 percent) still required case-by-case screening.[87] A similar screening also awaited those new majority foreign-owned subsidiaries that expected to invest outside of the 138 product groups (including the seventy-seven added during phase three) enumerated in the government's cumulative "positive lists." Only minority and equal-partnership joint ventures offered real prospects for growth, since the government had extended "automatic approval" to minority-foreign and equal-partnership joint ventures producing another 447 product groups on its positive list (in addition to the 193 already enumerated in phases one and two). Foreign multinationals remained unimpressed, however: during the eleven months of phase three, they established only forty-seven subsidiaries and joint ventures, totaling less than $9 million, in all product groups designated for automatic approval.[88] Again, such limited investment did little to increase either local production or intracompany trade by foreign multinationals.

The Japanese government continued to omit automobiles from its positive list, even though the Mitsubishi shock had occurred a full year earlier. To provide some corrective, during 1971, MITI finally (albeit reluctantly) deregulated foreign investment in automobiles and in five related industries. Only then, eight months into phase three, did the Japanese government finally approve Mitsubishi's 1969 application to establish a joint venture—but not until that company had agreed to sell Chrysler its 35 percent share

[87]As restricted in phase one, no single foreign shareholder could own more than 7 percent in an existing Japanese company, whose total foreign shareholdings could now reach 25 percent (up from 20 percent in phase one) only if that company operated in a nonrestricted industry. Otherwise, if that company operated in a restricted industry, total foreign shareholdings still (as in phase one) could not exceed 15 percent.

[88]Pearl, "Liberalization of Capital in Japan," p. 269.

in small increments over the next three years.[89] Once again, the government could limit foreign ownership, but it could not deny foreign access to the local market without the support of Japanese oligopolists.

From Public Regulations to Private Restrictions

For these oligopolists, private restrictions increasingly replaced government regulations as effective deterrents to foreign entry. Here, the structure of Japanese industry proved its value, as industrial organizations, especially former *zaibatsu*, brought together financial institutions, manufacturing enterprises, and trading companies. Again, consider the Japanese automobile industry, where Mitsubishi proved capable of simultaneously rejecting MITI's forced consolidation of the industry and spurning Chrysler's overtures for increased market access and managerial control. These, Mitsubishi controlled in at least two ways: First, contractual constraints on both foreign equity holdings and the dispersal of shareholdings prohibited Chrysler from increasing its shareholdings above 35 percent without Mitsubishi's approval, and they also obliged Chrysler to offer Mitsubishi the right of first refusal should Chrysler sell its shareholdings in the venture.[90] Second, cross-shareholdings among affiliated firms assured the former Mitsubishi *zaibatsu* unassailable control over all outstanding equity. Such cross-shareholdings were common in Japanese industry, and they grew dramatically during the decade preceding capital liberalization as one of several countermeasures to stifle unwanted foreign takeovers.[91] Indeed, cross-shareholdings helped to shape Mitsubishi's strategy, according to its chief negotiator: "We view this

[89]*Japan Economic Journal*, June 15, 1971.

[90]Mark Mason, *American Multinationals and Japan*, pp. 150–198.

[91]In fact, cross-shareholdings within the Mitsubishi group nearly doubled between 1964 and 1973, from 13 percent to 24 percent of the total outstanding equity recorded by Mitsubishi-related companies. While few other former zaibatsu could boast of such large cross-shareholding, all could boast of rapid growth; in Mitsui, for example, cross-shareholdings jumped from 9 percent in 1964 to 15 percent in 1973. For data, see Nakashima Shuzo, *Cross-Shareholdings and Enterprise Law [Kabushiki no mochiai to kigyou hou]* (Tokyo: Commercial Law Centre, 1990), table 6, p. 47.

relationship as one of Chrysler with the Mitsubishi group rather than as one between Chrysler and the Mitsubishi Motor Corporation."[92] For Mitsubishi, as for other Japanese conglomerates, cross-shareholdings and contractual provisions insured that their American partners would remain in the minority, able to exercise little managerial control.

Smaller Japanese automakers, with fewer private safeguards at their disposal, proved more reticent in pursuing foreign partners. Financially-troubled Isuzu, for example, approached GM only after Nissan had rejected Isuzu's overtures, and at the insistence of Isuzu's principal shareholders.[93] As in most Japanese business conglomerates (*keiretsu*), these large shareholders consisted of Isuzu's lead bank (Dai-Ichi) and a large trading company (C. Itoh) that exported Isuzu trucks, plus its largest suppliers of capital equipment (Hitachi) and of raw materials (Nippon Steel). Even then, Isuzu and its backers demanded that GM restrict its shareholdings to 34.2 percent for the first five years of the joint venture and below 50 percent subsequently. They could enforce these restrictions through cross-shareholdings and through other relations as buyers, creditors, and suppliers. Similarly, Toyo Kogyo's (Mazda's) principal creditor and major shareholder (Sumitomo Bank) forced a merger with Ford—but not until financial losses had forced Sumitomo to replace a reticent Mazda management, after almost a decade of on-again, off-again negotiations. Throughout, Sumitomo remained committed to retaining majority Japanese ownership of Mazda, and finally demanded that Ford both limit its initial acquisition to 25 percent of Mazda's equity and pledge never to seek a controlling interest in Mazda. Equally unlikely was a hostile takeover, given Japanese business practices. With the liberalization of government policy, just such private practices became the most effective restrictions on foreign investment in Japan.

As private restrictions replaced public regulations, the govern-

[92]Statement attributed to a vice president of Mitsubishi Heavy Industries (head of its passenger-car division), and quoted in Henderson, *Foreign Enterprise in Japan*, p. 264.

[93]For a postwar history of U.S. FDI in the Japanese auto industry through 1980, see Mason, *American Multinationals and Japan*, chap. 4, "The Screen Door: 1950–1970" and chap. 5, "The Inner Door: 1970–1980."

ment in August 1971 announced with little fanfare its fourth—
and, as the government stated at the time, its "final"—round of
capital liberalization. Still, foreign acquisitions of Japanese companies remained difficult: automatic approval did not extend to
individual foreign shareholdings in excess of 10 percent of total
equity (up from 7 percent earlier); larger individual acquisitions
still required case-by-case screening.[94] Fresh investments in new
projects, by contrast, enjoyed more liberal treatment, when the
government extended automatic approval to the establishment
of majority foreign-owned subsidiaries in another 228 product
groups—nearly twice the total number liberalized in the three
prior phases. Moreover, minority and equal-partnership joint ventures were no longer limited to product groups enumerated on a
positive list; they would now receive automatic approval unless
they sought to enter industries expressly proscribed in the government's new "negative list."[95]

Semiconductors appeared among the several industries where
50:50 joint ventures were now assured automatic approval. Motorola responded immediately by turning to Alps, a Japanese electronics manufacturer with which it had a long relationship.[96] As
far back as the early 1960s, Motorola had established a purchasing
office in Tokyo to buy from Alps (and others) electronic components for the consumer goods (principally TVs) and automotive
products (principally car radios) that Motorola manufactured in
the United States. By 1967, Motorola had expanded this relationship and established a joint venture with Alps to manufacture car

[94]Up from 7 percent in phase one, such individual foreign shareholdings in
existing enterprises could still not total more than 25 percent in nonrestricted
industries or 15 percent in restricted industries.

[95]During phase four, that negative list included data processing and six other
broad product groups, plus a still-undefined category of so-called new industries
requiring case-by-case screening.

[96]For this history of Motorola in Japan, see Clyde V. Prestowitz, Jr., *Trading
Places: How We Allowed Japan to Take the Lead* (New York: Basic Books, 1988);
David B. Yoffie, "Motorola and Japan (A)," Harvard Business School Case
no. 9-388-056; Chalmers Johnson, "MITI, MPT, and the Telecom Wars: How
Japan Makes Policy for High Technology," in Berkeley Roundtable on the International Economy, ed., *Creating Advantage: American and Japanese Strategies for Adjusting
to Change in a New World Economy* (Berkeley: BRIE, 1987); Mason, *American Multinationals and Japan*, pp. 199–242.

radios, also for export back to the United States. With the partial liberalization of semiconductors in 1971, Motorola again turned to Alps, this time to establish a semiconductor fabrication plant in Japan. By 1975, however, their joint venture failed, just as Japan fully liberalized foreign investment in the semiconductor industry. That liberalization and the Alps debacle together led Motorola to reconsider its entire strategy in the Japanese semiconductor industry. As a result, an expanded sales operation (1976), a design center (1978), and an equal-partnership joint venture to manufacture MOS wafers (in 1980, with Toko) soon followed.[97] Yet even with these several investments, Motorola's presence in the Japanese semiconductor industry remained limited into the 1980s as the company struggled to overcome the legacy of Japanese capital controls, whose deleterious effects lingered well after their formal abolition.

But at least Motorola had some presence in Japan, which is more than numerous other American multinationals could claim. With no more fear of a "foreign capital invasion," the Japanese government announced a fifth and (once again, according to the government) "final" phase of capital liberalization, beginning half-way through 1976. By then, several other American multinationals had taken advantage of the opportunity to invest in Japan. In fact, during the first decade of capital liberalization, ending in 1977, U.S. FDI in Japan actually grew sixfold, from $731 million to $4.6 billion (see Figure 2-1 above)—twice the rate apparent in other industrialized countries.[98] Nevertheless, despite such rapid growth, the absolute level of U.S. FDI in Japan seemed to have less in common with investments in other advanced economies than with the newly industrializing countries of Latin America. In fact, three such countries (Brazil, Mexico, and Venezuela) each continued to host more American multinationals than did Japan (through the

[97]As for other changes in Motorola's strategy: by 1974, Motorola had sold its consumer products division to Matsushita, as we shall see in chap. 3; by 1978, Motorola had terminated its joint venture with Alps manufacturing car radios, and then exited the car radio industry by 1980. Then, by 1982, Motorola acquired the remaining 50 percent of the manufacturing venture with Toko.

[98]Commerce Department, *U.S. Direct Investment Abroad, 1950–76*, table 1, p. 27; and *U.S. Direct Investment Abroad, 1977–81*, table 1, p. 1.

Figure 2-4. U.S. FDI in Japan by industry, 1977 vs. 1982

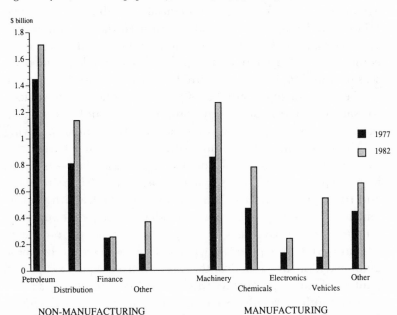

Sources: U.S. Department of Commerce, Bureau of Economic Analysis *U.S. Direct Investment Abroad: Balance of Payments and Direct Investment Position Estimates, 1977– 81* (Washington, D.C.: USGPO, Nov. 1986), table 1, p. 5; U.S. Department of Commerce, Bureau of Economic Analysis, "U.S. Direct Investment Abroad in 1983," *Survey of Current Business* (Aug. 1984), table 12, p. 29.

1970s), a preeminence Brazil retained for another decade. So, with U.S. FDI still at relatively low levels, Japan risked little when, in 1979, its government finally moved both to abolish the FIL and to amend the FECL—thus codifying the major changes wrought by twelve years of capital liberalization.[99] Effective March 1980, simple government notification replaced licensing applications as the essential precondition for foreign investment in Japan.

American automakers were among the most immediate beneficiaries of Japan's abolition of formal capital controls, with their investments growing faster than U.S. FDI in other Japanese in-

[99]The FECL was actually amended in December 1979, although these amendment (Law No. 65 of 1979) did not take effect until December 1980, a full year later.

dustries (see Figure 2-4).[100] In 1977, a new bank-imposed management team took charge of financially troubled Toyo Kogyo (Mazda) and reopened negotiations with Ford, following a five-year hiatus. By 1980, these negotiations granted Ford a 25 percent equity stake in Mazda. In exchange for cash, technology, and overseas distribution, Ford thus secured limited access to the Japanese market and a Japanese supplier of parts, components, and vehicles for sale in America. Still, Ford's progress in Japan failed to keep pace with GM's expanding investments. That company, having concluded another joint venture with Isuzu in 1976, emerged as a principal financier of its still-troubled Japanese affiliate—as well as its principal customer, consuming 40 percent of Isuzu's total car and truck production by 1981. In that year, GM and five of its affiliates (including its German subsidiary, Opel) renewed their long-term supply contracts for parts and components from Isuzu. Also in 1981, GM acquired a 5.3 percent stake in a second Japanese automaker, Suzuki, in a deal that also involved equity swaps and joint marketing agreements with Isuzu. As a result, Isuzu and Suzuki jointly developed small cars for sale in both the United States and Japan. Again in 1981, GM also acquired 20 percent in a Japanese supplier (Kyoritsu) of automobile electronics, the first of several moves that increased GM's purchase and export of Japanese-made parts, principally to America. Thus, for GM and Ford, minority-owned Japanese affiliates became important offshore sources of imported cars, sub-assemblies, and components (see Figure 2-5).

Offshore Sourcing

For U.S. automakers in Japan, direct investment and a related trade imbalance actually grew in tandem: between 1977 and 1982, a sixfold increase in auto investments (see Figure 2-4), nearly all in minority U.S. affiliates, brought a sixfold increase in U.S. imports from these affiliates (according to Figure 2-5). No other American investors in Japan shipped so aggressively back to their home market; in fact, total U.S. imports shipped by *all* other such inves-

[100]For the recent history of Ford and GM in Japan, see Mason, *American Multinationals and Japan,* chap. 5; and Joseph L. Badaracco, Jr., "General Motors' Asian Alliances," Harvard Business School Case, no. 9-388-094 rev. 5/88.

Figure 2-5. U.S. investment-related trade with Japan, 1977 vs. 1982

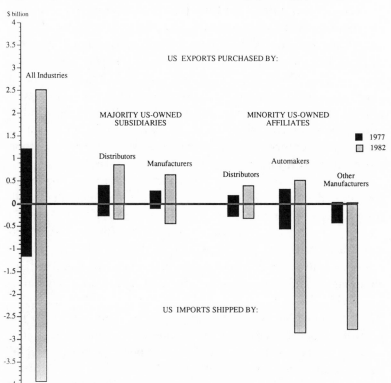

Sources: U.S. Commerce Department, Bureau of Economic Analysis, *U.S. Direct Investment Abroad, 1977* (Washington, D.C.: USGPO, 1981), tables II.I.3, II.I.19, III.I.3, and III.I.19, pp. 154, 158, 338, 354; U.S. Commerce Department, Bureau of Economic Analysis, *U.S. Direct Investment Abroad, 1982* (Washington, D.C.: USGPO, April 1984), tables II.G.3, II.G.20, III.G.3, III.G.20, pp. 127, 131, 266, 283; U.S. Commerce Department, International Trade Administration, Office of Trade and Investment Analysis, *U.S. Foreign Trade Highlights: 1982* (Washington, D.C.: USGPO, 1983).

tors barely exceeded $1 billion. Moreover, except for U.S. subsidiaries in Canada, U.S. affiliates in no other country contributed so greatly to American auto imports.[101] For minority U.S.-owned

[101]Commerce Department, *1977 Benchmark*, Tables II.I.3, II.I.19, III.I.3, and III.I.19, pp. 154, 158, 338, 354; U.S. Commerce Department, Bureau of Economic Analysis, *U.S. Direct Investment Abroad, 1982* (Washington, D.C.: USGPO, April 1984), Tables II.G.3, II.G.20, III.G.3, III.G.20, pp. 127, 131, 266, 283; U.S. Com-

automakers in Japan, the United States had become a fast-growing market, contributing one-fifth of their combined sales during 1982—twice their contribution in 1977. Most (three-fifths) of these American sales came during 1982 from intracompany shipments to their U.S. parents, either GM, Ford, or Chrysler. In reverse, however, the "Big Three" exported very little from the United States to their Japanese affiliates. As a result, as we see from Figure 2-5, minority U.S.-owned automakers during 1982 sold $2.8 billion more in the United States than they bought from the United States—a difference equal to nearly 15 percent of America's total trade deficit with Japan.

Outside the auto industry, however, American multinationals contributed more to U.S. exports, and actually generated small trade surpluses for the United States (see Figure 2-5), following a strategy of intracompany trade common to other industrialized countries.[102] In such countries, and in Japan, majority subsidiaries became the most important final markets and intermediary channels for U.S. exports. In fact, between 1977 and 1982, majority subsidiaries in Japan doubled their purchases of U.S. exports (from $1.2 billion to $2.5 billion), and thus kept pace with the growth of total U.S. exports to Japan—leaving them with a constant 12 percent contribution to U.S. exports to Japan.[103] This contribution, however, still fell well below the share (21 percent) recorded in other industrialized countries. Such different contributions reflected two simple facts: First, majority subsidiaries, the principal market for intracompany trade, accounted for over three-quarters of all sales by American multinationals—more than twice their share (32 percent) in Japan. And second, outside Japan, manufacturing subsidiaries accounted for a larger share of both U.S. FDI and intracompany trade than they did in Japan. Thus, the lower incidence of majority subsidiaries in Japanese manufac-

---

merce Department, International Trade Administration, Office of Trade and Investment Analysis, *U.S. Foreign Trade Highlights: 1982* (Washington, D.C.: USGPO, 1983).

[102]For cross-national comparisons, see the citations in note 101.

[103]For overall U.S. trade, see U.S. Commerce Department, International Trade Administration, Office of Trade and Investment Analysis, *U.S. Foreign Trade Highlights: 1989* (Washington, D.C.: USGPO, Sept. 1990), pp. 31, 36.

turing continued to deny American multinationals the same degree of market access they otherwise exploited to sell their exports in other industrialized countries.

Nevertheless, the growth of majority subsidiaries in Japan did allow American multinationals to sell more locally than they and other U.S. exporters shipped to Japan, again following a strategy common to other industrialized countries. In Japan, during 1982, majority subsidiaries accounted for one-third (32 percent) of the sales by all U.S. investors, up from one-quarter in 1977.[104] Nearly all (over 90 percent) of these sales came from the local market, where during 1982 they reached $24 billion—more than the $21 billion shipped to Japan that same year by all U.S. exporters. Yet majority subsidiaries actually produced locally few of the goods that they sold locally. Indeed, domestic sales of locally manufactured goods (valued at $5.9 billion during 1982) continued to lag far behind U.S. manufactured exports to Japan (valued at $10.0 billion). In most industrialized countries, the ratio of local production to U.S. exports was reversed, with locally produced sales two-and-a-half times larger than U.S. manufactured exports to these markets.[105] In such advanced economies, American multinationals generally managed to manufacture more goods abroad for sale locally than U.S. exporters shipped from America. Once again, the lower incidence of majority subsidiaries, especially in Japanese manufacturing, reduced the access of American multinationals to the Japanese market. In this instance, limited local production by manufacturing subsidiaries granted American multinationals even less market access than enjoyed by (otherwise constrained) U.S. exporters to Japan.

Decontrol and De-Liberalization

After 1982, U.S. FDI in Japanese manufacturing increased dramatically (see Figure 2-6), led by investments in chemicals. Within

---

[104]Commerce Department, *1977 Benchmark*, table II.I.3 and II.I.19, pp. 154, 158; Commerce Department, *1982 Benchmark*, table II.D.3 and III.E.1, pp. 111, 225.

[105]For sales data, see citations in note 104; for trade data see Commerce Department, *U.S. Foreign Trade Highlights, 1989*, p. 31.

Figure 2-6. U.S. FDI in Japan by industry, 1982 vs. 1988

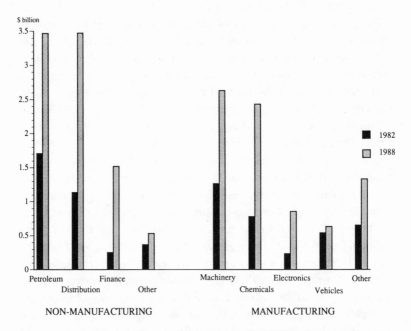

Sources: U.S. Department of Commerce, Bureau of Economic Analysis, "U.S. Direct Investment Abroad in 1983," *Survey of Current Business* (Aug. 1984), table 12, p. 29; U.S. Department of Commerce, Bureau of Economic Analysis, "U.S. Direct Investment Abroad: Detail for Position and Balance of Payments Flows, 1989," *Survey of Current Business* (Aug. 1990), table 44, p. 95.

chemicals, pharmaceuticals proved especially attractive when the Japanese government moved to cut health-care costs by decontrolling pharmaceutical prices during the early 1980s. By then, Japanese national health insurance was reimbursing patients for up to 90 percent of their medical expenses.[106] To help determine these expenses, the Ministry of Health and Welfare regularly updated an official list of prices at which it would reimburse patients

[106]For an overview of government policies, see Michael R. Reich, "Why the Japanese Don't Export More Pharmaceuticals," *California Management Review* 32 (Winter 1990): 124–150.

for prescriptions. The doctors themselves filled prescriptions at the regulated price, using drugs that they had purchased at a discount from pharmaceutical companies, and pocketed the difference. Here, a pharmaceutical company's profits depended to a considerable extent on keeping discounts to a minimum while maintaining a high official price. But between 1980 and 1984, the government sought to reduce health care costs by cutting official prices by 40 percent.[107] Not all pharmaceutical companies were equally affected by these changes, however. Banyu and other Japanese producers of product lines for which there were numerous substitutes felt the most pain, while Merck and other producers of pharmaceutical products with only limited substitutes fared better, since the government had spared from price controls those products new to the Japanese market. Often such products were directed at Japan's rapidly aging population, a market segment that also appealed to foreign companies. Merck was especially responsive to this confluence of demographic changes and government policies; its earlier licensee and subsequent acquisition target, Banyu, was not.[108]

Merck preferred to acquire an existing company, rather than exercise other expansion options, for reasons that also appealed to other American investors. For example, dollar-to-yen appreciation in 1983–84 diminished the profitability of U.S. exports, while also reducing the dollar cost of investments in Japan. Given the volatility of exchange rates, Merck preferred a speedy acquisition to a long-term investment program. Other reasons that favored acquisition were largely peculiar to pharmaceuticals. The speed of the transaction, for example, was enhanced by Merck's already extensive business relations with Banyu. Like other American pharmaceutical companies, Merck principally had exported technology to Japan prior to 1982. In fact, between 1978 and 1982,

[107]To make matters worse for the companies, new user fees for repeated visits to physicians reduced the number of prescriptions; for a further description of such policy changes, see Encarnation, "Cross-Investment," pp. 137–138.

[108]For the evolution of the Merck-Banyu acquisition, see ibid.; W. Karl Kester, *Japanese Takeovers: The Global Contest for Corporate Control* (Boston: Harvard Business School Press, 1991), esp. pp. 145–164; Timothy A. Luehrman, "Merck-Banyu," Harvard Business School Case no. 9-287-061.

over one-half of all drugs officially approved by the Japanese government were manufactured using foreign technology.[109] Finally, several reasons favoring an acquisition over a new investment were peculiar to this specific deal. For example, Banyu already relied heavily on Merck for technology. Moreover, Banyu's large existing marketing network (including 1600 detail personnel) made the company an attractive takeover target—especially since, in the near-absence of retail pharmacies, tens-of-thousands of doctors and hundreds of hospitals together served as the principal dispensers of prescription drugs. Moreover, Banyu sat on large cash balances, which made financing the deal all the more attractive. For all of these reasons, Merck quickly implemented its decision soon after the Japanese government had liberalized the pharmaceutical industry.

While liberalization provided a necessary precondition to acquisition, few other foreign companies joined Merck in executing this entry strategy. Acquisitions have generally played a minuscule role in the growth of U.S. investment in Japan, as opposed to their larger place in the comparable growth of American multinationals elsewhere.[110] For industrialized countries outside Japan, market entry through acquisition is often the most common investment strategy pursued by the Americans. But differences in capital markets have accounted for Japan's exception to the general rules of multinational behavior. In itself, the dearth of Japanese acquisitions in the United States testifies to the fact that standard business practices in Japan continue to prefer new investment to acquisition. Of course, such corporate preferences were supported for many years by formal capital controls that expressly denied foreign

[109]Japanese Federation of Pharmaceutical Manufacturers, Insurance Drug Price Research Council, *Pharmaceutical Industry and Price Standard* (Osaka: JFPM, May 1984), p. 19.

[110]According to statistics provided by W. T. Grimm and Company, U.S. corporations seldom entered the Japanese market through the acquisition of an existing company, in marked contrast to their entry strategy in other industrialized countries. For example, between 1979 and 1983, during the five-year period of the Merck acquisition, Japan (recording 8 U.S. acquisitions) trailed well behind the United Kingdom (169 acquisitions), Canada (127), West Germany (53), France (53), Switzerland (25), and the Netherlands (24). Even newly industrializing Brazil and Mexico recorded more U.S. acquisitions (13 in Brazil, 11 in Mexico) than did Japan.

investors any opportunity to enter Japan through merger and acquisition. But even the formal dissolution of these public regulations left standard business practices unchanged.

That dissolution also left other government practices in place—as Motorola would soon discover in the telecommunications industry.[111] In Japan, the Ministry of Posts and Telecommunications (MPT) and its affiliate, the National Telephone and Telegraph Company (NTT), tightly regulated market entry. For Motorola, such entry actually began in 1975, when the company opened a sales office in Tokyo to market American-made two-way radios to police departments and other government agencies (as well as to taxi companies and other private enterprises). Similar efforts to import U.S.-made cellular phones proved less successful, however. Indeed, differences in industry standards actually placed Motorola in direct competition with NTT, which soon faced a rival cellular telephone network (DDI, itself a consortium of large Japanese companies led by Kyocera) that offered to customers Motorola equipment incompatible with the nationwide NTT system. Regulators in MPT, however, refused to allocate to the competing Motorola system *any* frequency within the lucrative Tokyo-Nagoya corridor, thus denying Motorola a major market. The ensuing dispute, as well as similar ones over frequencies and standards, inhibited the importation of U.S.-made pagers. Eventually, NTT did become Motorola's principal buyer—but only reluctantly, and only after repeatedly and unsuccessfully suggesting to Motorola that it establish a joint venture with one of NTT's "Big Four" traditional suppliers. Rather, Motorola went outside the family and eventually (in 1987) concluded long-term contracts with Toshiba and Matsushita—but not with any Big Four supplier—for pocket pagers to be sold in the Japanese market.[112] With Toshiba, also in

[111]For the history of Motorola in Japan in this paragraph and the next, see Prestowitz, *Trading Places*; Yoffie, "Motorola and Japan (A)"; Johnson, "MITI, MPT, and the Telecom Wars"; Mason, *American Multinationals and Japan*, chap. 5.

[112]Motorola had long-standing relations with both companies: Toshiba had been a supplier of electronic components to Motorola as early as the late 1950s, and Matsushita had acquired Motorola's consumer electronics division in 1974. Neither company, however, figured among the "Big Four" telecommunications suppliers that NTT favored.

1987, Motorola expanded this relationship to include an equal-partnership joint venture for the manufacture of semiconductors in Japan. Here, Motorola secured access to Toshiba's process technology for the manufacture of D-RAMs, as well as to Toshiba's large internal market for semiconductors—all in exchange for Motorola's product technology in microprocessors. In addition, Motorola gained potentially valuable political allies in Japan—especially Toshiba, plus Kyocera and Matsushita—all the more important in a country where the government functions as Motorola's principal regulator, buyer, and competitor.

Back home with the U.S. government, meanwhile, Motorola was maneuvering to become the *cause célèbre* of the 1980s—much as Texas Instruments had done two decades earlier.[113] In fact, by 1979, Motorola was lobbying to keep the politically sensitive telecommunications industry high on the U.S. government's agenda for trade talks with Japan. Finally, Motorola's strategy paid off, for in 1980 the United States concluded the first of what would become several telecommunications accords with the Japanese government—all designed in part to improve Motorola's access to the Japanese market. Simultaneously, Motorola appealed to the U.S. government by filing successful dumping cases against Japanese competitors exporting pagers (in 1982) and cellular telephones (in 1984). In 1985, Motorola joined the U.S. Semiconductor Industry Association in a series of what were both dumping suits and lobbying activities designed to redress growing imbalances in bilateral semiconductor trade. In combination, these actions helped to convince the U.S. government that it should look more closely at Japanese competitive practices—not in the United States alone, but in Japan as well. There, a 1986 semiconductor trade accord set 20 percent as the target market share for foreign-affiliated sales by 1991. And in telecommunications, the 1989 talks over structural impediments plus the threat of unilateral U.S. trade sanctions (under "Super 301") together secured a Japanese agreement to increase foreign access to the home market. Motorola credited its political strategy for opening up the crucial Tokyo-Nagoya market

[113]To illustrate, see "Cover Story: The Rival Japan Respects," *Business Week*, Nov. 13, 1990, pp. 108–118.

to its allied cellular telephone system, and for increasing sales of Motorola pagers and semiconductors in Japan. But that political strategy would surely not have produced the desired results without having had Motorola's formidable firm-specific assets to back it up.

From Strong Dollar to Strong Yen

Like Motorola, numerous other American multinationals expanded their direct investments in Japan even as yen appreciation raised the dollar price of local assets. In fact, between 1982 (at the dollar's zenith for the decade) and 1988 (at the dollar's nadir), the stock of U.S. FDI in Japan actually doubled, from $6.6 billion to $16.9 billion (see Figure 2-1). That stock finally surpassed levels found in most other industrialized countries where, over the same period, U.S. FDI generally grew at a rate slower than it did in Japan.[114] In fact, by 1988, only five industrialized countries—Canada, the United Kingdom, Germany, Switzerland, and the Netherlands—hosted larger stocks of U.S. FDI than did Japan. Such comparisons can be misleading, of course, since most American multinationals invested large and undervalued (compared to more recent U.S. FDI in Japan) sums in these and other industrialized countries, all with economies less than one-half Japan's size. Nevertheless, by 1988 the sales of American multinationals in Japan matched—and often exceeded—comparable sales in other industrialized countries.[115] Thus, when measured by the value of U.S. FDI abroad, Japan had joined the ranks of those advanced economies that commonly hosted American multinationals.

However, when measured by the internal operations of such investment—beginning with levels of majority ownership—Japan no longer invited comparisons with other industrialized countries,

[114]Indeed, across industrialized countries, U.S. FDI in 1988 was only one-and-a-half times larger than comparable stocks in 1982; see Commerce Department, "U.S. Direct Investment Abroad: 1985," table 44, p. 95; Commerce Department, "U.S. Direct Investment Abroad: 1989," table 44, p. 95.

[115]U.S. Commerce Department, Bureau of Economic Analysis, *U.S. Direct Investment Abroad: Operations of U.S. Parent Companies and their Foreign Affiliates, Preliminary 1988 Estimates* (Washington, D.C.: USGPO, July 1990), Tables 6, 16, 18, 29, 52, 53, n.p.

but with economies far less industrialized than Japan. Certainly, over the 1980s, much of the new U.S. FDI in Japan entered majority subsidiaries, as Motorola, Merck, and numerous other American multinationals took advantage of the abolition of formal capital controls. In fact, by 1988 majority subsidiaries contributed nearly two-fifths (38 percent) of all sales by American multinationals in Japan, up from one-quarter (25 percent) a decade earlier (see Figure 2-7). Minority affiliates accounted for the remainder, with relative sales (62 percent) closer to their share in developing India (87 percent) than to their proportion in highly industrialized Germany (24 percent).[116] In Germany and most other industrialized countries, majority subsidiaries consistently accounted for upwards of three-quarters of all sales recorded by American multinationals. Moreover, in total value, subsidiaries' sales in Canada, the United Kingdom, Germany, France—again, each with economies one-third to one-half Japan's size—exceeded the total sales of majority subsidiaries in Japan. By failing to generate comparable sales, the lower incidence of majority subsidiaries in Japan worked to deny American multinationals the same market access they otherwise enjoyed in other industrialized countries.

In such advanced economies, American multinationals typically sold more goods locally through majority subsidiaries than they and other U.S. exporters shipped to these markets. So too in Japan, where subsidiaries' local sales generated far more revenues than did U.S. exports during 1988. At least as far back as 1977, local sales by majority subsidiaries just barely surpassed all U.S. exports to Japan. But over the next decade, local sales began to exceed U.S. exports by a wider margin—even after the devaluation of the dollar and its beneficial impact on prices of U.S. exports. Indeed, by 1988 majority subsidiaries relied on the Japanese market for over 87 percent of their total sales of $53.4 billion—a value of local sales far in excess of U.S. exports (of $37.7 billion) to Japan.[117] Yet, the resulting ratio between local sales and U.S ex-

---

[116]Ibid.

[117]For sales data, see ibid.; for trade data, see Commerce Department, *U.S. Foreign Trade Highlights, 1989*, p. 31.

Figure 2-7. American access to the Japanese market, 1977–88

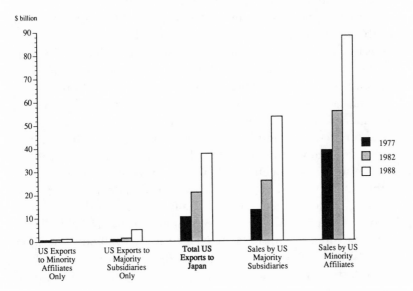

Sources: U.S. Commerce Department, Bureau of Economic Analysis, *U.S. Direct Investment Abroad, 1977* (Washington, D.C.: USGPO, 1981), tables II.F.5, II.I.3, II.I.19, III.F.5, III.I.3, and III.I.19, pp. 138, 154, 158, 282, 338, 354; U.S. Commerce Department, Bureau of Economic Analysis, *U.S. Direct Investment Abroad, 1982* (Washington, D.C.: USGPO, April 1984), tables II.D.3, II.G.3, II.G.20, III.D.3, III.G.3, III.G.20, pp. 111, 127, 131, 215, 266, 283; U.S. Commerce Department, Bureau of Economic Analysis, *U.S. Direct Investment Abroad: Operations of U.S. Parent Companies and their Foreign Affiliates, Preliminary 1988 Estimates* (Washington, D.C.: USGPO, July 1990), tables 6, 16, 18, 29, 52, 53, n.p.; U.S. Commerce Department, International Trade Administration, Office of Trade and Investment Analysis, *U.S. Foreign Trade Highlights: 1989* (Washington, D.C.: USGPO, Sept. 1990).

ports, even after a decade of growth, remained much closer to the ratio found in developing countries. By contrast, in industrialized countries at least since 1966, subsidiaries' sales have remained three times larger than U.S. exports. But never in Japan, where majority subsidiaries enjoyed slightly more market access than did U.S. exporters.

As in the cases of Merck and Motorola, many of these majority subsidiaries actually produced locally the same goods that they sold in Japan.[118] Such local manufacturing, in fact, has recently grown more rapidly than have all other domestic sources of revenue. To illustrate: Between 1977 and 1982, majority subsidiaries doubled both their total sales (see Figure 2-7) and their local production, thus leaving unchanged the sales contribution of that production. Similarly, between 1982 and 1988, total subsidiaries' sales doubled again, while over this same period the value of local production actually quadrupled, financed by a three-fold increase of U.S. FDI in Japanese manufacturing. As a result, during 1988, U.S. manufacturers actually contributed two-fifths of total sales by majority subsidiaries in Japan—up from only one-quarter as late as 1982— and roughly equivalent to their proportionate contribution in other industrialized countries. However, despite such large and rapid growth, domestic sales of locally manufactured goods (valued at $17.4 billion during 1988) continued to lag behind U.S. manufactured exports to Japan (valued at $22.0 billion). Such a lag was also apparent during 1988 in developing countries, where U.S. manufacturers continued to export twice as many manufactured goods as they produced and sold locally through majority subsidiaries.[119] Once again, that ratio was actually reversed in most industrialized countries, where locally produced sales remained at least one-and-a-half times larger than U.S. manufactured exports to these markets. There, but still not in Japan, local production by majority subsidiaries continues to grant American multinationals far greater market access than that enjoyed by U.S. exporters of manufactured goods.

After yen appreciation, however, these and other U.S. exporters increasingly established majority subsidiaries in order to create final markets and intermediate channels for their own shipments from America. Such intracompany trade has grown faster than U.S. exports as a whole. As a result, by 1988, shipments by Merck, Motorola, and other U.S. parents to their majority subsidiaries in Japan generated one-seventh of all U.S. exports to Japan—nearly three times their share as late as 1982. Despite such growth, intra-

[118]Data in this paragraph and the next from the same sources cited in note 117.

[119]During 1988, in developing countries, U.S. manufactured exports equalled $82.8 billion, while local manufacturing and sales by majority U.S.-owned subsidiaries equalled $40.8 billion.

company trade with Japan contributed to U.S. exports in roughly the same proportion (one-seventh) as did shipments from U.S. parents to their majority subsidiaries in developing countries. By contrast, across industrialized countries, such intracompany trade, at least since 1966, has continued to generate one-third of all U.S. exports. Specifically, in shipments of manufactured goods, intracompany trade accounted for as much as one-half of all U.S. exports to advanced economies—except to Japan, where such trade during 1988 could not have contributed more than one-quarter of all U.S. manufactured exports. Thus, in most advanced economies—but not in Japan—majority subsidiaries granted American multinationals a significant degree of managerial control over their subsidiaries' decisions to source manufactured goods and other products from their U.S. parents.

What little intracompany trade did occur with Japan, U.S. exporters channeled through majority subsidiaries operating as Japanese wholesalers (see Figure 2-8)—again, following a strategy with few precedents in other industrialized countries. In such advanced economies, U.S. parents during 1988 shipped roughly two-thirds of their intracompany trade through majority subsidiaries engaged in manufacturing. By contrast, in Japan, these U.S. parents shipped roughly the same share of their intracompany trade through subsidiaries engaged *not* in manufacturing but in wholesaling. Such differences in strategy reflected wide variation in the marketing barriers to entry that U.S. exporters encountered across industrialized countries. Suggesting that these barriers were significantly higher in Japan, American multinationals concentrated one-fifth of their foreign investments (stocks) in Japanese wholesaling (see Figure 2-6)—twice the level they invested in that sector in other industrialized countries. Moreover, between 1982 and 1988, wholesaling attracted more new U.S. FDI than did any other sector of the Japanese economy, as American multinationals, after the appreciation of the yen, moved quickly to establish distribution channels for their increased exports to Japan. By 1988 American investments in Japanese wholesaling reached and then surpassed investments in the petroleum industry, which until that date had served as the largest repository of U.S. FDI in Japan. Yet despite their large size and rapid growth, such investments in Japanese

Figure 2-8. U.S. investment-related trade with Japan, 1982 vs. 1988

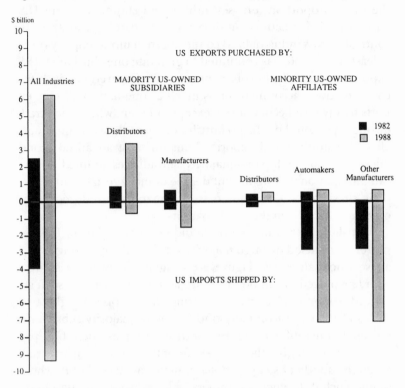

Sources: U.S. Commerce Department, Bureau of Economic Analysis, *U.S. Direct Investment Abroad, 1982* (Washington, D.C.: USGPO, April 1984), tables II.G.3, II.G.20, III.G.3, III.G.20, pp. 127, 131, 266, 283; U.S. Commerce Department, Bureau of Economic Analysis, *U.S. Direct Investment Abroad: Operations of U.S. Parent Companies and their Foreign Affiliates, Preliminary 1988 Estimates* (Washington, D.C.: USGPO, July 1990), tables 16, 18, 52, 53, n.p.; U.S. Commerce Department, International Trade Administration, Office of Trade and Investment Analysis, *U.S. Foreign Trade Highlights: 1989* (Washington, D.C.: USGPO, Sept. 1990).

wholesaling actually granted U.S. exporters far less market access than they enjoyed in the manufacturing sectors of other industrialized countries. The lower incidence of majority subsidiaries in Japanese manufacturing continued to deny American multinationals the same market access they otherwise exploited to sell their exports in other industrialized countries.

Minority affiliates in Japan also created much less opportunity for intracompany trade for U.S. exporters—yet conversely, these affiliates increased such trade for U.S. importers. During 1988, U.S. exports worldwide to minority affiliates were actually negligible, although these affiliates contributed one-quarter of total multinational sales. While the sales contribution of these affiliates was even larger in Japan, their contribution to U.S. exports was equally negligible. However, in reverse, Isuzu, Mazda, Mitsubishi, and other minority U.S.-owned automakers contributed sizably to U.S. imports—and to America's trade deficit with Japan. During 1988, they accounted for over one-tenth of that deficit, which came on the heels of a major investment drive by the U.S. parents of these minority auto affiliates. During the decade ending in 1988, the cumulative value of U.S. direct investments in Japanese automaking increased sevenfold, to $630 million from a mere $90 million in 1977 (compare Figure 2-4 with Figure 2-6). Little of this investment boosted U.S. auto exports, which remained small and stagnant over the decade, never exceeding $30 million; for Ford, GM, and Chrysler viewed their growing minority investments in Japan as offshore sources of U.S. imports, rather than as intermediate channels for U.S. exports. And they contributed one-tenth of America's persistent trade deficit with Japan.

Into the 1990s

Through 1989, American automakers and parts suppliers continued to invest in Japan, in response to the daunting Japanese challenge back in the U.S. home market. During that year, in fact, the Japanese auto industry accounted for fully three-quarters of all new U.S. investment in Japan.[120] With these fresh inflows counted, the cumulative total of all U.S. FDI in Japan through 1989 reached nearly $20 billion—double the total just four years earlier in 1985, when the exchange value of the U.S. dollar reached its apex against the Japanese yen (see Figure 2-1). Even the dollar's subsequent decline did little to dampen double-digit growth of

[120]For data on U.S. FDI in this paragraph, see Commerce Department, "U.S. Direct Investment Abroad: 1989," table 44, p. 95.

such American investment; and much of this growth, as we noted, actually represented mushrooming U.S. investment in the Japanese distribution system, where American multinationals directly sought to overcome high marketing barriers to entry. Here, they pursued a strategy that had no parallel for Americans. Indeed, by 1989 Japan accounted for fully 9 percent of all U.S. FDI in overseas distribution worldwide, even though Japan overall hosted barely 5 percent of total foreign direct investment by American multinationals. That modest national share remained large enough to boost Japan, for the first time, into the ranks of America's top five hosts for foreign direct investment—placing it just behind Switzerland (also with 5 percent of all U.S. FDI) and Germany (with 6 percent), but still well behind the United Kingdom (16 percent) and Canada (18 percent).

In these other industrialized countries, American multinationals currently pursue with good success common strategies of foreign investment and related trade. They expect initially to replicate these strategies in Japan: American multinationals increasingly invest in majority-owned subsidiaries, through which they produce and distribute more goods and services *locally* than all U.S.-based exporters ship to Japan. Despite such critical changes, however, strategic differences still emerge when American multinationals in Japan are compared with American multinationals in other industrialized countries: the use of U.S. FDI is strikingly at variance. Specifically, in Japan, most American investment remains locked in minority U.S. affiliates, which continue to contribute significantly to America's imports from Japan but seem unable to create sufficient distribution channels for sizable U.S. exports. While such differences have undoubtedly diminished over time, American multinationals in Japan operate even today at a competitive disadvantage relative to U.S. subsidiaries in other industrialized countries.[121] And, as we shall see in the next chapter, at a competitive disadvantage relative to Japanese multinationals in the United States.

[121]For industry-by-industry evidence in explicit support of this general conclusion, see American Chamber of Commerce in Japan, *Trade and Investment in Japan: The Current Environment* (Tokyo: ACCJ, June 1991), esp. pp. 66–111.

CHAPTER THREE

Japanese in the United States

In the United States, the Japanese have implemented nearly every trade and investment strategy that has been denied to American multinationals in Japan. Unlike those Americans, Japanese multinationals typically invest in majority subsidiaries, which then serve as final markets and intermediary channels for most of their parents'—and Japan's—exports to America. These exports, while large, pale in comparison to U.S. sales generated locally by Japanese subsidiaries: these U.S. sales have grown to nearly three times larger than comparable local sales recorded in Japan by majority U.S. subsidiaries. Indeed, the United States has emerged as the most attractive overseas destination for Japanese multinationals, accounting worldwide for nearly one-half their total foreign sales.[1] Meanwhile, Japanese subsidiaries in America have also become the largest source of U.S. exports to Japan, principally shipments to multinational parents back home. As we shall see below, Japanese subsidiaries in America export more to Japan than do *all* other U.S.-based exporters combined, including the parents of American multinationals with affiliates in Japan. Despite such differ-

---

[1]Japan, Ministry of International Trade and Industry, Industrial Policy Bureau, International Business Affairs Division, *The 19th Survey of the Overseas Business Activities of Japanese Enterprises [Dai jyukyu-kai wagakuni kigyo no kaigai jigyo katsudou]* (Tokyo: Ministry of Finance Printing Bureau, 1990), pp. 72–73, 82–83; Japan, Ministry of Finance, *Statistics for the Approval/Notification of Overseas Direct Investment [Taigai chyokusetsu-toshi no kyoka todokede zisseki]* (Tokyo: Ministry of Finance Printing Bureau, selected years).

ences, Japanese subsidiaries in the United States share one important characteristic with U.S. affiliates in Japan: both produce
locally slightly more than their parents (and other nationally based
exporters) ship across the Pacific.

Such limited local production, as I have argued in the previous
chapter, testifies to the continued inability of American multinationals to secure access to the Japanese market. In the U.S. market,
however, limited local production by the Japanese testifies both to
their continuing reluctance to jettison an otherwise successful trading strategy, and to their more recent emergence as foreign direct
investors. Here, the earlier evolution of American multinationals in Europe and European multinationals in the United States
proves instructive.[2] In Europe, American multinationals have long
invested in local production to gain far greater market access than
U.S. exporters could secure. But in the United States, as we shall
see below, local production by European investors did not exceed
shipments from European exporters until the 1970s. And not until
the 1980s did the ratio of local production to national exports by
the Europeans in the United States match that of the Americans in
Europe. The latecomer Japanese, by contrast, have only recently
matched their exports to America with local U.S. production, falling a full decade or two behind the Europeans, and close to a half-
century behind the Americans. Moreover, unlike either the Europeans or (especially) the Americans, the Japanese have not yet seen
their growth in local production appreciably alter the value of their
exports, even though the composition of that trade has begun to
change. Thus, in this larger evolutionary process, Japanese multinationals have proved to be the slowest to replace their original—
and winning—strategy of simply investing to trade.[3]

[2] For the evolution of American multinationals, see: Raymond Vernon, *Sovereignty at Bay: The Multinational Spread of U.S. Enterprises* (New York: Basic Books, 1971); Mira Wilkins, *The Maturing of Multinational Enterprise: American Business Abroad from 1914 to 1970* (Cambridge: Harvard University Press, 1974). For the evolution of European enterprises, especially in the United States, see Mira Wilkins, *The History of Foreign Investment in the United States to 1914* (Cambridge: Harvard University Press, 1989); Larry G. Franko, *The European Multinationals: A Renewed Challenge to American and British Big Business* (Stamford, Conn.: Greylock, 1976).

[3] The notion of investing to trade is a common theme in the literature on Japanese multinationals; see, for example, Wakasugi Ryuhei, *International Trade, Foreign*

To explain why Japanese multinationals in the United States evolved as they did, this chapter analyzes differences in the strategic investment policies pursued by the home and host country. The preceding chapter discussed the way in which Japanese government regulations and private restrictions combined to prevent American multinationals from freely investing and trading in Japan, especially in those industries where increasing returns to scale and scope serve to narrow competition to a few global competitors. Two such industries, automobiles and electronics, will again be examined in some detail in the present chapter. We shall see how Japanese oligopolists in these industries, unimpeded by foreign competition at home, have moved to exploit their advantages in the United States, where they were able first to trade and then to invest—doing both with much greater freedom than the Americans have ever enjoyed in Japan. For the Japanese, in fact, the biggest threat to their freedom to invest in the United States came not from U.S. policy, but from the strict capital controls imposed back home by the Japanese government. Those controls actually proved integral to Japan's strategic investment policy: inside Japan, by prohibiting capital outflows, the government insured sufficient financing for industries requiring large investments; while outside Japan, the government directed limited investments, both upstream to secure stable sources of raw materials and downstream to establish distribution channels for Japanese manufactures. When exports of electronics, automobiles, and related manufactures were finally threatened by U.S. trade restric-

---

Direct Investment, and Japanese Industrial Organization, [Boueki chokusetsu toushi to nihon no sangyou soshiki] (Tokyo: Toyo Keizai Shimposha, 1989), esp. pp. 119–27; Komiya Ryutaro, *The Contemporary Japanese Economy [Gendai nihon keizai],* (Tokyo: University of Tokyo Press, 1988), esp. pp. 221–295; Sekiguchi Sueo, *New Developments in Foreign Investment [Kaigai toushi no shintenkai]* (Tokyo: Nihon Keizai Shinbun-sha, 1979); Ozawa Terutomo, *Multinationalism, Japanese Style: The Political Economy of Outward Dependency* (Princeton: Princeton University Press, 1979), esp. pp. 227–228; Kojima Kiyoshi, *Direct Foreign Investment: A Japanese Model of Multinational Business Operations* (London: Croon Helm, 1978); Michael Yoshino, *Japan's Multinational Enterprises* (Cambridge: Harvard University Press, 1976), esp. chap. 5; Tsurumi Yoshihara, *The Japanese Are Coming: A Multinational Spread of Japanese Firms* (Cambridge: Ballinger, 1976); Sekiguchi Sueo and Matsuba Mitsuji, *Japan's Direct Investment [Nihon no chokusetsu toushi]* (Tokyo: Nihon Keizai Shinbun-sha, 1974).

tions—then and only then did some liberalization of capital controls become part of Japan's strategy.

Trade restrictions have long been powerful determinants of those foreign investments designed to supply local, as opposed to export, markets.[4] This is true everywhere except in Japan, where capital controls have acted to limit foreign investment in protected local markets. In the United States, however, there have been few such capital controls; instead, import restraints and exchange-rate adjustments combine to form America's fledgling strategic investment policy. But only recently. For, unlike Japan, the United States during most of the post-war period actively encouraged a free flow of both goods and capital across national borders. Such national asymmetries have served to grant Japanese competitors unequal access to U.S. markets, and now, that inequality cannot be easily reversed by changes in U.S. trade and foreign-exchange policies. Nowhere is this more apparent than in automobiles and electronics—two industries that together account for more than one-half of all U.S. imports from Japan and, as we shall see below, a correspondingly large share of all Japanese FDI in the United States.[5] Yet, before Japanese multinationals could even consider such investment, their government had to stop discouraging capital outflows. This requirement meant that the strategic investment policies of America and Japan actually evolved in two distinct stages (see Figure 3-1). Altogether, the evolution of Japanese policy may be described as neatly symbiotic: as America tilted away from liberal trade and toward selective protectionism, Japan leaned in the opposite direction, toward financial liberalization and away from capital controls.

During the first stage, the United States encouraged a free movement of finance across all borders; while at the same time, Japan imposed strict controls on both the inflow and outflow of

[4]For the impact of trade restrictions of foreign direct investment see, Grant L. Reuber et al., *Foreign Private Investment in Development* (Oxford: Oxford University Press for the Organization of Economic Cooperation and Development, 1973), esp. pp. 120–132; for a more recent analysis, see Stephen E. Guisinger et al., *Investment Incentives and Performance Requirements: Patterns of International Trade, Production, and Investment* (New York: Praeger, 1985), esp. pp. 48–54.

[5]U.S. Commerce Department, International Trade Administration, Office of Trade and Investment Analysis, *U.S. Foreign Trade Highlights: 1989* (Washington, D.C.: USGPO, Sept. 1990), pp. 100–101.

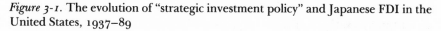

Figure 3-1. The evolution of "strategic investment policy" and Japanese FDI in the United States, 1937–89

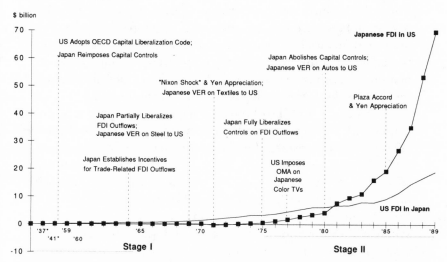

Sources: For the events highlighted, see Chapter 3 below; for data on U.S. FDI, see Figure 2-1; for data on Japanese FDI in the United States, see U.S. Commerce Department, *Selected Data on Foreign Direct Investment in the United States, 1950–79* (Washington, D.C.: USGPO, 1984), table 9, p. 17; U.S. Commerce Department, "Foreign Direct Investment Position in the United States: Detail for Position and Balance of Payments Flows," *Survey of Current Business* (various years).

capital. These asymmetries actually predated the Second World War, and they remained largely intact for some four decades. Consequently, beginning with roughly equal book values during the late 1930s, Japanese FDI in the United States by the early 1970s had grown to only one-tenth the size of otherwise restricted U.S. FDI in Japan. In fact, among foreigners investing directly in the United States, both the Japanese and the Germans began at a level of rough parity before the Second World War; yet by the early 1970s, total German FDI in America had grown to six times larger than all Japanese FDI in the United States.[6] What little they did invest, the Japanese concentrated in majority subsidiaries that op-

[6]See, for example, U.S. Commerce Department, *Selected Data on Foreign Direct Investment in the U.S., 1950–79* (Washington, D.C.: USGPO, 1984), table 9, p. 17.

erated either as marketing agents in America of imported products shipped by their parents, or as suppliers of U.S. food and raw materials destined for final processing and marketing by their parents in Japan. Initially, Japanese trading companies, supported by related financial, insurance, and shipping intermediaries, controlled much of this intracompany trade. But over time, Japanese manufacturers increasingly sought to establish in the United States their own subsidiaries, acting independently and serving as dedicated importers and distributors of their parents' products. Together with trading intermediaries, these Japanese manufacturers soon began to exercise unprecedented control over America's trade with Japan. While across the Atlantic, American and European multinationals invested to produce locally more in each other's market than they (and others) exported to these markets, Japanese manufacturers kept such production at home. There, in Japan, the exploitation of both scale and scope economies was aided by limited overseas investments, both upstream (in U.S. sourcing) and downstream (in U.S. marketing).

Beginning in the mid-1970s, the strategic investment policies of America and Japan entered a second stage, marked by both a proliferation of U.S. trade barriers and a liberalization of Japanese capital controls. These changes meant that earlier investment asymmetries dramatically reversed during the 1980s, when Japan finally surpassed Germany (and every other capital exporter except the United Kingdom) as America's largest source of foreign direct investment.[7] Indeed, Japanese FDI in the United States actually grew to four times the total of all U.S. FDI in Japan (see Figure 3-1). Now, the Japanese concentrated much of their new investment in majority subsidiaries engaged in local production, which by 1988 finally reached parity with U.S. imports of Japanese manufactured goods. Most of these goods consisted of either electronics or automobiles, where final products and individual components together contributed roughly three-quarters of America's 1988 trade deficit with Japan. Electronics and automobiles, in turn,

[7]U.S. Commerce Department, "Foreign Direct Investment Position in the United States: Detail for Position and Balance of Payments Flows, 1989," *Survey of Current Business* (Aug. 1990): 46.

accounted for most Japanese direct investment, initially in U.S. wholesaling and later in manufacturing. While these manufacturing investments did consume a growing share of U.S. imports from Japan, most such imports continued to be channeled through wholesaling subsidiaries, where intracompany shipments from Japanese parents contributed the greatest part of all bilateral trade. Intracompany shipments also dominated U.S. exports to Japan, as Japanese trading companies shipped food and raw materials from majority subsidiaries in the United States to their parents back home. Indeed, in contrast to American and European multinationals criss-crossing the Atlantic, the Japanese engaged in far more intracompany trade, and less in local production. Nevertheless, for Japanese manufacturers in the United States, the continuing growth of local production, plus increasing shipments between parents and subsidiaries, supports one of my central propositions: that foreign direct investment has exceeded simple trade as the principal means available to Japanese multinationals seeking access to the U.S. market.

Of course, liberalization of Japanese capital controls and proliferation of U.S. trade barriers have also served to stimulate various competitive forces, including both the powerful demands of buyers and the special gaming strategies of oligopolistic rivals.[8] Both forces are characteristic of the Japanese, and the two are highly interrelated. A few concentrated buyers may, for example, exert considerable influence over the foreign investment decisions of their multiple suppliers, especially when buyers demand products that either must be customized to local conditions or that can be substituted easily by local producers. In turn, these buyers may actually imitate the behavior of their competitors, especially in only

---

[8]The so-called follow-the-leader hypothesis is best tested in Frederick T. Knickerbocker, *Oligopolistic Reaction and Multinational Enterprises* (Boston: Graduate School of Business Administration, Harvard University, 1973). The so-called exchange-of-hostage hypothesis is best tested in E. M. Graham, "Transatlantic Investment by Multinational Firms: A Rivalistic Phenomenon?" *Journal of Post-Keynesian Economics* 1 (Fall 1978), pp. 82–99. For a review of this logic and supporting empirical research, see Richard E. Caves, *Multinational Enterprise and Economic Analysis* (Cambridge: Cambridge University Press, 1982), pp. 97–100, 106–107. Tsurumi, *The Japanese Are Coming*, pp. 88–95, provides empirical support for this logic using data on Japanese foreign investments.

moderately concentrated industries with high levels of horizontal and vertical interdependence among oligopolists. Such industries are especially common in Japan. There, as elsewhere, companies often make foreign investment decisions by following an industry leader or other industrial rivals, or by punishing a rival for an aggressive move made elsewhere. Thus, a risk-averse manager will often match a competitor's moves in order to reduce the probability that the competitor will later jeopardize the future of that manager's own company. According to this reasoning, it is better for both companies to move sequentially—even at the risk that both might suffer losses—than for a single company *not* to move and thereby risk a competitor's net gain. Yet such "oligopolistic competition" plus the "buyer power" that these competitors exercise over their multiple suppliers required a liberalization of Japanese controls on capital outflows before they could be fully implemented in liberal America.

STAGE I: REGULATED OUTFLOWS, LIBERALIZED INFLOWS

"While American companies in Japan were in the technologically advanced sectors and prominently in manufacturing, Japanese business in America aimed at aiding Japanese commerce. . . . The evidence indicates that a large percentage of U.S.-Japanese trade was financed by Japanese banks, insured by Japanese insurance companies, arranged by Japanese trading firms, and carried on Japanese ships. All of these needed representatives in the United States to carry on these functions."[9] This capsule conclusion, written by Mira Wilkins expressly to contrast national patterns of foreign direct investment and related trade during the 1930s, stood as largely accurate for at least four decades. During that extended period, Japanese government policy and corporate actions consistently sought to conserve scarce financial resources and production technology at home while also attempting to secure abroad both markets for such production and sources of raw materials. Except during the Second World War, that Japanese

[9]Mira Wilkins, "American-Japanese Direct Foreign Investment, 1930–1952," *Business History Review* 56 (Winter 1982), pp. 517, 510.

strategy persisted until the 1970s, and it remained largely un-affected by either U.S. government policies or the actions of American multinationals operating in Japan.

Prewar Legacies

The employing of foreign investment to promote international trade has long characterized Japanese business activity in the United States, beginning with their first investments, mainly in the financial sector.[10] The Yokohama Specie Bank, Ltd., Japan's chief foreign exchange bank, established a wholly owned branch in New York during the same year (1880) that the bank was incorporated in Japan. Subsequently, the Yokohama Bank established four additional American branches, all on the Pacific coast. As late as the 1930s, these several branches together represented the largest Japanese direct investment in the United States, where they financed over one-half of all U.S. exports to Japan. Fifteen other Japanese banks with wholly owned branches in America financed much of the remaining bilateral trade—which also relied on wholly owned branches of three Japanese insurance companies for marine indemnity. Together, these banks and insurance companies accounted for over one-half of the $41 million invested directly in the United States by Japanese corporations—a total sum that approached the $47 million invested in Japan by all American multinationals (see Figure 3-1 above).[11] More specifically, Japanese investment in the U.S. financial sector roughly equalled U.S. FDI in the Japanese manufacturing sector. Most of these American manufacturers, when they invested in Japan, actually substituted for U.S. exports; yet most Japanese financial institutions invested in America principally to promote U.S. exports.

While Japanese financial institutions invested the most dollars in

[10]Unless otherwise noted, the following discussion of prewar legacies relies heavily on the pioneering work of Mira Wilkins; see ibid., pp. 498–510; "Japanese Multinational Enterprise before 1914," *Business History Review* 60 (Summer 1986): 218–223; *History of Foreign Investment in the United States*, esp. pp. 159–61, 174, 336–337, 460–461, 516–517, 526–527.

[11]U.S. direct investment in Japan probably peaked at $61.4 million in 1930, while Japanese investment in the United States probably peaked at $41.0 million in 1937 following a sharp increase that year; see Wilkins, "American-Japanese Investment," tables 2 and 3, pp. 506–507.

the United States, Japanese trading companies and other distributors accounted for the greatest number of wholly owned subsidiaries, with the second largest total of dollar investments. In the United States, Mitsui Busan represented the most important Japanese trading company, opening in New York its first American branch in 1879, followed by two additional branches on the U.S. west coast. After a slow and shaky start, these Mitsui branches at their peak (around 1914) handled more than one-quarter of Japan's trade with the United States, while also serving as a major conduit for the transmission of U.S. technology to Japan. After Mitsui, Mitsubishi became the second-largest Japanese trading company in the United States, and possibly the most diversified. Indeed, Mitsubishi's three American branches exported to Japan a broad range of U.S. products, including unprocessed raw materials (fats, cotton), processed inputs (steel, steel scrap, fertilizer, petroleum, pulp, newsprint), capital goods (machinery built to Japanese specifications), and consumer goods (canned seafood, canned fruits). In reverse, Mitsubishi's American branches imported a more limited range of Japanese products, notably silk and cultured pearls. In such two-way trade, Mitsui and Mitsubishi typically acted as agents for the sellers, and especially for U.S. exporters; at times, they also acted on their own account, relying on intracompany trade, both among foreign subsidiaries and with their Japanese parents. Such trade often involved steamship affiliates: the Mitsui Line, in fact, served mainly as a department of the trading company, while Mitsubishi's line (Nippon Yusen Kaisha, or NYK) separately established more American branches (in total, seven) than did the parent trading company. Once again, these Japanese direct investments controlled bilateral trade, with two-thirds of all Japanese imports and three-quarters of all Japanese exports transported during the 1930s on Japanese-flag carriers.

The tight relationship that had grown between Japanese FDI and bilateral trade was sharply interrupted in July 1941, when Japanese troops invaded Indochina. President Roosevelt froze all Japanese assets in the United States and brought all bilateral flows of both capital and goods under U.S. government control. After Pearl Harbor, the U.S. Treasury confiscated enemy assets, placing some under the Alien Property Custodian and liquidating others.

Japanese banks and insurance companies proved prime targets for liquidation, since none seemed likely to show a profit in the absence of trade with Japan, and none seemed essential to either the local economy or the Allied war effort (all in marked contrast to U.S. FDI in Japan). Of twenty-eight enemy-owned banks and insurance companies liquidated during the war by the Alien Property Custodian, nineteen belonged to the Japanese, including the Yokohama Specie Bank, the largest single liquidation. By the end of the war, the Custodian had liquidated 169 Japanese corporations—but only after concluding that "the complete elimination of German and Japanese ownership of properties in the United States was in the national interest."[12] After the war, such properties were of little help to the Japanese in any case, since the Allied Occupation directly handled all Japanese trade until mid-1947.[13] Thereafter, Japanese firms slowly reemerged as substantial financial, insurance, trading, and shipping intermediaries between the United States and Japan. So modest were these early reinvestments, however, that the U.S. Commerce Department, in its first post-war survey of foreign direct investment in the United States, concluded that Japanese FDI during 1950 merited inclusion under the rubric "other areas"—a distinction that Japan would retain until 1959.[14]

Postwar Japanese Controls

The continued paucity of Japanese FDI in the United States for more than two decades after the Second World War could not be blamed solely on the U.S. liquidation of prewar assets, however. As we have seen in the previous chapter, capital controls back home severely constrained fresh Japanese outflows. Those capital controls rested on legislation promulgated in 1949, during the Allied

[12]Quoted in Wilkins, "American-Japanese Investment," p. 514.
[13]Tsurumi, *The Japanese Are Coming*, p. 135.
[14]To illustrate, see Commerce Department, *Foreign Direct Investment in the U.S.: 1950–79*, table 1, pp. 2–3; for more detailed accounting of "other areas," see U.S. Commerce Department, Office of Business Economics, *Foreign Investments of the United States: Supplement to the Survey of Current Business* (Washington, D.C.: USGPO, 1953), Appendix table 4, p. 44.

Occupation; indeed, the same Foreign Exchange Control Law (FECL) that tightly regulated American multinationals investing in Japan also specified that every Japanese investment abroad had to be approved by the Ministry of Finance (MOF), typically in close consultation with the Ministry of International Trade and Industry (MITI), and with other agencies charged with guiding specific industries.[15] Under this regime, applications for foreign investment never received automatic government approval, but instead required time-consuming negotiations between prospective Japanese investors and those government ministries responsible for nurturing Japanese industry. In general, MOF, MITI, and other such ministries looked more favorably on investment applications that either promoted Japanese exports of manufactured goods or secured Japanese imports of vital raw materials. At the same time, these ministries looked askance at any proposed investments which might threaten Japanese producers back home (with whom they maintained close contact) or which were so large as to interfere with the government's industrial and macroeconomic policies. These policies aimed at reindustrializing war-ravaged Japan, a task that strict capital controls made easier by keeping scarce capital at home. Those investments that did receive permission to go abroad typically generated, through exports, more foreign exchange for Japan than they consumed in their overseas operations. By contrast, the few approved investments that did drain foreign exchange usually supplied Japan with raw materials essential for industrial growth; thus, they contributed to Japan's persistent (at least through 1964) current account deficits. As a result, through 1959, after a decade of capital controls, Japanese FDI in America reached $80 million (see Figure 3-1)—barely 1 percent of all foreign direct investment in the United States—a level well below its prewar high (2 percent in 1937).[16]

During the second decade of capital controls, the relative contribution of Japanese multinationals to total foreign investment in

[15]For further discussion of this interaction, see Dennis J. Encarnation and Mark Mason, "Neither MITI nor America: The Political Economy of Capital Liberalization in Japan," *International Organization* 44 (Winter 1990): 30–38.

[16]For postwar investment, see Commerce Department, *Foreign Direct Investment in the U.S.: 1950–79*, table 1, pp. 2–3; for prewar investment, see Wilkins, "American-Japanese Investment," table 3, p. 507.

America improved little. In fact, between 1959 and 1969, Japanese FDI in the United States doubled in absolute terms (see Figure 3-1 above), as did all foreign direct investment in America—thus leaving constant the relative financial contribution (roughly 1 percent) of Japanese multinationals. What did change was the relative importance of foreign investment for Japanese manufacturers. The 1950s saw the return of several prewar investors—most notably, those Japanese trading companies that served principally as intermediaries for U.S. exports of raw materials and food back to a reindustrializing Japan. Not until the late 1950s did several newcomers arrive, and newcomers continued to enter the United States throughout the next decade. Primarily, they were Japanese manufacturers seeking to establish in America their own subsidiaries, independent of traditional trading companies, to serve as dedicated importers and distributors of their parents' products. In only a very few industries (most notably, cotton textiles after 1957) did voluntary export restraints and other such trade barriers interfere with this strategy of investing to trade. Otherwise, America remained open to most imports and related investments from Japan. For example, to sell vehicles and parts, Toyota (1957), Honda (1959), and Nissan (1960) in rapid succession invested in U.S. wholesaling.[17] So did Matsushita (1959), Hitachi (1959), Sony (1960), NEC (1962), and Toshiba (1965)—all in electronics. For many of these emergent multinationals, moreover, American sales offices produced immediate dividends. During 1964, for example, Honda achieved top ranking (by both value and volume) in U.S. motorcycle sales; while for that year, Nissan gained a tenth-place ranking in U.S. auto imports[18] (Honda did not begin to ship cars to America until 1969). Thus, while Japanese multinationals invested in the United States no more aggressively than did other foreigners, their industrial origins shifted significantly, as large Japanese manufacturers began to establish their own trading outposts.

By 1964, moreover, the Japanese government had begun to

[17]For the evolution of these investments, see Economic World, *Directory of Japanese Companies in the U.S.A., 1987–89* (NY: Economic Salon, Ltd., 1990); The Oriental Economist, *Japanese Overseas Investment: A Complete Listing by Firms and Countries, 1984–85* (Tokyo: The Oriental Economist, 1984).

[18]For U.S. sales data, see Economic World, *Japanese Companies in the U.S.A.,* pp. 371, 399.

promote Japanese investments in America and elsewhere abroad, through the use of tax incentives and subsidized loans—all integral components of Japan's larger export-promotion strategy.[19] That strategy benefitted greatly from U.S. foreign economic policy, for the Kennedy Round of trade negotiations under the GATT (1963–72) significantly reduced tariffs on those manufactured products exported by developed countries. Indeed, beginning in 1964, Japan recorded the first of a continuous series of postwar trade surpluses. With the United States, the first such surplus appeared in 1965, fed by net exports from Honda, Matsushita, and others. During that same year, Japan joined the OECD, after securing (as noted in Chapter 2) numerous exemptions from that organization's capital liberalization code. Any further liberalization of Japanese capital controls, however, was deferred until 1968, when Japan had freed itself (as most observers then agreed)[20] from persistent deficits on its current account—thanks in large part to its trade surpluses with the United States. There, also beginning in 1968, a sudden spurt of import competition was leading American producers—especially in steel and noncotton textiles—to demand protection from their government. In steel, Japan almost immediately (1969) agreed to voluntary export restraints (VERs), but in noncotton textiles similar negotiations dragged on until 1971, when Japan finally imposed VERs.[21] Thus, at the beginning of a new decade, America began escalating its negative response to Japan's strategy of export promotion.

Caught in these trade disputes, and emboldened by growing current account surpluses, the Japanese government soon lifted controls on capital outflows—moving quickly here, in marked contrast to its much slower, carefully phased liberalization of capital

[19]For this strategy, see Lawrence Krause and Sekiguchi Sueo, "Japan and the World Economy," in Hugh Patrick and Henry Rosovsky, ed., *Asia's New Giant: How the Japanese Economy Works* (Washington, D.C.: Brookings Institution, 1982), p. 454; see their note 52 for further details.

[20]See, for example, Komiya Ryutaro and Itoh Motoshige, "Japan's International Trade and Trade Policy, 1955–1984," in Inoguchi Takashi and Daniel I. Okimoto, eds., *The Political Economy of Japan, Volume 2: The Changing International Context* (Stanford: Stanford University Press, 1988), esp. p. 188.

[21]As noted above, limits on cotton textiles had begun more than a decade earlier, in 1957.

inflows.[22] In 1969, the Bank of Japan began to grant its first automatic approvals for Japanese direct investments abroad, thus signaling the end of MOF's case-by-case screening. While initially, these investments had to be small (less than $200 thousand) to qualify for automatic approval, that ceiling was first raised the following year (to $1 million) and then completely eliminated during 1971. In that year, Japan enjoyed an unprecedented $6 billion surplus on its current account, just as the United States suffered its first global trade deficit in 78 years. The resulting "Nixon shocks," which effectively ended the Bretton Woods regime of fixed exchange rates, precipitated a rapid revaluation of the yen against the dollar that reduced the relative price of dollar-denominated investment in America. Now seeking to defend the yen against further revaluation, the Japanese government actively encouraged imports and capital outflows, while it also discouraged exports and capital inflows. In particular, for Japanese multinationals investing abroad, the government introduced new low-interest loans with greater foreign-exchange allocations, and expanded tax incentives. But the greatest incentive came in June 1972, when the Japanese government fully liberalized all remaining restrictions on direct investment overseas.[23]

This dramatic Japanese liberalization, however, still left in place certain government powers—defined by the Foreign Exchange Control Law—to reimpose controls on capital outflows whenever it wished. In fact, soon after liberalization, the government did invoke these powers when, by late 1973, a fourfold increase in crude oil prices sent the Japanese economy into its first postwar recession, and its current account into deficit. First, to help finance that deficit, and also to encourage investments at home, the Japanese government reimposed earlier restrictions on real estate purchases abroad.[24] But this move proved insufficient to slow the out-

[22]For the step-by-step evolution of capital liberalization on FDI in flows and outflows, see Krause and Sekiguchi, "Japan and the World Economy," Appendix, esp. pp. 454–458.

[23]The Japanese often refer to 1972 as the *gannen* (the very first year) of foreign direct investment; see Komiya Ryutaro and Wakasugi Ryuhei, "Japan's Foreign Direct Investment," *Annals of the American Academy of Political and Social Sciences* 513 (Jan. 1991), p. 51.

[24]Krause and Sekiguchi, "Japan and the World Economy," p. 457.

flow of Japanese FDI; so, employing "administrative guidance," MITI and other ministries sought to postpone already-approved investments in most other sectors (except for natural resources and energy-intensive industries). Of course, once the recession was well under way, such guidance was less necessary, since steep losses at home delayed private investments abroad. These delays proved temporary, however; and once the nation's economy recovered from the oil-price shock, the government returned to its policy of promoting outflows of Japanese FDI.

Investment Outflows and Trade Surpluses

Liberalization of capital outflows freed Japanese multinationals to invest directly in the United States (as Figure 3-1 shows). During the entire decade ending in 1969, such investment barely doubled, from $80 million (in 1959) to $176 billion. But then over the next five years, Japanese FDI in America doubled again, to $345 million in 1974. Moreover, such dramatic growth paralleled a much larger overall increase of foreign investment in the United States. European multinationals, for example, also doubled their direct investments in America between 1959 and 1969, and doubled them again by 1974.[25] By that time, they too were being aided by an appreciation of European currencies against the dollar. So the Europeans remained well ahead of the Japanese, whose direct investments continued to contribute less than 2 percent of all FDI in the United States—a share that had not changed appreciably since 1959 (at least), and a consistent percentage as far back as 1937.

Yet an increasing share of that still-limited Japanese investment now entered U.S. manufacturing, spurred both by liberalized capital controls at home and by heightened trade conflicts abroad. In fact, Japanese manufacturing investments in the United States actually quadrupled in just two years (1972–74), building on a very small base—while European multinationals posted their gains across a broader spectrum of U.S. industries.[26] Between 1968 and

[25]Commerce Department, *Foreign Direct Investment in the U.S., 1950–79*, table 1, pp. 2–3.

[26]Ibid., table 9, p. 17.

1972 (as noted above), in several contested industries American producers felt particularly aggrieved by stepped-up competition from Japanese imports. Beginning with highly visible protests over steel and textiles, protectionist actions in the United States spread to a wide range of products: from footwear to metal tableware, from specialty steels to fasteners, from individual electronic components to fully assembled electric machinery, from sheet glass to consumer electronics. Here, "the response of the Japanese color television producers is worth noting," according to Itoh Motoshige and Komiya Ryutaro.[27] "They partially replaced exports of their products by direct investment and production in the United States [just as they also] invested in some NICs [newly-industrializing countries] and exported sets produced there to the United States." (We will examine Japanese investments and related trade in the East Asian NICs in Chapter 4.) Indeed, during the 1972–74 acceleration of Japanese investment in U.S. manufacturing, Sony opened three new American plants in rapid succession, beginning with color TV assembly (1972), then integrating backward into color TV tube production (1973), and finally diversifying laterally into the production of hi-fi speakers (1974).[28] Not to be outdone by Sony, archrival Matsushita belatedly entered U.S. manufacturing through its 1974 acquisition of Motorola's color television business. That acquisition was one of a dozen completed that year by the Japanese, who slowly and reluctantly began imitating America's more aggressive European investors.[29] (At home, Japanese acquisitions, while also limited, were nonetheless more common, especially acquisitions of financially distressed suppliers and other affiliated companies.)[30] Instead, new (so-called greenfield) ven-

[27]Komiya and Itoh, "Japan's Internation Trade and Trade Policy," p. 198.

[28]For the evolution of these investments, see Economic World, *Directory of Japanese Companies in the U.S.A.;* The Oriental Economist, *Japanese Overseas Investment, 1984–85.*

[29]According to statistics provided by W. T. Grimm and Company, Japanese acquisitions of U.S. companies during 1974 (totaling 12) continued to fall well behind those of the Canadians (42 acquisitions) and the British (36), but moved just ahead of both the Germans and the Swiss (10 each). All told, the year saw 173 major acquisitions.

[30]W. Carl Kester, *Japanese Takeovers: The Global Contest for Corporate Control* (Boston: Harvard Business School Press, 1991), esp. pp. 4–17; James C. Abegglen, *The Strategy of Japanese Business* (Cambridge: Ballinger, 1984), pp. 125–139; Economist

tures provided Japanese multinationals with a common form of entry to markets, not only in the United States but elsewhere in the world.

Having made several sizable investments in largely wholly owned subsidiaries, Sony, Matsushita, and other Japanese multinationals could generate locally more U.S. sales than they and other Japanese exporters produced through trade. In fact, during 1974, local sales accounted for nearly three-quarters of the $40 billion in revenues generated by all Japanese subsidiaries in the United States—a sum well above the $12.3 billion of U.S. imports from Japan.[31] Put differently, local sales were two-and-a-half times larger than such imports, close to the 3:1 ratio of local sales to U.S. imports that characterized European multinationals in the United States. Again, these Europeans produced locally much that they also sold locally: their subsidiaries engaged specifically in U.S. manufacturing recorded 1974 sales nearly equal to U.S. imports of European manufactured goods (see Figure 3-2). If we add to this figure the value of additional assembly operations by European subsidiaries engaged principally in U.S. wholesaling, then the total value of local production exceeds all U.S. imports from Europe. By contrast, Japanese subsidiaries in the United States engaged in far less U.S. production: during 1974, U.S. imports of Japanese manufactured goods were ten times larger than the local sales of Japanese subsidiaries engaged principally in U.S. manufacturing. Even when we add to these local sales the assembly operations of subsidiaries engaged principally in U.S. wholesaling, the total value of Japanese production in the United States still remains below U.S. imports of manufactured goods from Japan. Thus, local production remained peripheral to the Japanese core investment strategy in America.

Intelligence Unit, *Japanese Overseas Investment: The New Challenge*, Special Report No. 142 (London: Economist Intelligence Unit, 1983), pp. 109–114, 123–128; Sarkis J. Khoury, *Transnational Mergers and Acquisitions in the United States* (Lexington, Mass: Lexington Books, 1980).

[31]U.S. Commerce Department, Bureau of Economic Analysis, *Foreign Direct Investment in the United States*, vol. 2: *Report of the Secretary of Commerce, Benchmark Survey, 1974* (Washington, D.C.: USGPO, April 1976), table E-10, p. 60.

Figure 3-2. U.S. production, imports, and distribution: EC vs. Japan, 1974

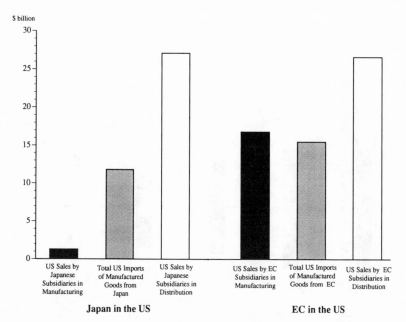

$ billion

US Sales by Japanese Subsidiaries in Manufacturing	Total US Imports of Manufactured Goods from Japan	US Sales by Japanese Subsidiaries in Distribution

Japan in the US

US Sales by EC Subsidiaries in Manufacturing	Total US Imports of Manufactured Goods from EC	US Sales by EC Subsidiaries in Distribution

EC in the US

Sources: U.S. Commerce Department, Bureau of Economic Analysis, *Foreign Direct Investment in the United States, Volume 2, Report of the Secretary of Commerce, Benchmark Survey, 1974* (Washington, D.C.: USGPO, April 1976), table K-5, p. 139; U.S. Department of Commerce, International Trade Administration, Office of Trade and Investment Analysis, *U.S. Foreign Trade Highlights* (Washington, D.C.: USGPO, various years).

The Japanese invested principally to sustain and control their trade. During 1974, for example, Japanese subsidiaries in the United States served as final markets and (especially) intermediary channels for over four-fifths of all U.S. imports from Japan (see Figure 3-3). That share was more than twice the relative contribution of European subsidiaries to U.S. imports from Europe. For both the Europeans and the Japanese, such trade remained largely intracompany, from overseas parents to their subsidiaries in America.[32] Typically for both, but especially for the Japanese, these

[32]Ibid.

Figure 3-3. Investment-related U.S. trade with Japan and the EC, 1974

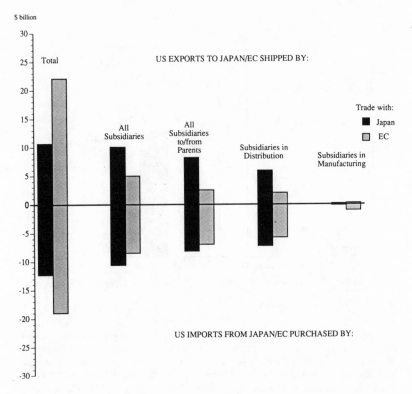

Sources: U.S. Commerce Department, Bureau of Economic Analysis, *Foreign Direct Investment in the United States, Volume 2, Report of the Secretary of Commerce, Benchmark Survey, 1974* (Washington, D.C.: USGPO, April 1976), tables E-7, E-8, E-16 and E-17, pp. 57–58, 66–67; U.S. Department of Commerce, International Trade Administration, Office of Trade and Investment Analysis, *U.S. Foreign Trade Highlights: 1982* (Washington, D.C.: USGPO, 1983).

subsidiaries were engaged principally in U.S. wholesaling. Indeed, through very limited investments in distribution, Japanese exporters still managed to channel more than two-thirds of all U.S. imports from Japan—imports that consisted of (in rank order by value) motor vehicles, metals, and machinery. Here, the sales subsidiaries of Honda (motorcycles), Hitachi Metals (steel), and Matsushita (electrical products) excelled. In reverse, Mitsui, Mitsubishi, and other Japanese trading companies bought (again, in order by value) U.S. food and inedible raw materials from their wholesaling subsidiaries in the United States. During 1974, these shipments by wholesaling subsidiaries back to their Japanese parents accounted for over four-fifths of all U.S. exports to Japan—and their combined value represented nearly five times the relative contribution of European multinationals to U.S. exports bound for Europe (see Figure 3-3). With such unprecedented control, Japanese subsidiaries also contributed over half of America's small but rapidly growing trade deficit with Japan.

STAGE II: LIBERALIZED CAPITAL OUTFLOWS, REGULATED MERCHANDISE INFLOWS

After 1975, the United States began to run burgeoning trade deficits with Japan. Interrupted only by the oil price shocks of 1979–80, these deficits climbed exponentially, from $5 billion in 1976, to $10 billion in 1980, and then to a postwar high of $57 billion during 1987. After that date, trade deficits began to decline modestly, yet already their size and persistence had precipitated a fundamental shift in America's strategic investment policies by setting off a new round of U.S.-Japan trade negotiations. During this second round, voluntary export restraints (VERs) and orderly marketing agreements (OMAs) proliferated, beginning in electronics and reaching automobiles—two industries that together accounted for over three-quarters of America's trade deficit with Japan.[33]

During this second round, as the United States moved to control the inflow of Japanese goods, Japan also altered its strategic investment policy, by fully liberalizing Japanese direct investment abroad.[34] These and other long-term capital outflows were sup-

[33]For a discussion of VERs and OMAs, see Komiya and Itoh, "Japan's Trade Policy," p. 197; for the industry composition of U.S. trade deficits, see Commerce Department, *U.S. Foreign Trade Highlights, 1989*, pp. 100–101.

[34]For the evolution of capital liberalization, see Krause and Sekiguchi, "Japan and the World Economy," Appendix, esp. pp. 454–458.

posed to offset trade surpluses (like those with the United States), as the Ministry of Finance pursued its stated objective of "balancing the basic balance." In pursuit of this objective, MOF removed in 1975 the same capital controls it had reimposed the previous year, under pressure from the first oil-price shock; and then MOF initiated yet another loan program, through the Export-Import Bank of Japan, to assist those Japanese investors going abroad.[35] Finally, in 1979, Japan (as we have noted in Chapter 2) moved directly to amend the FECL, and thus to codify all major changes wrought by twelve years of capital liberalization. Effective in March 1980, a simple notification to the Bank of Japan replaced the earlier licensing applications as the essential precondition for all Japanese FDI abroad. Now, capital liberalization at home had finally freed Japanese multinationals to respond in the United States to competitive pressures—especially those pressures arising from both the structure of particular industries and the unpredictable behavior of foreign-exchange markets.

Parallel Growth

Just as America's trade deficits with Japan grew exponentially, so too did Japan's direct investment in the United States. After 1959, a decade was required for Japanese FDI in America to double; but for this FDI to double again, only one-half that time had to pass, the five years between 1969 and 1974. And thereafter, Japanese FDI in the United States doubled every year-and-a-half, at least through the end of the decade (see Figure 3-1 above). By contrast, throughout the 1970s, European multinationals continued to double their direct investments in America every five years.[36] Thus between 1974 and 1979, Japanese multinationals outpaced their European counterparts, and began contributing an ever-growing

[35]Chalmers Johnson, *MITI and the Japanese Miracle: The Growth of Japanese Industrial Policy, 1925–1975* (Stanford: Stanford University Press, 1982), pp. 275–304. According to the *Far Eastern Economic Review* (June 13, 1985, p. 83), outstanding loans in the program grew fourfold in seven years, from ¥4 billion in 1977 to ¥58 billion in 1983.

[36]Commerce Department, *Foreign Direct Investment in the U.S., 1950–79*, table 1, pp. 2–3.

share of all foreign direct investment in the United States. In fact, during the latter half of the 1970s, that share actually pierced an apparent 2 percent ceiling which long had characterized (at least since 1937) Japanese FDI in America. Indeed, by 1979, Japanese multinationals were contributing upwards of 6 percent of the cumulative value of foreign direct investment in the United States—a share comparable to those of the French and the Swiss, but still well below the shares invested by multinationals from Germany, Canada, the United Kingdom, and the Netherlands.

Of this new Japanese investment, most entered U.S. wholesaling, where Japanese manufacturers joined existing trading companies, by establishing wholly owned importers and distributors for their parents' products. In fact, those Japanese subsidiaries that derived the bulk of their income from wholesaling accounted, after 1978 and through the next decade, for over one-half of all Japanese FDI in America.[37] With that huge investment, Japanese multinationals managed to retain unprecedented control over their burgeoning trade with the United States. By 1980, Japanese subsidiaries in America—nearly all operating as wholesalers—distributed over three-quarters of all U.S. imports from Japan, and they shipped well over two-thirds of all U.S. exports to Japan (see Figure 3-4). For all U.S. exports, the relative contribution of Japanese multinationals had declined since 1974 (from 84 percent to 71 percent in 1980; compare Figure 3-3 and Figure 3-4) but still remained at least twice as large as that of European subsidiaries in the United States. Similarly, for U.S. imports, the relative contribution of Japanese multinationals had also declined slightly since 1974 (from 82 percent to 78 percent in 1980), as America's trade with Japan skyrocketed. Still, this trade remained at least twice the constant share of trans-Atlantic shipments distributed in the United States by European subsidiaries. In fact, these Europeans proved very likely to trade with unaffiliated European importers and exporters, while Japanese subsidiaries depended on their par-

[37]The investment data reported in Dennis J. Encarnation, "Cross-Investment," in Thomas K. McCraw, *America versus Japan* (Boston: Harvard Business School Press, 1986), table 4-2, p. 120; idem, "American-Japanese Cross-Investment," in Stephan Haggard and Chung-in Moon, eds., *Pacific Dynamics: The International Politics of Industrial Change* (Boulder: Westview Press, 1989), table 8.2, p. 212.

Figure 3-4. Investment-related U.S. trade with Japan and the EC, 1980

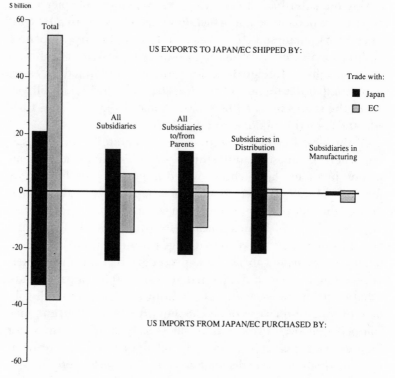

Sources: U.S. Commerce Department, Bureau of Economic Analysis, *Foreign Direct Investment in the United States, 1980* (Washington, D.C.: USGPO, Oct. 1983), tables G-19, G-21, G-23, G-33, G-35, and G-37, pp. 159, 161, 163, 173, 175, 177; U.S. Department of Commerce, International Trade Administration, Office of Trade and Investment Analysis, *U.S. Foreign Trade Highlights: 1982* (Washington, D.C.: USGPO, 1983).

ents for nearly all of their two-way trade with the United States (see Figure 3-4). That intracompany trade, when totaled for 1980, contributed an astounding $9.5 billion to America's $10 billion trade deficit with Japan—a sum far in excess of their 1974 contribution ($0.8 billion out of $1.6 billion). Thus between 1974 and 1980 America's trade deficit with Japan soared, thanks in large part to intracompany trade between the subsidiaries and parents of Japanese multinationals.

Nevertheless, Japanese multinationals still managed to generate locally far greater U.S. sales than they and other Japanese exporters produced through trade. In fact, during 1980, local sales continued (as they had in 1974) to account for over three-quarters of the $91 billion of 1980 revenues generated by Japanese multinationals in America—a value well above the $31 billion of U.S. imports from Japan that year.[38] Since 1974, even though these local sales have doubled in value, their growth still has failed to keep pace with the increase in U.S. imports from Japan. As a result, the ratio of local sales to U.S. imports actually declined from 2.5:1 (in 1974) to 2:1 (in 1980). For European multinationals in the United States, by contrast, that ratio nearly doubled between 1974 and 1980, from 3:1 to nearly 6:1. Moreover, for the Europeans, much of that growth in local sales came from increases in local production, which by 1980 had grown to at least twice as large as U.S. imports of European manufactures (see Figure 3-5)—up sharply from near-parity with those imports in 1974 (see Figure 3-2). Such parity did not characterize the local production by Japanese multinationals until 1980, and then only after one included the estimated value of the additional assembly operations performed by Japanese subsidiaries engaged principally in U.S. wholesaling. Otherwise, for subsidiaries engaged principally in manufacturing, local sales between 1974 and 1980 remained at one-tenth the size of U.S. imports of Japanese manufactured goods (see Figure 3-5)—even though both figures tripled over this period. To feed this remarkable growth in local sales, Japanese investments in subsidiaries engaged principally in U.S. manufacturing also tripled between 1974 and 1980, when they accounted for one-fifth of all Japanese FDI in the United States.

Here, the electronics industry attracted the greatest attention; in 1980, it accounted for over one-quarter of all Japanese FDI in U.S. manufacturing.[39] In fact, more Japanese electronics manufacturers invested in local U.S. production between 1978 and 1979 than had invested in the United States for three decades prior to 1978—

[38]For U.S. sales, see U.S. Commerce Department, Bureau of Economic Analysis, *Foreign Direct Investment in the United States, 1980* (Washington, D.C.: USGPO, Oct. 1983); for U.S. trade, see idem, *U.S. Foreign Trade Highlights*, pp. 100–101.

[39]Actually, 28 percent; see Ministry of Finance, *Statistics for the Approval of Overseas Investment*, various years.

Figure 3-5. U.S. production, imports, and distribution: EC vs. Japan, 1980

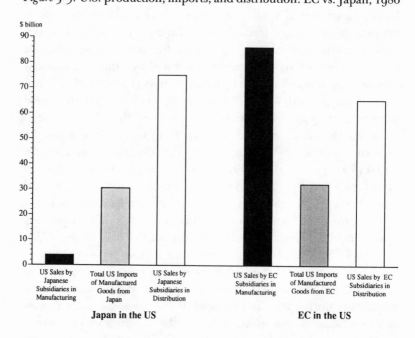

Sources: U.S. Commerce Department, Bureau of Economic Analysis, *Foreign Direct Investment in the United States, 1980* (Washington, D.C.: USGPO, Oct. 1983), table E-5, p. 103; U.S. Department of Commerce, International Trade Administration, Office of Trade and Investment Analysis, *U.S. Foreign Trade Highlights: 1982* (Washington, D.C.: USGPO, 1983).

a claim that could be made by no other Japanese industry. Most of these manufacturers began investing in U.S. wholesaling during the late 1960s to sell color television sets exported from Japan.[40] As these sales grew, Zenith and other U.S. producers (often acting in concert with labor unions) waged what David Yoffie has described as a "political war on Japan," using "every conceivable avenue of attack" through the U.S. courts, the Congress, and the federal bureaucracy—but with no immediate success.[41] Unimpeded by

[40]Abo Tetsuo et al., *Local Production of Japanese Automobile and Electronics Firms in the United States* (Tokyo: University of Tokyo, Institute of Social Science, March 1990), pp. 97–100.

[41]David Yoffie, *Power and Protectionism: Strategies of the Newly Industrializing Countries* (New York: Columbia University Press, 1983), p. 215.

trade restrictions, U.S. imports of Japanese-made color TVs continued to climb, until by 1976 they had captured just over one-third of the U.S. color TV market.[42] Also during that year, Sanyo (through its acquisition of Whirlpool's majority shareholdings in a joint venture with Sears)[43] joined Sony and Matsushita in local U.S. assembly of color TVs. Despite all such investment, Japanese-made sets continued to flood into the country, leading the U.S. International Trade Commission (ITC) to rule in 1977 that Japanese exporters had seriously injured U.S. industry.

Although the ITC recommended that tariffs be imposed, the Carter Administration preferred to negotiate with Japan an Orderly Marketing Agreement (OMA), which declared that, for three years beginning July 1977, Japanese exports of color TVs to America would be limited to 60 percent of their 1976 total. Omitted from this OMA were U.S. imports of "subassemblies," for both American and Japanese trade negotiators wanted to encourage Japanese multinationals to invest in U.S. assembly plants that would, at least initially, require such imports. Indeed, a separate sideletter to the agreement exempted all color TV sets that could claim more than 50 percent U.S. content;[44] the remainder of that content ordinarily would consist largely of subassemblies and other components (e.g., semiconductors) imported from Japan or elsewhere in East Asia. Freed from capital controls at home, Toshiba, Mitsubishi, and Hitachi were quick to respond to these new U.S. incentives, and in the first year of the OMA (1977) the Japanese invested in three color TV-assembly plants.[45] Prior to these investments, in 1976, U.S. imports of Japanese subassemblies were valued at $74 million; by 1979, two years after these color TV plants opened in America, such imports had tripled to $215 million.[46] Yet even though local content did grow to exceed 50 percent, reaching in some plants as much as 75 percent—all in accordance with the

[42]Abo, *Local Production*, pp. 97.

[43]For the details of this acquisition, see Robert H. Hayes and Kim Clark, "Sanyo Manufacturing Corporation—Forrest City, Arkansas," Harvard Business School Case no. 9-682-045.

[44]For the contents of this sideletter, see Abo, *Local Production*, pp. 97–100.

[45]For the evolution of these multinationals, see Economic World, *Japanese Companies in the U.S.A., 1987–89;* The Oriental Economist, *Japanese Overseas Investment, 1984–85.*

[46]Yoffie, *Power and Protectionism*, p. 217.

sideletter to the 1977 OMA—a recent Japanese study of the 1986 operations of these TV plants concludes nevertheless that "key components procured directly from Japan or indirectly, namely via Southeast Asian countries and Mexico [still], constitute one of the crucial factors in securing the product quality of all Japanese affiliates' plants."[47] Thus, the twin forces of capital liberalization in Japan and trade protectionism in America converged during the late 1970s to stimulate U.S. investments by Japanese manufacturers—and thereby to alter the composition, value, and direction of related trade.

Industry Pressures

The potent convergence of these government policies in the late 1970s also unleashed certain competitive pressures that arise from the structure of industries, including the power of buyers to influence the investment decisions of their suppliers. Since Japanese color TV manufacturers made greater use of integrated circuits than did their American competitors,[48] their new investments in the United States put added pressure on Japanese semiconductor producers to follow. Acting as the industry leader, NEC became the first Japanese firm (in 1978) to produce semiconductors in America.[49] Even before the OMA on color TVs, one-third of NEC's semiconductor sales came from exports, and one-third of those exports were destined for the U.S. market. Since most of these sales consisted of commodity-like products with ready substitutes, suppliers found that they had to follow existing buyers overseas if they wished to maintain the relationship—as Japanese component manufacturers had already done in East Asia (as we shall see in Chapter 4).[50] Similarly, in the United States, when Sanyo, Toshiba, Hitachi, and Mitsubishi completed the long list of Japanese consumer electronics companies—beginning with Sony and Matsu-

[47]Abo, *Local Production*, pp. 114–115.

[48]Ibid., pp. 97–98.

[49]Unless otherwise noted, for data in this paragraph and the next three paragraphs, see Encarnation, "Cross-Investment," pp. 128–133.

[50]For the earlier evolution of these manufactures to East Asia, see Yoshihara Kunio, *Japanese Investment in Southeast Asia* (Honolulu: University Press of Hawaii, 1978), pp. 133–178.

shita—that set up local production, NEC moved to America with them. Customization of parts also encouraged suppliers to locate in close geographic proximity to those buyers who required it, a common condition in industrial and communications electronics. For example, IBM and AT&T, both major buyers of semiconductors and other electronic components, demanded customization for the production of computers and telecommunication equipment. Here again, the growing need for close and repetitive interaction among engineers from both semiconductor suppliers and their buyers—American and (increasingly) Japanese—added pressure on NEC, a premier component supplier, to invest heavily in the United States.

But the actual timing of NEC's investment in America followed the threat of new U.S. trade restrictions (modeled on those in consumer electronics) that appeared in 1975, when American semiconductor manufacturers charged NEC and other Japanese producers with selling capacitors in violation of U.S. antitrust provisions.[51] During the following year, such protectionist pressures escalated when American manufacturers formed the Semiconductor Industry Association (SIA), at least partially in response to growing Japanese competition. Already by 1976, Japanese semiconductors accounted for almost 7 percent of total sales in the large U.S. market—a share roughly comparable in dollar value to the 12 percent of total sales supplied by American producers in the smaller Japanese market.[52] That comparability soon ended, however, after American producers failed to invest in increased domes-

[51]For the specifics of this case, see *The Economist*, Dec. 8, 1984, pp. 75–76; for a general overview of the political economy of protectionism in semiconductors, see Daniel I. Okimoto, "Political Context," in Daniel I. Okimoto et al., eds., *Competitive Edge: The Semiconductor Industry in the U.S. and Japan* (Stanford: Stanford University Press, 1984), esp. pp. 93–94, 100, 105–106, 122–129.

[52]The production data in this paragraph are derived from the following sources (in order): Japan, Ministry of International Trade and Industry, *The Semiconductor Industry and Japanese Government Policies* (Tokyo, 1983), p. 3; U.S. Congress, Joint Economic Committee, *International Competition in Advanced Industrial Sectors: Trade and Development in the Semiconductor Industry* (Washington, D.C.: USGPO, 1983), pp. 105–106; U.S. Congress, Office of Technology Assessment, *International Competitiveness in Electronics* (Washington, D.C.: USGPO, 1983), p. 141; Machinery Promotion Association, Economic Research Center (Kikai shinkou kyoukai keizai kenkyuujo), *International Comparison of the Semiconductor Industry in Japan and the U.S.* (Tokyo: MPA, 1981), p. 51.

tic capacity (during the 1974–75 recession) to supply growing U.S. demand specifically for memory semiconductors (especially 16K DRAMS). Instead, after 1977, the balance of trade in semiconductors shifted to favor the Japanese, leading the SIA to press successfully for an orderly marketing agreement. That agreement did little to stymie the Japanese, however: by 1979 they had captured 43 percent of the U.S. market for 16K chips—even in the face of a yen-to-dollar appreciation that had begun during the previous year. Such appreciation also threatened additional Japanese shipments, but reduced the yen cost of foreign investment; so NEC shifted strategy and moved quickly in 1978 to acquire a financially troubled U.S. company (Electronic Arrays) that already traded with NEC. Yet, even as late as 1978, such acquisitions remained less common than new "greenfield" investments for Japanese multinationals—again, in marked contrast to the entry strategies of America's European investors.[53]

Once NEC made the first move in 1978, its Japanese competitors proved especially likely to imitate their industry leader in their U.S. investments. They followed NEC in rapid succession: Hitachi and Fujitsu acted in 1979; Toshiba, in 1980; Hitachi again, in 1981; Mitsubishi, in 1983.[54] During 1982, NEC also constructed a new U.S. manufacturing plant—its second investment in semiconductors—but this time imitating the "greenfield" investments of its competitors. Such imitative rivalries among Japanese oligopolists stood in marked contrast to the foreign investments of American multinationals in Japan: After IBM's entry in 1971, as we have seen in Chapter 2, no other U.S. semiconductor producer succeeded in establishing manufacturing operations in Japan until the 1980s, well after capital liberalization, when both Motorola and Fairchild reentered Japan. To account for the different patterns of American and Japanese investment in semiconductors, existing research

[53]According to statistics provided by W. T. Grimm and Company, only four Japanese multinationals entered the U.S. market during 1978 through the acquisition of an existing American company, in marked contrast to British (62 acquisitions), Canadian (49), and German (27) investors.

[54]For the evolution of these multinationals, see Economic World, *Japanese Companies in the U.S.A., 1987–89;* The Oriental Economist, *Japanese Overseas Investment, 1984–85.*

suggests that such imitative strategies appear most often in moderately concentrated industries—not in the less concentrated ones, where rivals seem unaware of any interdependence; nor in the very concentrated industries, where rivals often knowingly collude.[55] In Japan, the semiconductor industry has remained more highly concentrated than in the United States. In 1978, for example, the top four Japanese companies—NEC, Hitachi, Fujitsu, and Toshiba—collectively controlled 63 percent of the open market for integrated circuits. NEC alone held 18 percent of the market. The comparable figure in America for the top four companies was lower, at 49 percent, in part because of U.S. antitrust policies. Indeed, such policies proscribed IBM and AT&T from entering the open market. Japanese government policies, by contrast, actively encouraged increased industrial concentration. MITI actually prohibited specialized manufacturers of integrated circuits from entering the semiconductor industry, thus promoting the entry of those large, diversified electronics companies that had more in common with each other than did their American rivals.[56]

Of course, common industry structures can be expected to breed similar corporate strategies. In Japan, the largest semiconductor manufacturers were themselves horizontally diversified electronics companies of roughly comparable size. For the top six Japanese companies, semiconductors averaged 7 percent of total sales in 1979—compared to 70 percent for the top nine U.S. semiconductor companies.[57] Unlike most of their American coun-

[55] Knickerbocker, *Oligopolistic Competition*, chap. 6; the following estimates of market shares in the Japanese and American semiconductor industries were reported in Machinery Promotion Association, *Semiconductor Industry*, p. 96; and Semiconductor Industry Association, *International Microelectronic Challenge* (Menlo Park, Calif.: SIA, 1981), p. 35.

[56] For the role of Japanese policies in promoting concentration generally, see Richard E. Caves and Uekusa Masu, *Industrial Organization in Japan* (Washington, D.C.: The Brookings Institution, 1976), pp. 141–154; for the semiconductor industry specifically, see Machinery Promotion Association, Economic Research Center (Kikai shinkou kyoukai keizai kenkyuujo), *Survey Report on the Semiconductor Industry in Japan and the U.S.* (Tokyo: MPA, 1980), p. 122.

[57] For the internal and external sales of Japanese semiconductor companies reported in this paragraph and the next, see Joel Stern, "International Structural Differences in Financing," in Semiconductor Industry Association, eds., *An American Response to the Foreign Industrial Challenge in High Technology Industries* (Menlo

terparts, Japanese companies competed elsewhere in other consumer and industrial product areas, as well as in semiconductors.
With Japanese production concentrated in only a few diversified
conglomerates, each of which consumed a small-to-moderate proportion of its own production, cross-purchasing strategies became
common among large Japanese companies. In 1979, for example,
the top six companies, which produced over one-half of all semiconductors, consumed at least 60 percent of all noncaptive domestic production. In the U.S. semiconductor industry, by contrast, a
large proportion of noncaptive sales flowed from Intel and other
full-line semiconductor companies, which themselves consumed
little of their competitors' production. With a few captive makers,
several full-line companies, and many smaller specialized producers, competitors in the United States were far more diverse than
those in Japan. Cross-purchasing, like vertical and horizontal integration, contributed to the "follow-the-leader" behavior that characterized Japanese semiconductor producers—and other industrial oligopolies in Japan as well—leading them all to invest directly
in America.

With the pressures from industry structures and government
policies all converging at the turn of the decade, Japanese FDI in
the United States soared—nearly tripling between 1979 and 1982
(see Figure 3-1). Along the way, during 1981, the book value
(stock) of all such Japanese investments surpassed the cumulative
value (stock) of all U.S. FDI in Japan; and only three years later,
Japanese stock in America stood at nearly twice the value of U.S.
stock in Japan. Moreover, during the early 1980s, the United States
replaced Southeast Asia as the principal target for new direct investments, with over two-fifths of all annual investment outflows
from Japan now destined for America.[58] As in bilateral trade,
American-Japanese cross-investment had thus created another
new asymmetry—and once again, an asymmetry that worked to
favor Japan.

Park, Calif.: SIA, 1980), pp. 133–134; Office of Technology Assessment, *International Competitiveness in Electronics*, p. 138; Joint Economic Committee, *International
Competition*, p. 68.

[58]Ministry of Finance, *Statistics for Overseas Direct Investment*, selected years.

Local Production

Such asymmetries first became apparent in automobiles, beginning with trade. By 1980, Japanese-made automobiles were contributing nearly one-half of America's $12.2 billion yearly trade deficit with Japan, and they represented over one-third of total U.S. imports.[59] These auto imports—aided by the wholesaling subsidiaries of Japanese automakers in the United States—supplied over one-fifth of the U.S. market in 1980, nearly double their share just two years earlier. (By comparison, Volkswagen had become in 1978 the first foreign automaker actually to assemble cars in the United States—at the same time that the U.S. government moved to rescue Chrysler from financial collapse.) After 1978, U.S. demand for Japanese autos simply skyrocketed, as a second oil price shock brought a surge in the sales of fuel-efficient cars. That rapid increase was far greater than any experienced after the first (1973) oil shock, and it pushed auto production in Japan ahead of that in America.[60] Caught unprepared, GM (the U.S. industry leader) incurred its first financial loss in decades; with Ford, GM scurried to Japan and elsewhere in East Asia, now in search of joint ventures and other new sources of supply. Meanwhile back home, Ford and GM parted company politically, at a time when the Congress began to consider some twenty pieces of protectionist legislation.[61] While GM initially favored the maintenance of free trade, Ford immediately petitioned the U.S. International Trade Commission (ITC) for relief from the torrents of Japanese imports. Ford was also joined in a separate petition by the United Automobile Workers (UAW). The ITC denied both petitions, however, citing the U.S. recession—not surging imports—for the American automobile industry's demise. Such unfavorable government actions further galvanized U.S. industry: Chrysler now joined Ford and the UAW in demanding import restraints, and even GM began to call for Japan to impose voluntary export restraints. Thus, in an

[59]U.S. Commerce Department, *U.S. Foreign Trade Highlights: 1989,* pp. 100–101.
[60]Abo, *Local Production,* pp. 65–66.
[61]V. Krishna, "Voluntary Export Restraints (A): Japanese Automobiles, 1981–84," Harvard Business School Case no. 9-187-163.

attempt to find some effective response to exaggerated asymmetries in trade with Japan, U.S. automakers added the politics of protectionism to their existing global strategy.

Meanwhile, in Japan, automakers remained divided but largely at loggerheads with MITI.[62] Moving preemptively, Honda announced in January 1980, less than a year after initiating U.S. motorcycle production, that it would construct an auto assembly plant in the United States, to begin production during 1982. For Honda, long relegated to a distant third-ranking position in the Japanese market, this move opened a rare opportunity for growth in the face of U.S. protectionism—an opportunity made especially attractive in 1976, when the Honda Accord was acclaimed America's "Import Car of the Year." In February 1980, barely a month after Honda's announcement, MITI began encouraging Toyota and Nissan to restrict car exports to the United States[63]—with little success, even though UAW President Fraser visited Tokyo at that time to express similar demands and to invite Japanese investment in America. The U.S. trade representative would come next (in May) to Tokyo, but not before MITI had again approached Toyota and Nissan. During these April talks, the "Big Two" Japanese automakers voiced strong opposition both to any voluntary export constraints and to direct investments in the United States. Such investments were unwarranted, they told MITI, in a market characterized by high relative wages and poor labor-management relations, and where prevailing forecasts predicted that U.S. automakers would themselves begin compact-car production in America. These disincentives to investment did not appear to impede Japanese truck production in America, however; compared to automobiles, trucks demanded fewer precision parts and required fewer model changes. Accordingly, Nissan announced in April that it would begin constructing a pick-up truck assembly plant in the United States—at almost the same time that the U.S. trade representative arrived in Tokyo with his demand that Japanese automakers invest in America. Investment, he hypothesized, would both increase U.S. auto exports to Japan from these new trans-

---

[62]Unless otherwise noted, this paragraph and the next rely on Abo, *Local Production,* pp. 65–66, for the history of these negotiations.

[63]Yoffie, *Power and Protectionism,* p. 225.

plants and reduce U.S. imports of Japanese-made cars, by substituting for existing trade. Despite these arguments, the U.S. trade representative, like MITI, was ineffective in securing concessions from Toyota and Nissan for either trade or investment.

The balance in bargaining power shifted, however, once it appeared likely that a bipartisan coalition in the U.S. Congress would favor protectionist legislation. Such a coalition emerged in early 1981, when the Democratic chairman (Lloyd Bentson of Texas) and ranking Republican member (John Danforth of Missouri) of the Senate Finance Committee, both conservatives, introduced a bill that would limit U.S. imports from Japan to 1.6 million automobiles per year. With hearings scheduled for spring and a vote expected during summer 1981, this "Danforth Bill" added a new urgency to both sets of negotiations—those between the U.S. trade representative and MITI, and those between MITI and the Big Two Japanese automakers. In May, MITI announced an agreement on the temporary imposition of Japan's voluntary export restraint (VER) made retroactive to April 1981 (the beginning of the Japanese fiscal year) and continuing through March 1984 (with periodic renewals extending through 1992). Simultaneous with MITI's announcement, Senator Danforth withdrew his bill from the U.S. Senate, feeling that his intention to limit Japanese imports would be satisfied by the VER's first-year quota (1.68 million vehicles). That quota represented a 7.7 percent cutback from sales of the previous year, which MITI had allocated by using a formula based largely on historical market shares. Allocation virtually guaranteed to each of the largest Japanese exporters—Toyota, Nissan, and Honda (in that order)—a 4-6 percent share of the U.S. market, to which could be added all sales from American assembly plants. In fact, as encouragement for such manufacturing investments, the VER expressly omitted any mention of components, subassemblies, and knocked-down kits. From these unrestricted imports, the Japanese could construct complete automobiles— exactly what Ford and GM had done in Japan before the Second World War. For those American firms at that earlier time, and now for Japanese automakers, foreign investment could be used to circumscribe trade barriers on finished autos, by both increasing local production and altering the composition of related trade.

Faced with the prospect of indefinite government-imposed constraints on exports, then, Japanese automakers fundamentally altered their U.S. investment strategies.[64] Honda, the most export-dependent of Japan's top-three producers, set the trend: barely a year after the imposition of the VER, that company (in 1982) began assembling in Marysville, Ohio, its award-winning Accord model, becoming in the process the sixth largest (following VW) manufacturer of automobiles in the United States. The following year, Nissan began assembling pick-up trucks in Smyrna, Tennessee, and announced an expansion of this plant to include auto assembly, which began in 1985. That move, it now seems, served to accelerate Toyota's planned investment in U.S. manufacturing, as that Japanese industry leader finally moved to imitate the behavior of its oligopolistic rivals.[65] But unlike these Japanese rivals, Toyota had also opted to invest quickly (and rather inexpensively) in a 50:50 joint venture with GM. That venture, the New United Motors Manufacturing, Inc. (NUMMI), was managed day-to-day by Toyota, which planned to use NUMMI as a laboratory for learning to operate on an expended scale in America. Unimpeded by such concerns, Honda (during 1984–85) added a second production line to its Marysville plant, and then began constructing its first U.S. engine plant—just as Japan extended its expanded VER on automobiles (beginning in March 1984, with a slightly increased quota)[66]—the first of a series of such extensions, pushing limitations on trade into the 1990s. Despite these VERs, however, by 1986 North America had become Honda's largest national market, accounting for over one-half its worldwide sales. With these sales, Honda finally surpassed both Nissan (in 1984) and Toyota (in 1986) to claim the largest U.S. market share among Japanese automakers—and also to emerge as America's fourth largest automaker, having exceeded the production of (then French-owned) American Motors.[67]

[64]For an overview of these developments, see *The Economist*, Dec. 8, 1984, pp. 75–76. For the Toyota-GM venture, also see *New York Times*, Jan. 30, 1985, p. D1; the special report in *Business Japan*, April 1983, pp. 18–20.

[65]This motivation is explicitly examined in the *Wall Street Journal*, July 9, 1985, p. 2.

[66]That increase was 10 percent, to 2.3 million units.

[67]For market data, see *The Economist*, Dec. 8, 1984, pp. 75–76; *Fortune*, Oct. 28, 1985, pp. 30–33.

In their drive to increase U.S. production and sales, Honda and other Japanese automakers found ready allies among state and local governments eager to influence final plant-location decisions with a wide range of fiscal incentives, infrastructure expenditures, and marketing practices.[68] Competition often proved intense, especially because several states—including those located in the "rust belt"—were looking to foreign investment in new manufacturing plants as one way of reversing economic decline. Ohio, for example, won out over several other contenders by offering Honda an incentive package that included: a $2.5 million grant to develop the site; a $90 thousand reduction in annual property taxes; designation of the site as a foreign trade subzone with reduced duties; a guarantee that the federal government would make railroad improvements valued at $300 thousand; even free English tutoring at a nearby state university for Japanese expatriates and their children.[69] Meanwhile, Tennessee—Ohio's main competitor—proposed a comparable incentive package to Honda's rival, Nissan. Among many inducements, Tennessee spent $12 million for new roads to the Nissan plant, and $7 million to help train plant employees; the county government also reduced property taxes by another $1 million over the first ten years of the project. In all, Ohio and Tennessee, like other governments, tailored a package of incentives to the special needs of each potential investor, with those who offered the greatest potential for employment typically awarded the greatest assistance. By contrast, California found that it did not need to offer such incentives in order to remain the favorite site for Japanese investors; although that state's unitary tax—a popular subject for vitriolic debate—did emerge as an effective disincentive to Japanese investment there. Still, California felt compelled to join over 40 other U.S. states (and nearly a dozen municipalities) in opening investment offices in

[68]For a survey of the strategies pursued by governments competing for investment, see Dennis J. Encarnation and Louis T. Wells, Jr., "Sovereignty En Garde: Negotiating with Foreign Investors," *International Organization* 39 (Winter 1985), pp. 47–48; idem, "Competitive Strategies in Global Industries: A View from Host Countries," in Michael E. Porter, ed., *Competitive Strategies in Global Industries* (Boston: Harvard Business School Press, 1986).

[69]The competitive bids of Ohio and Tennessee are reviewed in The Economist Intelligence Unit, *Japanese Overseas Investment*, pp. 109–114.

Tokyo, where they all actively engaged in large-scale marketing campaigns designed to help the Japanese differentiate among possible investment sites.[70] While the most attractive targets for these American marketeers may have been Honda, Nissan, and other such large investors, U.S. states and municipalities also realized sizable employment gains from smaller American and Japanese suppliers, who felt compelled to invest—often without government incentives—in jurisdictions close to the multinational buyers they supplied.

Local Content

Oligopolistic competitors, of course, can exert considerable pressure on their existing suppliers to follow them overseas, as already demonstrated in consumer electronics. In automobiles as well, such "buyer power" operated to compel several Japanese parts suppliers to set up American production facilities, as a convenience to on-shore buyers engaged in manufacturing.[71] In fact, between 1984 and 1986—just as Honda opened a second production line, as Nissan began assembling cars, and as Toyota took over management of NUMMI—Japanese auto parts suppliers doubled their number in the United States, where they typically established wholly owned subsidiaries.[72] Back in Japan, most suppliers were small- to medium-sized companies not otherwise known for any rapid expansion overseas.[73] Just such rapid movement, however,

[70]State governments, in particular, have placed great emphasis on differentiating their jurisdictions among possible investment sites. Again, Ohio stands out: the Ohio Development Board represents the marketing arm of the state government, which not only grants incentives but also conducts complete marketing operations, with offices in Japan and Europe as well as at home. See Encarnation and Wells, "Competitive Strategies," pp. 267–289.

[71]This motivation is explicitly examined in *Wall Street Journal*, March 29, 1985, pp. 1, 20; and in *New York Times*, July 6, 1984, p. D4.

[72]U.S. General Accounting Office, *Foreign Investment: Growing Japanese Presence in the U.S. Auto Industry* (Washington, D.C.: GAO, March 1988), pp. 42–45.

[73]For data on company size, see ibid., *Growing Japanese Presence,* table 4.3, p. 43. According to Kojima Kiyoshi, small-scale investment has long been a hallmark of Japanese overseas operations, in marked contrast to U.S. investments; see his *Direct Foreign Investment: A Japanese Model of Multinational Business Operations* (London: Croom Helm, 1978). However, with the notable exception of Japanese auto parts suppliers, such a conclusion seems inappropriate to Japanese investments in the United States.

was necessary after a stagnant home market and Japanese VERs on automobiles had limited opportunities for growth. Yet in the United States, increased new sales still seemed possible, not only to transplanted Japanese automakers, but also to America's Big Three. For all these buyers, moreover, proximity to U.S. assembly plants seemed to be important.[74] For example, parts produced by nearby suppliers—whether American- or Japanese-owned—often proved to be less expensive than imports, especially after the dollar declined in value relative to the yen. Moreover, for Japanese assemblers in America, having suppliers conveniently nearby also facilitated the re-creation of the same just-in-time delivery system used in Japan—a system that U.S. automakers had begun to imitate. Less common to the Americans was the sharing of R&D costs among buyers and suppliers, a practice that Japanese automakers also hoped to transfer to the United States.[75] Finally, by utilizing suppliers close at hand—again, irrespective of their ownership—Japanese multinationals could satisfy an important political demand: these purchases could be classified as "local content," and as such, they would qualify to meet any content requirement that the U.S. Congress might impose.

For Japanese automakers, local content in America increased over time, thanks in part to the U.S. investments made by traditional Japanese suppliers; still, it peaked at a level well below that enjoyed by the Big Three American automakers. In 1987, each of the Big Three reported local content well above 85 percent.[76] By contrast, after five years of U.S. production, Honda had doubled its local content, from 30 percent (in 1982) to 60 percent (in 1987). Nissan, by comparison, started in 1985 with a higher level of local content (47 percent), thanks in part to its parallel experience in local truck production; but by 1987 that content had reached Honda's level, at just over 60 percent. That same upper ceiling also characterized local content in NUMMI during 1987, even though in 1985 it had stood at a high initial level (50 percent) as a result of GM's existing relations with suppliers. Moreover, those special relations also meant that NUMMI depended on Japanese subsid-

[74]See survey responses recorded throughout GAO, *Growing Japanese Presence.*
[75]Abo, *Local Production,* pp. 86–88.
[76]For local-content data in this paragraph, see GAO, *Growing Japanese Presence,* table 3.2, p. 31.

iaries in America to supply far less of its local content than did the other, more purely Japanese transplants. In fact, fewer than one-tenth of NUMMI's U.S.-based suppliers were Japanese-owned; while for Honda, Japanese subsidiaries in America accounted for nearly one-quarter of its U.S.-based suppliers.[77] Indeed, when Honda invested in Ohio, its Japanese-based suppliers of head-lights, auto fuel tanks, exhaust pipes, steering wheels, and auto engine parts also established plants within that state. More generally, at least one-quarter of all Japanese auto suppliers interviewed by the General Accounting Office reported that their U.S. investments had been encouraged by Japanese automakers, and that "ties to assemblers in Japan" (typically in the same *keiretsu*) accounted for their subsequent success in America.[78] Even with U.S. investments by their traditional suppliers, however, Japanese automakers still continued to import a greater proportion of their parts and components than did America's Big Three.

These giant U.S. automakers actually contributed to the growth of Japanese automobile production in America, especially after the 1985 appreciation of the yen.[79] In 1986, Mazda announced that it would acquire an existing American facility from Ford, its largest shareholder; production of automobiles began there the following year. Also in 1986, Mitsubishi announced that it would invest directly in the United States, forming a 50:50 joint venture (Diamond–Star Motors Corporation) with its largest shareholder, Chrysler; production of automobiles began in 1988. By then, Toyota had finally started production outside of its joint venture with GM, after constructing a new, wholly owned assembly plant in Kentucky. Simultaneously, GM's principal Japanese affiliate, Isuzu, formed a joint venture with Subaru to produce trucks and utility vehicles, beginning in 1989, and Honda began production at its second auto assembly plant. In that year as well, Japan moved to extend its VER on automobiles, setting an upper limit of 2.3 million vehicles—a quota that Japanese automakers ultimately failed to meet, just as they had failed in 1988. Yet, through 1988, seven

[77]Ibid., table 3.1, p. 30; for specific examples on Honda, see *Wall Street Journal*, March 29, 1985, pp. 1, 20; *New York Times*, July 6, 1984, p. D4.
[78]GAO, *Growing Japanese Presence*, pp. 45–46, including table 4.9.
[79]For the evolution of Japanese auto investments, see ibid.

Japanese automakers had collectively invested $5 billion in eight U.S. assembly plants (with capacity for 2 million cars) and three U.S. engine plants. With that huge investment as a lever, the Japanese now stood ready to displace American automakers from their own home market.

From Strong Dollar to Strong Yen

As dollar depreciation lowered the yen price of local U.S. assets, wave after wave of Japanese multinationals moved on the path of Honda and other automakers to multiply their direct investments in America. In fact, between 1982 (at the yen's nadir for the decade) and 1988 (at the yen's zenith), the cumulative stock of Japanese FDI in the United States grew more than fivefold, from $9.7 billion to $53.4 billion (see Figure 3-1). That Japanese sum surpassed levels of investment by Dutch, Canadian, and German multinationals, all of which had as late as 1982 larger FDI in America than did their Japanese counterparts.[80] In fact, by 1988, only one other country—the United Kingdom—could claim to have directly invested more in the United States than had Japan. Such comparisons can be misleading, of course, since other European and Canadian multinationals long ago invested large and now grossly undervalued sums, compared to more recent Japanese FDI in America. Nevertheless, by 1988, the total sales of Japanese multinationals in the United States actually exceeded comparable sales by multinationals based in *all* other countries—indeed, nearly twice the sales of the next group of contenders, from the United Kingdom.[81] Thus, when measured by the cumulative value of FDI stock, Japan had joined the upper ranks of those industrialized countries that commonly serve as home bases for multinationals with significant direct investments in the United States.

Again, like those multinationals based in advanced economies,

---

[80]U.S. Commerce Department, "Foreign Direct Investment Position in the United States: Detail for Position and Balance of Payments Flows, 1982," *Survey of Current Business* (Aug. 1983): 46.

[81]U.S. Commerce Department, Bureau of Economic Analysis, *Foreign Direct Investment in the United States: 1988 Benchmark Survey, Final Results* (Washington, D.C.: USGPO, Aug. 1990).

Japanese subsidiaries generated far greater revenues from local sales in America than did all Japanese exporters shipping goods and services to that market. Indeed, by 1987, Japanese subsidiaries relied on the U.S. market for nearly 90 percent of their total sales of $225.3 billion—a value of local sales far in excess of U.S. imports (of $89.8 billion) from Japan.[82] Moreover, the resulting 2:1 ratio of local sales to U.S. imports proved quite stable over the decade, extending back at least as far as 1980. And subsequently, the growth of local U.S. sales by Japanese subsidiaries kept pace with the growth of U.S. imports from Japan. After 1985, such parallel growth seemed highly unlikely: imports were threatened by yen appreciation, which in turn boosted Japanese FDI and associated sales in the United States. Nevertheless, those local sales remained twice as large as U.S. imports from Japan during the 1980s. Over that decade, by contrast, the subsidiaries of European multinationals sold locally in America four times more than European exporters shipped to the United States (see Figure 3-6). Simultaneously, the same 4:1 ratio also appeared on the other side of the Atlantic, where the majority subsidiaries of American multinationals sold locally four times more than U.S. exporters shipped to Europe.[83] But that 4:1 ratio did not hold for the Americans in Japan (as noted in Chapter 2), where majority subsidiaries during the 1980s enjoyed only slightly more market access than did U.S. exporters. Nor did that ratio hold for the Japanese in America, where—despite major adjustments in both exchange rates and investment inflows—local sales by subsidiaries retained the familiar 2:1 proportion to U.S. imports from Japan evident since 1980.

As in the cases of Honda and Nissan, many of these Japanese subsidiaries actually produced locally the same goods that they sold in the United States. Here, however, any accurate estimate of how much these subsidiaries manufacture in America is confounded by

[82]For sales data, see ibid; for trade data, see Commerce Department, *Foreign Trade Highlights: 1989*, p. 36.

[83]For sales data, see U.S. Commerce Department, Bureau of Economic Analysis, *U.S. Direct Investment Abroad: Operations of U.S. Parent Companies and Their Foreign Affiliates, Preliminary 1988 Estimates* (Washington, D.C.: USGPO, July 1990), tables 6 and 29, n.p.; for trade data, see Commerce Department, *Foreign Trade Highlights: 1989*, p. 31.

Figure 3-6. U.S. production, imports, and distribution: EC vs. Japan, 1987

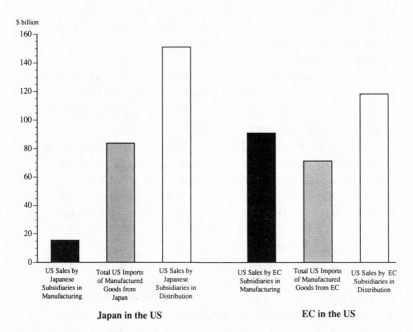

Sources: U.S. Commerce Department, Bureau of Economic Analysis, *Foreign Direct Investment in the United States: 1987 Benchmark Survey, Final Results* (Washington, D.C.: USGPO, Aug. 1990), table E-3, p. 77; U.S. Commerce Department, International Trade Administration, Office of Trade and Investment Analysis, *U.S. Foreign Trade Highlights: 1989* (Washington, D.C.: USGPO, Sept. 1990), p. 56.

the survey protocols employed by the U.S. Commerce Department: namely, Honda and other such manufacturers remain categorized as wholesalers so long as their distribution of U.S. imports generates more sales than do their U.S. production facilities. As a result, sales by Japanese subsidiaries listed as manufacturers serves only as a very conservative estimate of local production. At the other extreme, a more inclusive measure would add to this estimate the value of local sales generated by wholesaling subsidiaries—less the value of the imports marketed in the United States by these same wholesalers. Using *either* measure, we must conclude that local manufacturing has recently grown more rapidly than have all other sources of revenue, both for Japanese subsidiaries in America and for Japanese exporters back home—and under more inclusive assumptions, such local production must be reckoned to have recently reached parity with U.S. imports of Japanese manufactured goods.

Even measured conservatively, however, the value of local production certainly grew more rapidly than did total U.S. sales by either Japanese subsidiaries in America or Japanese exporters in Japan. During the 1970s, such growth remained rather modest: between 1974 and 1980, Japanese subsidiaries doubled their total U.S. sales, while tripling their stake in (officially classified) U.S. manufacturing, which yielded a slight increase in the sales contribution made by local production. That contribution markedly increased between 1980 and 1987: total subsidiaries' sales nearly tripled, while the value of (officially classified) manufacturing—financed by a threefold increase of Japanese FDI in U.S. manufacturing—grew sixfold (see Figure 3-6). Such growth, moreover, even when conservatively measured, brought a reduction in the ratio of local manufacturing to U.S. imports of Japanese manufactured goods, which first fell gradually (from 1:9 in 1974 to 1:7 in 1980) and then precipitously (to 1:3.5 in 1987). This ratio still meant, however, that domestic sales of goods manufactured in the United States by Japanese subsidiaries (valued conservatively at $24.8 billion during 1987) continued to lag far behind the value of U.S. manufactured imports from Japan (valued at $89.2 billion). That lag would not be eradicated until a more inclusive measure of local production was adopted—one that took into account the local value added to U.S. imports by Japanese wholesalers in America. Yet, even when this more inclusive measure had been employed, local production in 1987 barely exceeded U.S. imports of Japanese manufactured goods.

By contrast, both for Europeans in America and for Americans in Europe, the opposite held true: foreign trade still lagged far behind local production, even when such production was measured conservatively (see Figure 3-7). Already we have noted that this preeminence of local production over foreign trade was well under way as early as 1966—at least for the Americans. For the

Figure 3-7. Investment-related U.S. trade with Japan and the EC, 1987

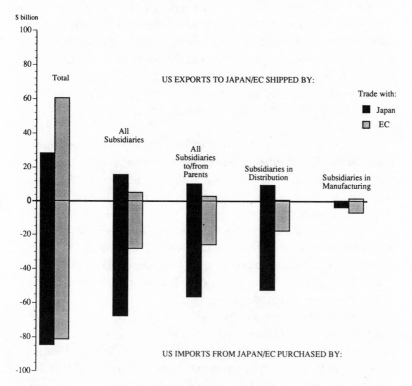

Sources: U.S. Commerce Department, Bureau of Economic Analysis, *Foreign Direct Investment in the United States: 1987 Benchmark Survey, Final Results* (Washington, D.C.: USGPO, Aug. 1990) tables G-24, G-26, G-28, G-30, G-32, and G-34, pp. 142–152; U.S. Commerce Department, International Trade Administration, Office of Trade and Investment Analysis, *U.S. Foreign Trade Highlights: 1989* (Washington, D.C.: USGPO, Sept. 1990), pp. 31, 36.

Europeans, even as late as 1974, their exporters shipped slightly more to the United States than their subsidiaries manufactured and sold locally in America. By 1980, however, that relationship had reversed: now, local production had become twice as large as all U.S. imports from European manufacturers, but that ratio of local production to U.S. imports had weakened during 1987 (see Figure 3-6). Still, local production remained considerably larger than did U.S. imports of manufactured goods.[84] On the other side of the Atlantic, however, that 2:1 ratio had actually strengthened during the 1980s, in the period of a strong dollar, as majority subsidiaries of American multinationals produced more in Europe than U.S. manufacturers shipped to that continent. Thus, in most advanced economies, both American and European multinationals generally managed to manufacture many more goods abroad for sale locally than they and other home-based exporters shipped across the Atlantic.

Local production and sales did not greatly outweigh foreign trade across the Pacific, however. As recently as 1987, American subsidiaries in Japan (as we have already seen) and Japanese subsidiaries in America (see Figure 3-6) produced locally only slightly more than home-based exporters shipped to these markets. And even after they had begun to produce more locally, Japanese multinationals still continued to establish new subsidiaries in the United States as both final markets and intermediate channels for their parents' shipments from Japan (see Figure 3-7). Such intracompany trade has at least kept pace with the rapid growth of direct U.S. imports from Japan. Indeed, at least since 1974, intracompany shipments to Japanese subsidiaries in the United States from their parents back home have remained a stable contributor of nearly four-fifths of all U.S. imports from Japan.[85] And that four-fifths contribution must be regarded as exceptional, especially when compared to intracompany trade across the Atlantic. Indeed, in the Japanese case, that figure was twice the (equally stable) share of U.S. imports from Europe generated by intracompany shipments to European subsidiaries in America; and it has remained twice the share of those U.S. exports to Europe generated by intracompany shipments to American subsidiaries in Europe.[86] Compared to the reverse flow of intracompany trade across the

[84]That ratio was closer to 3:1 using the more inclusive measure of local production outlined above.

[85]Actually, 84 percent in 1974, 78 percent in 1980, and 79 percent in 1987; compare Figures 3-3, 3-4, and 3-7.

[86]Compare Figure 3-7 with the data reported in Commerce Department, *U.S. FDI: 1988 Survey,* tables 6 and 29, n.p.

four-fifths contribution seems even more exceptional—being four times larger than the share of U.S. exports to Japan currently generated by intracompany shipments to American subsidiaries in Japan. When we limit our comparisons to intracompany ship-ments of manufactured goods, the merely slight decline in these exceptional figures still yields the same conclusion: compared to their American and European counterparts, Japanese multina-tionals have exercised a greater degree of managerial control over their subsidiaries' decisions to source manufactured goods and other products from their parents.

During 1988, Honda and other Japanese multinationals chan-neled nearly all—90 percent—of their intracompany trade through majority subsidiaries principally engaged in U.S. whole-saling. This means that Japanese wholesaling subsidiaries distrib-uted over three-quarters of all U.S. imports (principally manufac-tured goods) from Japan. Moreover, that three-quarters share has been very stable over time, dating back at least to 1974. Since then, neither the appreciation of the yen nor the growth of Japanese FDI in U.S. manufacturing has altered the importance of wholesal-ing subsidiaries in the trading strategies of Japanese multination-als. By contrast, both European multinationals in the United States and American multinationals in Europe have relied far more ex-tensively on subsidiaries engaged in manufacturing abroad as con-duits for their intracompany trade. For European multinationals, in particular, such trade has been more evenly divided between wholesaling and manufacturing subsidiaries in America—again, at least as far back as 1974. On the other side of the Atlantic, however, American multinationals have consistently, at least since 1966, relied on manufacturing affiliates to serve as final markets and intermediate channels for no less than two-thirds of their intra-company exports to Europe—but not to Japan, where we have seen that wholesaling has accounted for the lion's share of U.S. intracompany exports. In Japan, American multinationals have attempted to overcome high marketing barriers to entry erected by Japanese oligopolists by investing directly in downstream whole-saling. On the other side of the Pacific, these same Japanese oligop-olists later tried to re-create similar entry barriers by investing in

U.S. wholesaling. Thus, the Japanese have retained an unprecedented degree of downstream control over U.S. imports from Japan.

Upstream, meanwhile, Japan has also continued to exercise unprecedented control over U.S. exports to Japan: during 1987, Japanese subsidiaries in America shipped roughly three-fifths of all U.S. exports to Japan (see Figure 3-7). That share—while always large—actually declined after 1974, when Japanese subsidiaries in America shipped over four-fifths of all U.S. exports to Japan. Throughout the period, nearly all (some 93 percent during 1987) of these Japanese subsidiaries operated in the United States as wholesalers, exporting food, metals, and other (unprocessed and semiprocessed) materials to Japan. And throughout, the parents of these subsidiaries have been their principal buyers in Japan, accounting for two-thirds of all subsidiary shipments. By contrast, the parents of both European multinationals in the United States and American multinationals in Europe have relied far less extensively on their foreign subsidiaries as sources of supply.[87] For European multinationals, in particular, manufacturing and wholesaling subsidiaries in the United States together (and in rather equal measure) shipped during 1987 barely one-tenth of all U.S. exports to Europe (principally to their European parents). Even at its height (in 1974 and again in 1980), such trade made up barely one-sixth of all U.S. exports to Europe. As for U.S. imports from Europe, American subsidiaries (principally manufacturers) contributed just one-eighth of all such flows, a share that has remained relatively constant since 1966. Solely for the Japanese has investing to trade yielded unrivaled control, not only over downstream U.S. markets but also over upstream U.S. sources of Japanese supply.

Into the 1990s

On the eve of a new decade, at the end of 1989, Japanese FDI in the United States reached $69.7 billion—double the value just two

[87]For cross-national comparisons, see U.S. Commerce Department, Bureau of Economic Analysis, *Foreign Direct Investment in the United States: 1987 Benchmark Survey, Final Results* (Washington, D.C.: USGPO, Aug. 1990).

years earlier (see Figure 3-1). Mergers and acquisitions fueled much of that new investment, as the Japanese abandoned their earlier reticence to engage in such standard business practices in America. This change in attitude, however, proved to be relatively tardy: as recently as 1987 (the year of Sony's $2 billion acquisition of CBS Records) the Japanese still managed to account for only 7 percent of all foreign acquisitions of U.S. companies[88]—just the same share they had posted back in 1974, when Matsushita followed arch-rival Sony into U.S. manufacturing by acquiring Motorola's TV business. By 1989, however, that 1987 share had tripled, to one-fifth, led again by Sony, with its $3.4 billion acquisition of Columbia Pictures.[89] Indeed, by 1989, only British investors could boast of having acquired more U.S. companies than had the Japanese, who retained their second-place ranking behind the British through 1990. That year also brought Matsushita's grand, oligopolistic response to earlier moves by Sony, as Matsushita acquired Hollywood entertainment group MCA for $6.1 billion, in the largest Japanese takeover ever of an American enterprise. With that acquisition, Matsushita followed Sony into diversification from electronic hardware (VCRs) to entertainment software (movies). Even today, the ongoing Matsushita-Sony rivalry illustrates an important broader trend: Japanese multinationals have

[88]See the following statistics provided by W. T. Grimm and Company:

Domicile of foreign parent	Number of foreign acquisitions of U.S. companies			
	1987	1988	1989	1990
United Kingdom	78	114	89	82
Japan	15	35	53	38
Canada	28	37	50	33
France	19	25	17	26
West Germany	15	29	18	19
Switzerland	9	15	8	16
Netherlands	9	9	14	15
Other	–	–	–	–
Total	220	307	285	266

[89]For a review of these large acquisitions, see "Special Report: BT 100, the Definitive List of Japanese Direct Investors in America," *Business Tokyo,* May 1991, pp. 13–27.

begun to join both the Americans and the Europeans in viewing foreign acquisitions as an acceptable strategy for purposes of diversifying products and markets abroad.

This most recent step in the transformation of Japanese multinationals closely follows the same evolutionary path that has been well documented throughout the present chapter: in the United States, European and Japanese multinationals have come to pursue remarkably similar strategies regarding foreign investment and related trade—strategies that look very similar to those implemented by American multinationals outside Japan. All these multinational players invest in majority-owned subsidiaries, and they eschew minority shareholdings whenever they can. Through their subsidiaries, they report foreign (and especially local) sales far in excess of what their home countries export. Exports from these nations, in turn, have already begun to trail the values of foreign production by American, European, and Japanese subsidiaries abroad. In addition, these majority subsidiaries also trade extensively with their parents and with other overseas affiliates, to create new intracompany markets for foreign sales.

To be sure, some differences in strategy persist: the Japanese, for example, engage in intracompany trade far more frequently than do either the well established Europeans or the even better established Americans; just as both the Europeans and (especially) the Americans engage more actively in foreign production than do the newly emergent Japanese. Yet such differences, while noteworthy, have diminished greatly over time, as American, European, and Japanese multinationals increasingly confront similar political and economic environments. So, multinational strategies seem now, in the 1990s, closer to arriving at a common course than ever before—a course that first became apparent in East Asia, where (as we shall see in the next chapter) both the Americans and the Japanese can claim long histories of foreign investment and related trade.

CHAPTER FOUR

Americans and Japanese in East Asia

THE RIVALRY between American and Japanese multinationals is not confined to bilateral flows of trade and investment only. These rivals have expanded their competition multilaterally by drawing other geographic areas into the fray, most notably East Asia. To that complex of varied nations and markets, we direct special attention in this chapter. The countries in that vast region defy any easy classifications, but they have commonly been divided into three distinct categories:[1] the "Four NIEs," "the ASEAN Four," and the "Big Two." The Four NIEs (or newly industrializing economies) of East Asia consist of South Korea, Taiwan, Hong Kong, and Singapore—all countries that have attained a relatively high standard of living in a rather brief period of time.[2] While the Four

---

[1] A similar classification scheme, for example, is commonly used by the Japanese government in its analysis of regional trends in foreign direct investment; see Japan, Ministry of International Trade and Industry, Industrial Policy Bureau, International Business Affairs Division, *The 19th Survey of the Overseas Business Activities of Japanese Enterprises [Dai jyuukyuu-kai wagakuni kigyou no kaigai jigyou katsudou]* (Tokyo: Ministry of Finance Printing Bureau, 1990), pp. 72–83 (hereafter cited as MITI, *19th Overseas Survey*).

[2] For recent analyses of both processes and outcomes of economic development in the Four NIEs, see Stephan Haggard, *Pathways from the Periphery: The Politics of Growth in the Newly Industrializing Countries* (Ithaca: Cornell University Press, 1990), esp. pp. 51–161, 191–222; Frederic C. Deyo, ed., *The Political Economy of the New Asian Industrialism* (Ithaca: Cornell University Press, 1987); Gary Gereffi and Donald Wyman, eds., *Manufactured Miracles: Patterns of Industrialization in Latin America and East Asia* (Princeton: Princeton University Press, 1989); Stephan Haggard and Chung-in Moon, eds., *Pacific Dynamics: The International Politics of Industrial Change* (Boulder, Colo.: Westview Press, 1989).

NIEs are dispersed widely along Asia's Pacific Rim, the ASEAN Four (all members of the Association of Southeast Asian Nations) are geographically more concentrated, consisting of Thailand, Malaysia, Indonesia, and the Philippines. In common, they have generally achieved a lower level of economic development than have the Four NIEs, although they do possess more of those raw materials essential for industrial growth.[3] Finally, the Big Two—China and India—together contain within their borders over three-fifths of the world's population, living well below the economic standards of the ASEAN Four and (especially) of the Four NIEs.[4] Individually, each of these East Asian countries offers American and Japanese multinationals a varied set of competitive advantages to be exploited in the larger U.S.-Japan rivalry.

To pursue these competitive advantages, American and Japanese multinationals have implemented remarkably similar strategies in regard to foreign direct investment and related trade.[5] For as we shall see in this chapter, growing numbers of American and Japanese multinationals invest in majority foreign-owned subsidiaries, which they then tightly integrate through international (often intracompany) trade with both overseas buyers and upstream suppliers, back home and elsewhere abroad. To be sure,

[3]Compared to the Four NIEs, the ASEAN Four have attracted much less academic attention; for one of the few explicit cross-national comparisons to date, see Richard F. Doner, *Driving a Bargain: Automobile Industrialization and Japanese Firms in Southeast Asia* (Berkeley: University of California Press, 1990).

[4]For the political economy of India, see Dennis J. Encarnation, *Dislodging Multinationals: India's Strategy in Comparative Perspective* (Ithaca: Cornell University Press, 1989); for China, see Benjamin Gomes-Casseres, "Socialism and Modernization in China," Harvard Business School Case no. 9-388-115.

[5]This conclusion contradicts a large body of research that employs data from East Asia to argue the "uniqueness" of Japanese multinationals; see, in particular, the ongoing and pioneering work of Kojima Kiyoshi: "Japanese Direct Investment Abroad," Monograph Series 1, Social Science Research Institute, International Christian University, Tokyo, 1990; (with Terutomo Ozawa) "Japanese-Style Direct Foreign Investment," *Japanese Economic Studies* 14 (Spring 1986): 52–82; "Japanese and American Direct Investment in Asia: A Comparative Analysis," *Hitotsubashi Journal of Economics* 26 (June 1985): 1–35; *Japan's Foreign Direct Investment [Nihon no kaigai chokusetsu toushi]* (Tokyo: Bunshindo, 1985), esp. pp. 6–14; *Foreign Direct Investment [Kaigai chokusetsu toushi ron]* (Tokyo: Daiyamondo-sha, 1979); *Direct Foreign Investment: A Japanese Model of Multinational Business Operations* (London: Croom Helm, 1978); "Transfer of Technology to Developing Countries—Japanese Type versus American Type," *Hitotsubashi Journal of Economics* 17 (Feb. 1977): 1–14.

some differences in multinational strategy do persist: the Americans, for example, first shifted aggressively away from import substitution to export promotion, and they have retained their early leadership with proportionately larger shipments back home. Meanwhile, the Japanese have moved with greater aggressiveness to sell far more in the local and regional markets of East Asia, rather than through exports back to Japan—where their sales match exports to America. Yet such strategic differences clearly have diminished over time, as American and Japanese multinationals respond to so many of the same economic and political environments in East Asia.

East Asia's entry into the larger U.S.-Japan rivalry took place only recently, and it required fundamental changes in government policies across the entire region. Beginning with the Four NIEs, East Asian governments have abandoned their exclusive encouragement of local production as a substitute for imports, by agreeing to promote more export-oriented investments.[6] Only after this change in policy had taken place did East Asia begin to attract foreign direct investment from American multinationals at rates that exceeded the growth of such U.S. FDI elsewhere in the world. A single policy change, in short, made the region's richly abundant natural and human resources more enticing than ever—just at the time when American multinationals needed to find effective responses to a strong dollar and stiff import (especially Japanese) competition back home. Already these factors had begun to increase U.S. direct investments in Japan (as we have seen in Chapter 2); and now, they produced an even larger effect across the rest of East Asia (see Figure 4-1), where American multinationals worked to establish inexpensive sources of supply—principally, for export back home. By concentrating on this newly created trade, American multinationals brought East Asia directly into the existing U.S.-Japan rivalry.

Japanese multinationals, by comparison, proved much slower in response to East Asia's competitive challenge, even though they had long felt inclined to trade within a region made so attractive by

---

[6]For the evolution of trade and industrial policies across the Four NIEs, see Haggard, *Pathways from the Periphery*, esp. pp. 51–125.

Figure 4-1. United States and Japan: Bilateral and East Asian FDI, 1950–89

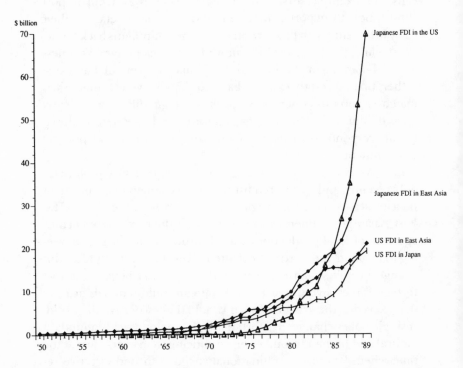

Sources: For data on U.S. FDI to both Japan and East Asia, see Figure 2-1; for data on Japanese FDI to the United States, see Figure 3-1; for data on Japanese FDI to East Asia, see Japan, Ministry of Finance, *Statistics for the Approval/Notification of Overseas Direct Investment* *[Taigai chokusetsu-toushi no kyoka todokede jisseki]* (Tokyo: Ministry of Finance Printing Bureau, selected years).

its geographic proximity, its sizable downstream market, and its abundant promise as an upstream source of raw materials.[7] For Japanese multinationals to accelerate their East Asian investments, however, another substantial change in government policy had to occur—not in the policies of East Asian host governments, but in

[7]On the early evolution of Japanese FDI in East Asia, the most important detailed analysis remains Yoshihara Kunio, *Japanese Investment in Southeast Asia* (Honolulu: University Press of Hawaii, Monographs of the Center for Southeast Asian Studies, Kyoto University, 1978).

Japan instead. Specifically, the Japanese government needed to liberalize its tight restrictions on capital outflows before Japanese multinationals could act. When they did act, they first matched and then surpassed otherwise modest U.S. investments in East Asia. Meanwhile, that requisite change in Japan's strategic investment occurred at roughly the same time when the Four NIEs were beginning their own transformation from import substitution to export promotion. Simultaneously, across the Pacific, the United States began to move away from free trade toward protectionism, especially restraints on Japanese exports. With the encouragement of these policy changes at home and abroad, then, the East Asian investments of the late-comer Japanese quickly caught up with, and then surpassed, those of the first-mover Americans.

East Asia's shift from import substitution to export-led growth fostered a much tighter cross-national integration of that region's diverse economies.[8] Initially, of course, export promotion meant that East Asia focused on foreign markets in industrialized countries, aided by the direct investments and related trade of both American and Japanese multinationals. Increasingly, however, powerful forces of national specialization encouraged intraregional shipments of raw materials and intermediate components, with final products destined to sell not only in industrialized countries, but in other markets as well, especially those located elsewhere in East Asia. Here, sharp differences in natural endowments, human resources, government policies, market sizes, and relative prices all contributed to a growing differentiation among the Four NIEs, ASEAN Four, and Big Two as possible sites for foreign investment and related trade. Once again, American and Japanese multinationals played prominent roles, now by using their several subsidiaries as integrated buyers and suppliers spread across the region. A strong yen and U.S. protectionism, plus the

[8]On regional integration in East Asia, see Edward J. Lincoln, "Japan's Rapidly Emerging Strategy toward Asia," a paper prepared for the Research Programme on Globalization and Regionalisation, Organization for Economic Cooperation and Development, Paris, February 1991; Dennis J. Encarnation, "An Emerging Yen Bloc? Japanese Investment and Related Trade in East Asia," a paper prepared for the Research Institute, Ministry of International Trade and Industry, Tokyo, Japan, April, 1990.

pressures of oligopolistic competition and strong buyers—in short, the same factors that worked so effectively to increase Japanese direct investments in the United States—all operated to accelerate the movement of Japanese multinationals to East Asia. And as they moved there, so did the Americans—albeit in smaller numbers (see Figure 4-1), and still engaged in finding some effective response to both a strong dollar and the evolving Japanese challenge at home in the U.S. market. As a larger result, nearly every country in the region would eventually discover that the U.S.-Japan rivalry had infiltrated its national borders. East Asia, in short, was subsumed into the global rivalry between the Americans and the Japanese.

THE AMERICAN CHALLENGE

Historically, American multinationals have invested only a small amount of their total capital in East Asia. Prior to the Second World War, in fact, that region hosted barely 5 percent of all U.S. FDI worldwide—less than any other region of the world except Africa.[9] Within East Asia, the principal hosts were mainland China, the Philippines, and the Netherland East Indies (later, Indonesia). Here, the United States long harbored colonial ambitions in China's large domestic market, while the Philippines became a virtual U.S. territory, one blessed with plentiful natural resources, many of which also became available in greater abundance in the Netherland East Indies. The temptations seemed clear, and by 1929 each of these three East Asian economies hosted more U.S. FDI than did Japan, where only a few select multinationals were as yet making market inroads.[10]

After the Second World War, and for the next two decades, East Asia's share of total U.S. FDI actually declined, to less than 3 per-

[9]U.S. Commerce Department, Office of Business Economics, *U.S. Business Investments in Foreign Countries: A Supplement to the Survey of Current Business* (Washington, D.C.: USGPO, 1960), esp. table 4, p. 92.

[10]For a detailed analysis of these investments, see U.S. Commerce Department, Bureau of Foreign and Domestic Commerce, *American Direct Investments in Foreign Countries, 1929* (Washington, D.C.: 1932), pp. 25–28, 38.

cent, as American multinationals concentrated their ever-growing foreign investment elsewhere in the world.[11] Still, compared to Japan, the rest of East Asia continued to host more U.S. FDI (see Figure 4-1). By 1950, in fact, newly independent India, still writhing from the chaos of partition, hosted greater American investment than did war-ravaged, U.S.-occupied Japan. And through 1960, the still-developing Philippines could make a similar claim, in comparison with now-resurgent Japan. Indeed, as late as 1966, the Philippines and India together hosted over one-half of all U.S. FDI in East Asia (see Figure 4-2), with a combined value nearly equal to all U.S. FDI in Japan. Thus, within East Asia, Americans multinationals consistently concentrated their limited investments in a very few countries, where little of this early postwar investment came as a direct response to the U.S.-Japan rivalry. To the contrary: American multinationals invested in East Asia principally to supply local markets hosting their investments. As late as 1966, for example, these host-country markets contributed fully three-quarters of all foreign sales generated by American multinationals in East Asia (see Figure 4-3). The remaining production, all exported, found limited markets back in the United States. American subsidiaries in East Asia simply shipped most of their exports to third countries, principally located elsewhere in the region.[12] Still, when combined, exports during 1966 contributed barely one-quarter of all foreign sales by U.S. affiliates operating in East Asia.

To encourage host-country sales, the Philippines and India—like Japan—erected steep trade barriers, which through the 1960s induced prospective American exporters to invest in foreign production in order to supply protected local markets (see Figure 4-3). These import-substitution policies proved especially potent, in fact, for attracting foreign investment into manufacturing, which accounted for more U.S. FDI in East Asia than did wholesaling, finance, and all other service industries combined (see Figure 4-2). And within manufacturing, over three-quarters of this 1966 in-

[11] U.S. Department of Commerce, Bureau of Economic Analysis, *Selected Data on U.S. Direct Investment Abroad, 1950–76* (Washington, D.C.: USGPO, February 1982), table 1, pp. 1–16.

[12] U.S. Commerce Department, Bureau of Economic Analysis, *U.S. Direct Investment Abroad, 1966: Final Data* (Washington, D.C.: USGPO, 1975), table L-6, p. 202.

Figure 4-2. U.S. FDI in East Asia by country and industry, 1966 vs. 1977

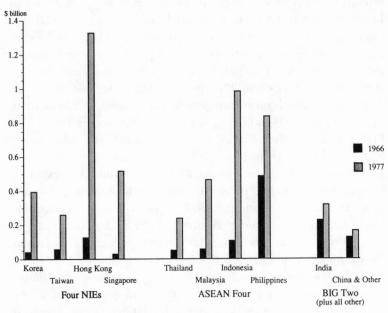

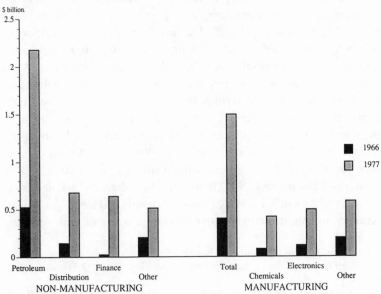

Sources: Same as Figure 2-1.

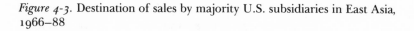

Figure 4-3. Destination of sales by majority U.S. subsidiaries in East Asia, 1966–88

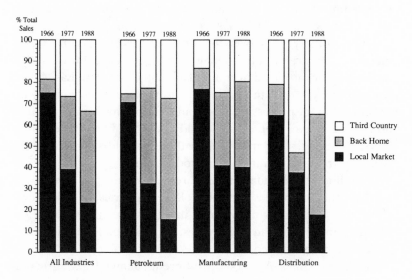

Sources: U.S. Commerce Department, Bureau of Economic Analysis, *U.S. Direct Investment Abroad, 1966: Final Data* (Washington, D.C.: USGPO, 1975), esp. table L-2, p. 198; U.S. Commerce Department, Bureau of Economic Analysis, *U.S. Direct Investment Abroad, 1977* (Washington, D.C.: USGPO, 1981), table III.H.1, p. 318; U.S. Commerce Department, Bureau of Economic Analysis, *U.S. Direct Investment Abroad: Operations of U.S. Parent Companies and their Foreign Affiliates, Preliminary 1988 Estimates* (Washington, D.C.: USGPO, July 1990), table 34, n.p.

vestment entered the large, protected markets of India and the Philippines, where American multinationals concentrated their investments in chemicals and machinery (especially electronics).[13] As in Japan, so too elsewhere in East Asia: IBM and other U.S. machinery manufacturers more often generated overseas sales through foreign production than through international trade.[14]

In addition, both India and the Philippines—which *unlike* Japan, could boast of considerable natural resources—took the lead

[13]Ibid., p. 17.

[14]Specifically, for IBM, see Joseph M. Grieco, *Between Dependency and Autonomy: India's Experience with the International Computer Industry* (Berkeley: University of California Press, 1984).

in coaxing those U.S. enterprises contemplating either foreign trade or local sales to invest in search of new supplies. Here, petroleum retained its original position as the primary attraction for U.S. investments in East Asia: in fact, through 1966, the petroleum industry drew over two-fifths of the East Asian investments of American multinationals (see Figure 4-2). During 1966, the Philippines attracted over one-half of all U.S. FDI in East Asian petroleum, as American multinationals invested heavily in downstream refining, processing, distribution, and marketing. Similar downstream investments had already brought Exxon and other U.S. oil companies to Japan—but without the added allure of East Asia's upstream exploration and production.

In addition to abundant natural resources and protected local markets, the Philippines and India offered American multinationals certain advantages unavailable in either Japan or other East Asian countries. In the Philippines, for example, America's colonial legacy continued to provide a comfortable environment for U.S. companies. A markedly different colonial legacy greeted American multinationals investing in India, however. There, rapid industrialization to supply the world's second largest population attracted large amounts of new money. Elsewhere, however, large populations did not alone provide sufficient incentive for U.S. FDI: a combination of autarchic policies and political upheavals in populous mainland China and (to a lesser extent) Indonesia served to cancel their national attraction as potential hosts to American multinationals (see Figure 4-2). And elsewhere in East Asia, adverse political risk stunted the growth of U.S. FDI, as Vietnam-related insurrections (in Thailand, Malaysia, and Indonesia), territorial secession (in the Malaysian federation, with the loss of Singapore), and thorny questions of constitutional legitimacy (in Taiwan and Korea) all dampened the attractiveness of import substitution across the region. In this context, the Philippines with its relatively small but stable local market seemed all the more attractive, and continued through the mid-1960s to host the largest share of U.S. FDI. Only next came populous India where, during the preceding decade, U.S. FDI already had experienced its greatest period of growth. Thus, each of these countries demonstrated the continued—although limited—seduction of East Asia's import-substitution policies to American multinationals.

Over the next decade, however, import-substitution lost most of its earlier appeal, thanks to fundamental changes in the international political economy. Here, the years 1971 to 1973 provided a watershed: in 1971, America suffered its first global trade deficit in 78 years, at the same time that Japan was enjoying an unprecedented surplus. The resulting "Nixon shock," as we saw in preceding chapters, added new and unexpected volatility to foreign-exchange markets, by bringing the Bretton Woods regime of fixed rates to an end. Subsequently, the Japanese yen (and other major currencies) rapidly appreciated against the U.S. dollar until 1973, when a fourfold increase in crude oil prices reversed the dollar's rapid decline. Of course, a strong dollar not only contributed to America's growing trade deficits (to date, 1975 remains the last year in which the United States recorded an overall surplus), but it also served to accelerate U.S. FDI in East Asia. Between 1966 and 1977, direct investments by American multinationals in East Asia quadrupled (see Figure 4-1), from $1.3 billion to $5.5 billion—a growth rate well ahead of the threefold increase in all U.S. FDI worldwide, and a total sum greater than that in Japan.[15]

In marked contrast to these American investments in Japan, most new U.S. FDI in East Asia served to boost national exports, as American multinationals acted to link that region directly to the larger U.S.-Japan rivalry. Between 1966 and 1977, exports by U.S.-owned subsidiaries in East Asia grew to exceed host-market sales; so that by 1977, shipments to markets outside of the host country contributed fully three-fifths of all sales by American multinationals investing in East Asia (see Figure 4-3). Of these shipments, exports back to the United States accounted for the largest share, contributing at least one-third of total sales in 1977, up from less than one-tenth in 1966. Most of this home-bound trade came from

[15]For data on U.S. FDI through 1976, see Commerce Department, *U.S. Direct Investment Abroad, 1950–76*, table 1, pp. 1–16; for data subsequently, see U.S. Commerce Department, Bureau of Economic Analysis, *U.S. Direct Investment Abroad: Balance of Payments and Direct Investment Position Estimates, 1977–81* (Washington, D.C.: USGPO, February 1986), table 1, p. 1.

U.S. FDI in the petroleum industry and manufacturing (especially electronics), and nearly all (over nine-tenths) of this trade was shipped intracompany, by majority subsidiaries in East Asia to their U.S. parents.[16] Thus, for American multinationals, foreign investments in majority subsidiaries served to link East Asia directly to their parents' operations back in the United States— where these new (and presumably less expensive) sources of supply provided at least a partial response to U.S. trade competition with Japan and other countries.

Exports to other foreign markets also increased, albeit less dramatically. By 1977, these third-country markets consumed another one-quarter of all sales by majority U.S. subsidiaries in East Asia, up from one-sixth a decade earlier. Over these years, Japan emerged as the largest third-country market, especially for U.S. subsidiaries engaged in the East Asian wholesaling and petroleum industries.[17] By contrast, those U.S. subsidiaries principally engaged in East Asian manufacturing exported much less to Japan: barely 5 percent of their total sales. Outside Japan, manufacturing subsidiaries typically exported to other U.S. affiliates of the same American multinational; but as we saw in Japan, few such U.S. affiliates existed because of the peculiar difficulties faced by American multinationals that tried to gain access to the Japanese market. In the absence of additional investment in Japan, then, U.S. FDI in East Asian manufacturing proved of relatively little value to American multinationals seeking to increase their penetration of the Japanese market through (typically, intracompany) trade. In Japan, again, the Americans found themselves effectively shut out.

Once American multinationals began diversifying their investments to increase their East Asian exports, the earlier predomi-

---

[16]U.S. Commerce Department, Bureau of Economic Analysis, *U.S. Direct Investment Abroad, 1977* (Washington, D.C.: USGPO, 1981), table II.A.18, p. 123 and table III.A.18, p. 242 (hereafter cited as Commerce Department, *1977 Benchmark*).

[17]Ibid., for all industries, exports to Japan during 1977 consumed 11 percent of all sales by American multinationals operating in East Asia, while other countries in the region consumed an additional 7 percent (Europe bought another 4 percent). For manufacturing industries, however, intraregional shipments to other East Asian countries outside of Japan actually led third-country exports, consuming 10 percent of all sales by U.S. MNCs operating in that region (while Japan and Europe each consumed an additional 4 percent of these sales).

nance of the Philippines and India disappeared. Indeed, by 1977, Hong Kong and Indonesia had actually emerged preeminent (see Figure 4-2); together they hosted two-fifths of the cumulative stock of all U.S. FDI in East Asia. Such a shift in geographic concentration signaled a major change in the principal inducements for foreign direct investment. Hong Kong, now the greatest East Asian host for American multinationals, boasted of no outstanding natural resources other than its welcome harbor; nor did it offer a large, protected market. Rather, Hong Kong traded its abundant skilled labor, modern infrastructure, and open-trade policies for fully one-quarter of the total stock of all U.S. FDI in East Asia through 1977.[18] By that date, moreover, Hong Kong certainly did not stand alone in its spirited pursuit of export-led growth: Singapore and (to a lesser extent) Malaysia had also abandoned import substitution following their break-up in 1968, and they both took places among the most important new sites for U.S. direct investments, followed by export-oriented Korea and Taiwan. Such policies had a particular appeal to American manufacturers, who located two-fifths of their East Asian investments in the Four NIEs (see Figure 4-2), led by Hong Kong—which had also established its even greater lead in trade-related services. Through 1977, Hong Kong alone attracted over one-third of all U.S. FDI in East Asian wholesaling, and over one-half of all U.S. FDI in finance.[19] So large were these service investments in Hong Kong and elsewhere that by 1977 they exceeded U.S. investment in East Asian manufacturing (see Figure 4-2). Since these services were essential for trade, their growth signaled a major shift in the foreign-investment strategies of American multinationals—away from import substitution and toward export promotion.

Still, import substitution exercised an appeal especially for American manufacturers, who continued to channel at least two-fifths of their East Asian investments into the Philippines and India combined (see Figure 4-2). Nor did this geographic shift in U.S. investments mean that East Asia's natural resources were

---

[18]For an analysis of Hong Kong's strategy, see Haggard, *Pathways from the Periphery*, pp. 100–126.

[19]Commerce Department, *U.S. Direct Investment Abroad, 1977–81*, table 1, p. 1.

losing their charm. To the contrary: Between 1966 and 1977, the petroleum industry continued to attract the largest share—still over two-fifths—of the East Asian investment of American multinationals (see Figure 4-2 above). What did change, however, was the placement of that investment, with far larger sums now entering upstream exploration and extraction, especially in Indonesia, where U.S. oil companies concentrated one-third of their total FDI in East Asia.[20] In particular, the oil price shocks of 1972–73 and Indonesia's acceptance as a member in the OPEC cartel explained much of this increased investment in oil exploration and extraction. And these price shocks also generated additional pressures on both oil producing and oil consuming nations in the region to increase their exports.

As a sharp contrast, consider India, where the retention of import-substitution policies did little to increase U.S. FDI; there, by 1977, national strategy advocated dislodging IBM, Coca-Cola, and other foreign multinationals.[21] As Chapter 3 demonstrated, trade restrictions can act to stimulate those foreign direct investments destined to supply large local markets, just as they did in the United States. But in India, as in Japan, domestic capital controls actually limited the inflow of such investment, as well as helping to control the level of foreign ownership. In fact, during 1977, majority U.S.-owned subsidiaries contributed barely one-fifth of the total sales recorded by all American multinationals investing in India.[22] By comparison, across East Asia as a whole, majority U.S. subsidiaries accounted for over four-fifths of total 1977 sales recorded by all American multinationals. But unlike India, most other East Asian countries hosting U.S. FDI (with the notable exception of South Korea) imposed less stringent capital controls.[23] In the absence of these controls, moreover, American multinationals clearly preferred to invest in majority U.S. subsidiaries, in order to secure unrivaled managerial control over both the integration and the

[20]Ibid.

[21]For an overview of this strategy, see Encarnation, *Dislodging Multinationals*, esp. pp. 25–37; Grieco, *Between Dependency and Autonomy*.

[22]Commerce Department, *1977 Benchmark*, tables II.F.5 and III.F.5, pp. 138, 282–283.

[23]For data on capital controls, see ibid., table II.I.3, pp. 139–140.

coordination of their foreign investment and related (often intra-company) trade.

During the 1980s, that U.S. preference for majority ownership remained strong, even as American multinationals continued their rush to East Asia. Between 1977 and 1988, in fact, U.S. FDI tripled (see Figure 4-1), from $5.5 billion to $18.9 billion—a growth rate that remained well ahead of the twofold increase in U.S. investments worldwide.[24] As a result, by 1988 East Asia hosted nearly 6 percent of all direct investment by American multinationals—far more than Japan could boast, and nearly twice the world share recorded by East Asia just a decade earlier. In Japan, most of that U.S. investment remained locked in minority U.S.-owned affiliates, while in East Asia (and elsewhere in the world), majority subsidiaries still contributed over three-quarters of the total sales recorded by American multinationals.[25] Simply, these Americans avoided investments in countries that restricted majority ownership. Korea, for example, implemented strict capital controls that limited foreign ownership—so much so that majority U.S.-owned subsidiaries during 1988 accounted for barely one-fifth of the total sales of all American multinationals in Korea.[26] In India, that share was even lower; as a result, India attracted virtually no new U.S. FDI between 1977 and 1988 (see Figure 4-4), just as Korea ranked lowest among the Four NIEs (and below most of the ASEAN Four) as a host to American investments. Thus, neither large protected markets (India) nor export-oriented policies (Korea) could effectively overcome the deleterious effects of capital controls on U.S. direct investment.

By contrast, government policies that promoted foreign trade

---

[24]Commerce Department, *U.S. Direct Investment Abroad, 1977–81*, table 1, p. 1; U.S. Commerce Department, Bureau of Economic Analysis, "U.S. Direct Investment Abroad: Detail for Position and Balance of Payments Flows, 1989," *Survey of Current Business* (August 1990), p. 63.

[25]U.S. Commerce Department, Bureau of Economic Analysis, *U.S. Direct Investment Abroad: Operations of U.S. Parent Companies and their Foreign Affiliates, Preliminary 1988 Estimates* (Washington, D.C.: USGPO, July 1990), tables 6 and 29, n.p. (hereafter cited as Commerce Department, *U.S. FDI: 1988 Survey*).

[26]For a comparison of capital controls in both India and Korea, see Encarnation, *Dislodging Multinationals*, esp. pp. 204–215; for sales data, see Commerce Department, *U.S. FDI: 1988 Survey*, tables 6 and 29, n.p.

Figure 4-4. U.S. FDI in East Asia by country and industry, 1977 vs. 1988

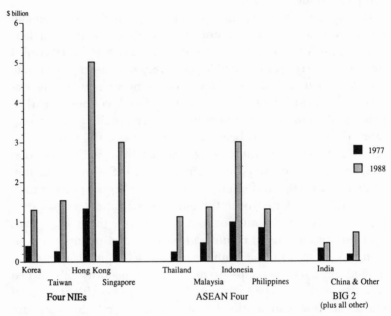

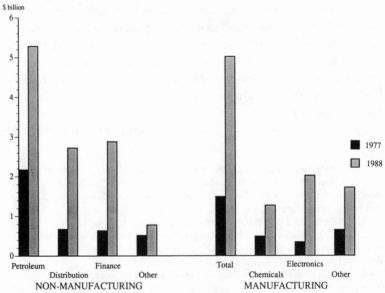

Sources: Same as Figure 2-1.

and encouraged capital flows proved especially attractive to U.S. investors. Nowhere was this more apparent than in Hong Kong, where American multinationals still concentrated fully 25 percent of their foreign investment in East Asia. One-third of that total East Asian investment supplied trade-related services: mainly finance, followed by overseas distribution (principally, the purchasing agents of both American manufacturers and retailers). These service investments had grown rapidly over the previous decade, as U.S. trade with East Asia accelerated. In truth, most of that investment growth took place in Hong Kong, where by 1988 American multinationals concentrated one-half of all U.S. FDI in East Asian finance (up from one-third in 1977), and two-thirds of all such investment in distribution (twice its share a decade earlier).[27] In turn, Hong Kong depended on these services to generate most (80 percent) of its U.S. FDI, as the Crown Colony solidified its dominant position as the regional center for a broad range of American multinationals that provided trade-related services.[28]

Similarly, during the 1980s, Indonesia improved its relative standing as the East Asian center for the U.S. petroleum industry, the source of most (over 85 percent) of that country's investment from the United States. In fact, during 1988 Indonesia accounted for one-half of all U.S. FDI in East Asian petroleum (up from one-third in 1977), mostly in exploration and extraction.[29] Since petroleum attracted 25 percent of all U.S. FDI in East Asia, Indonesia's dominant position in that industry meant that the country could continue to boast of its ranking as the second largest host for all American investment in East Asia. But that rank now was threatened (see Figure 4-4): between 1977 and 1988, manufacturing (with one-third of all U.S. FDI in East Asia) had surpassed petroleum as the principal repository of American investments in East Asia, as human resources finally eclipsed natural resources as East Asia's principal attraction to American multinationals. Moreover, within manufacturing, electronics surpassed chemicals, adding further to the major regional shift from raw-materials-intensive industries to labor- and technology-intensive sectors.

[27]Commerce Department, "U.S. Direct Investment Abroad, 1989," p. 63.
[28]For Hong Kong's dependence on foreign direct investment, see Haggard, *Pathways from the Periphery,* pp. 191–222.
[29]Commerce Department, "U.S. Direct Investment Abroad, 1989," p. 63.

With this rise of manufacturing—especially in electronics—Singapore catapulted to the front ranks, to stand alongside Indonesia, claiming the second-largest share of U.S. FDI in East Asia (see Figure 4-4). Just a decade earlier, Singapore had ranked fourth (next to Malaysia) among East Asian hosts to U.S. FDI. But by 1988, this island nation had in place a sophisticated economic bureaucracy, an ultra-modern infrastructure, and a highly educated workforce—all of which became the envy of East Asia.[30] These incentives were attractive to American manufacturers, who were further encouraged by both an absence of restrictive capital controls and the presence of lucrative investment incentives. As a result, by 1988 Singapore hosted over one-fourth of all U.S. FDI in East Asian manufacturing (up from 1/14th a decade earlier), followed by Taiwan with another one-fourth.[31] In Singapore, moreover, over one-third of that manufacturing investment worked to produce electronics, while Malaysia harbored another one-sixth. As a result of these U.S. investments, Singapore became the regional center for American electronics companies.[32]

These high-tech companies invested in East Asia principally to export back home to the United States. In fact, as early as 1977, such exports generated fully three-fifths of all East Asian sales by U.S. electronics subsidiaries, and through 1988 that share remained constant.[33] Much of this trade emerged as a response to Japanese competition in consumer electronics. It began in 1968, when General Electric (GE) opened its first offshore TV-parts plant, in Singapore.[34] There, low-cost labor assembled American-made components, an activity that was encouraged by U.S. trade

[30]For an analysis of these factors in Singapore's economic development, see Haggard, *Pathways from the Periphery,* pp. 101–115, 146–151.

[31]Commerce Department, "U.S. Direct Investment Abroad, 1989," p. 63.

[32]For additional data on the electronics industry in Singapore during the 1980s, see Daniel Todd, *The World Electronics Industry* (London: Routledge, 1990), esp. pp. 245–263; United Nations, Centre on Transnational Corporations, *Transnational Corporations and the Electronics Industries of ASEAN Economies* (New York: United Nations, 1987), esp. tables 9–11, pp. 26–31.

[33]Commerce Department, *1977 Benchmark,* tables III.I.19, III.I.23, pp. 354, 358.

[34]For a benchmark study of such investments, see Richard W. Moxon, "Offshore Production in the Less-Developed Countries By American Electronics Companies" (DBA thesis, Harvard University, Graduate School of Business Administration, 1973), appendix 4, pp. 143–148.

policy (Section 807), which called for import duties to be paid only on value added offshore (and not on the U.S. components now being reimported in the assembled product).[35] Once GE had moved, RCA and Zenith (both in 1969) followed swiftly by making their own investments in offshore assembly,[36] thus demonstrating the same oligopolistic behavior that would later characterize Japanese electronics companies in the United States and East Asia. GE's move also prompted a quick response from U.S. suppliers, who in turn acted in rapid succession:[37] in Singapore and then Malaysia, for example, several American semiconductor producers—Fairchild (in 1968), Texas Instruments (in 1969), National Semiconductor (in 1970), and Motorola (in 1973)—invested in labor-intensive assembly operations close to their powerful buyers. Thus, the demands of buyers, the special gaming strategies of oligopolistic rivals, intense import competition from the Japanese, liberal U.S. trade policies—all of these factors acted together to push and pull American multinationals to East Asia.[38]

Even so, through 1977, the combined value of U.S. electronics investments in East Asia remained quite small—but it rose rapidly during the 1980s (see Figure 4-4), as a strong dollar and intense import competition led American electronics companies to invest aggressively in East Asia in search of low-cost sources of supply. No longer did these investors simply import and then assemble U.S.-made components into low-technology products for reexport back to the United States, however. Instead, American subsidiaries in East Asian greatly diversified their sources of supply, by shifting the direction of trade toward other countries in the region. This shift signaled a larger trend: a movement toward greater regional integration, accelerated by foreign investment and related trade.

[35]For the impact of U.S. trade policy on U.S. FDI and related trade in East Asia, see U.S. Congress, Office of Technology Assessment, *International Competitiveness in Electronics* (Washington, D.C.: USGPO, 1983), pp. 116–119, 134–137, 434–435.

[36]Ibid., p. 118; Moxon, *Offshore Production*, appendix 4, pp. 143–148.

[37]Dieter Ernst, *The Global Race in Microelectronics: Innovation and Corporate Strategies in a Period of Crisis* (Frankfurt: Campus Verlag, 1983), esp. table 5.3 and 5.4, pp. 158–159; United Nations, *The Electronics Industries of ASEAN Economies*, esp. table 8, pp. 21–22.

[38]For a similar analysis of these factors, see Office of Technology Assessment, *International Competitiveness in Electronics*, pp. 192–193.

Nowhere was this movement more apparent than in the semi-conductor industry, where by 1978 Malaysia had emerged as the world's second-largest exporter—thanks largely to U.S. investments and trade, both encouraged by Malaysian government policy.[39] Initially, in 1978, the United States was Malaysia's largest overseas market and largest offshore supplier, as American semiconductor companies tightly linked U.S. parents to their overseas affiliates. A decade later, however, Malaysia's dependence on American-made components had been cut in half (from 60 to 30 percent of semiconductor imports), and its dependence on the U.S. market had been partially reduced (from 62 to 54 percent of semiconductor exports). What did not change was the role played by Singapore as the second-largest market and source of supply, thanks again in large part to the cross-investments and bilateral trade of American semiconductor companies operating in both Malaysia and Singapore.[40] By 1988, Singapore was joined by other countries in the region: Korea rose meteorically to become Malaysia's fourth-largest supplier, closely following Japan; while Hong Kong now consumed the third-largest share of Malaysian semiconductor exports, with Japan following far behind. Such intraregional trade, as well as Japan's relative trading position, seemed likely to improve once Japanese semiconductor companies completed their rush to join the Americans in Malaysia—and elsewhere in East Asia.[41]

THE JAPANESE RESPONSE

"In the American case," writes Mira Wilkins, "early foreign investment went disproportionately to geographically nearby

[39]For surveys of the semiconductor industry in Southeast Asia, see United Nations, *Electronics Industries of ASEAN Economies*, pp. 16–24; Joseph Grunwald and Kenneth Flamm, *The Global Factory: Foreign Assembly in International Trade* (Washington, D.C.: Brookings, 1985). In this paragraph, all national data on the value and direction of semiconductor trade (SITC 7763 and 7764) come from the Organization for Economic Cooperation and Development, *OECD Microtables, Series B: Foreign Trade Statistics by Country* (Paris: OECD, various years).

[40]During 1988, Singapore consumed over 15 percent (the same share recorded in 1978) of all Malaysian semiconductor exports, and supplied 13 percent (down from 17 percent in 1978) of Malaysian semiconductor imports.

[41]For the rush of Japanese semiconductor companies to East Asia, see Todd, *World Electronics Industry*, pp. 268–271.

areas—Canada, Mexico, and the Caribbean—and to culturally nearby ones—Great Britain. The earliest Japanese foreign investments were, likewise, in geographically close and relatively familiar regions."[42] This capsule conclusion, based on remarkably similar national patterns of foreign direct investment well before the Second World War, remained accurate—at least for the Japanese—for at least three decades after the war. Indeed, by 1914, according to the best available prewar data, East Asia hosted the greatest share of Japanese FDI, with China (including Manchuria) the principal destination.[43] As we noted above, American multinationals also concentrated their East Asian investments in China before the war; but the value of those investments probably remained well below that of the Japanese. Most such Japanese investment either set up textile mills, principally to supply the local Chinese market, or established trade-related services comparable to the trade, finance, insurance, and shipping operations simultaneously established in the United States.[44]

These industry patterns would reemerge after the war, but on a smaller scale, and not immediately. Indeed, for decades afterward, Japanese direct investment in East Asia remained quiescent and narrowly circumscribed for at least two reasons: first, Japanese capital controls greatly restricted all FDI outflows; and second, powerful postwar anti-Japanese feelings pervaded the entire Asian region, especially Korea, where no Japanese could invest until

[42]Mira Wilkins, "Japanese Multinational Enterprise before 1914," *Business History Review* 60 (Summer 1986): 207. Wilkins's observation helps to explain the attention expressly given East Asia by Japanese scholars. In addition to Kojima and Yoshihara (notes 5 and 7 above), see the following works: Sekiguchi Sueo, ed., *ASEAN-Japan Relations: Investment* (Singapore: Institute of Southeast Asian Studies, 1983); Ozawa Terutomo, *Multinationalism, Japanese Style: The Political Economy of Outward Dependency* (Princeton: Princeton University Press, 1979), esp. pp. 227–228; Hikoji Katano et al., *Japan's Direct Investment to ASEAN Countries* (Kobe: Research Institute For Economics and Business Administration, Kobe University, 1978).

[43]Ibid., tables 1–2, p. 209 and note 41, p. 217. Japanese direct investments in China ranged in value between $153 million and $190 million, which by 1914 was less than three-quarters of all Japanese FDI worldwide. Meanwhile, by 1929 (the first year for which comparable data are available), U.S. FDI in China had reached $114 million; see Commerce Department, *American Direct Investments in Foreign Countries*, 1929, table IV, p. 26.

[44]Wilkins, "Japanese Multinational Enterprise before 1914," pp. 207–218, 227–231; also see William D. Wray, *Mitsubishi and the N.Y.K., 1870–1914: Business Strategy in the Japanese Shipping Industry* (Cambridge: Harvard University Press, 1984).

formal diplomatic relations between that nation and Japan were reestablished in 1965. Across East Asia as a whole, in consequence, annual FDI outflows from Japan between 1950 and 1970 seldom exceeded $300 million.[45] Of this annual sum, the largest share—roughly one-fifth—typically went to Southeast Asia, where natural-resource industries were especially attractive. During the 1960s, for example, the Japanese invested in oil (Indonesia), iron ore (India, Malaysia, and the Philippines), copper ore (Malaysia and the Philippines), and natural gas (Brunei). Indeed, the Japanese government often encouraged such investment—which it did formally in 1971—with the legislative approval of special tax provisions for foreign investments in strategic resources.[46]

By contrast, few Japanese multinationals entered manufacturing in East Asia—again, in accordance with Japanese government policy. Before 1960, in fact, the Japanese government approved only 9 manufacturing investments: four in Thailand, three in Taiwan, and one each in Hong Kong and Singapore.[47] Over the following decade, no Japanese investor sought Japanese government approval for a manufacturing plant in Korea, or in the Philippines until 1967; nor in Indonesia until 1968. Subsequently, however, Japanese investments in East Asia took on new importance, as U.S.-Japan trade tensions heightened. Indeed, between 1968 and 1972 (as I noted in Chapter 3) American producers in several contested industries felt particularly aggrieved by stepped-up competition from Japanese imports. In the United States, protectionist actions began with the highly visible protests over steel and textiles, and then spread to a wide range of products: from footwear to metal tableware, from specialty steels to fasteners, from individual electronic components to fully-assembled electric machinery, from sheet glass to consumer electronics.[48] Just such

[45]Komiya Ryutaro and Wakasugi Ryuhei, "Japan's Foreign Direct Investment," *Annals of the American Academy of Political and Social Sciences* 513 (Jan. 1991), tables 1–2, pp. 52–53.

[46]Lawrence Krause and Sueo Sekiguchi, "Japan and the World Economy," in Hugh Patrick and Henry Rosovsky, ed., *Asia's New Giant: How the Japanese Economy Works* (Washington, D.C.: Brookings Institution, 1982), pp. 447 and 456.

[47]For country-by-country data in this paragraph, see Yoshihara, *Japanese Investment in Southeast Asia*, tables 2.2 and 3.1, pp. 18, 65.

[48]For an overview of these trade conflicts, see Komiya Ryutaro and Itoh Motoshige, "Japan's International Trade and Trade Policy, 1955–1974," in Inoguchi

U.S.-Japan trade conflicts put increased pressure on Japanese manufacturers of these products; finally, it forced them to invest outside Japan if they wished to escape American protectionism.

In the overall story of Japanese FDI, one year, 1972, represents an historical watershed. At home, in fact, the Japanese often refer to 1972 as the *gannen* (the very first year) of foreign direct investment.[49] During that year, the Japanese government fully liberalized most capital controls affecting the outflow of direct investment; and during 1972, annual outflows of Japanese FDI finally exceeded $2 billion. On a macroeconomic level, of course, Japan could easily afford this hefty sum, having recently recorded an unprecedented surplus in its current account. Moreover, such foreign direct investment now seemed essential for Japanese exporters facing higher relative prices; for them, double-digit increases in Japanese wages during the early 1970s were exacerbated in 1971 by the yen's rapid appreciation against the U.S. dollar. And because the values of most Asian currencies remained closely tied to the dollar, labor-intensive Japanese industries suffered a major cost disadvantage relative to their Asian competitors.

To overcome these disadvantages, the Japanese had to become more competitive; so producers moved to establish factories in East Asia, where a strong yen now worked in their favor by substantially reducing the initial costs of investment. Indeed, between 1972 and 1974, Japanese textile manufacturers and electronics producers staged an investment rush to East Asia.[50] During these three years, they managed to establish (principally in the former Japanese colonies of Korea and Taiwan) more than one-half of all Japanese-approved textile and electronics projects set up in East Asia since the war. Most of these projects were majority Japanese-owned: in textiles, the median foreign equity holding was 51 percent, while in electronics such shareholding reached figures as high as 66 percent—an industry-wide average. Both figures re-

---

Takashi and Daniel I. Okimoto, eds., *The Political Economy of Japan, Volume 2: The Changing International Context* (Stanford: Stanford University Press, 1988), pp. 197ff.

[49]Komiya and Wakasugi, "Japan's Foreign Direct Investment," p. 51.

[50]Unless otherwise noted, data in this paragraph on Japanese investments in East Asian textiles and electronics from Yoshihara, *Japanese Investment in Southeast Asia*, tables 4.4, 4.8, 5.1, and 5.6, pp. 112–166.

mained lower in countries (e.g., Korea) that maintained strict capital controls. From these subsidiaries during 1974, Japanese textile manufacturers and electronics producers each exported well over one-half of their total East Asia production.[51] They shipped these exports in roughly equal measure to markets back home and in third countries (mainly the United States), and then they sold the remainder of their East Asian production in the local host-country market. Thus, by 1974, Japanese textile manufacturers and electronics producers operated in East Asia in much the same way American multinationals did: both invested, when possible, in majority subsidiaries, principally to secure less expensive foreign sources of supply, much of which they later exported. This procedure, in large part, represented the multinationals' response to growing tensions in the U.S.-Japan rivalry.

At the same time, however, the Japanese have actively pursued foreign investment and related trade strategies unfamiliar to the Americans. Specifically, Japanese manufacturers have sometimes teamed up with Japanese trading companies (*sogo shosha*), which already could claim extensive experience across the region.[52] In East Asia, this strategy emerged with special clarity in the textile industry: by 1974, at least three such sogo shosha—C. Itoh, Marubeni, and Mitsui—had invested aggressively in East Asian textiles, typically through multi-party joint ventures with Japanese manufacturers. (Indeed, the inclusion of several partners in a single joint venture was a rather common Japanese strategy, which seemed to insure majority Japanese shareholdings.) In establishing these subsidiaries, Japanese trading companies showed particular biases: while C. Itoh and Marubeni spread their investments among Japan's three largest textile manufacturers—Toray, Teijin and Toyobo—Mitsui concentrated its investments in Toray alone. Yet in all of these joint ventures, the sogo shosha pursued a single overriding objective, according to Yoshihara Kunio: "If in-

<hr>

[51] Japan, Ministry of International Trade and Industry, Industrial Policy Bureau, *The 3rd Survey of the Overseas Business Activities of Japanese Enterprises [Dai san-kai wagakuni kigyou no kaigai jigyou katsudou]* (Tokyo: MITI, 1974), table 4-1-1, p. 85 (hereafter cited as MITI, *3rd Overseas Survey*).

[52] Indeed, that experience dates back to the turn of the century; see Wilkins, "Japanese Multinational Enterprise before 1914," esp. pp. 208–218, 229–231.

vestment was to establish a spinning mill, the participating trading company wanted to be its chief supplier of fiber; if it was to set up a fiber plant, the trading company wanted to be its chief supplier of chemical raw materials; if investment was to build an export base, it wanted to market the goods."[53] In this way, Japanese trading companies considered their East Asian investments as growing markets for trade arbitrage, useful for creating new markets for both Japanese and East Asian exports.

While sogo shosha were often crucial to Japanese investments in East Asian textiles, they remained notably absent from electronics and most other industries. This fact leads Yoshihara to conclude:

> The trading company is little involved in the marketing of electrical machinery, automobiles, and general machinery, and its overseas investment in these products is small. But in such homogenous products as textiles, iron and steel, and chemicals, whose marketing it handles, overseas investment is large. *Contrary to the widely held view that the trading company is an active investor in most industries, its investment is highly selective.* In the field of products which are differentiated or which require customer service, involvement as either marketer or investor tends to be small. [Emphasis added][54]

Largely unaided by Japanese trading companies, Japanese electronics producers flocked to East Asia, led by NEC (as early as 1958), followed by Matsushita and Sanyo (both by 1961), Sharp (1962), Hitachi (1967) and finally, Fujitsu and Sony (1973).[55] Typically, these companies imitated their American competitors, by initially investing in East Asia to supply local host-country markets. During 1972, for example, local host-country sales contributed over three-fifths of the total sales reported by all Japanese electronics affiliates manufacturing in East Asia.[56] After that fateful year, when U.S. protectionism suddenly escalated, "the response

---

[53]Yoshihara, *Japanese Investment in Southeast Asia*, tables 4.9, 4.10, and 4.11, pp. 122–125.

[54]Ibid., pp. 169–170.

[55]For the evolution of these Japanese multinationals, see the Oriental Economist, *Japanese Overseas Investment: A Complete Listing by Firms and Countries, 1984–85* (Tokyo: The Oriental Economist, 1984).

[56]MITI, *3rd Overseas Survey*, table 4-1-11, p. 106.

of the Japanese color television producers is worth noting," according to Komiya Ryutaro and Itoh Motoshige.[57] "They partially replaced exports of their products by direct investment and production in the United States [just as they also] invested in some NICs [newly-industrializing countries] and exported sets produced there to the United States." Indeed, during 1972–74, when Sony and Matsushita began producing color TVs in the United States, they and other Japanese electronics companies moved to shift all of their monochrome TV production to East Asia.[58] With that shift came a tighter integration of East Asia into the increasingly hostile U.S.-Japan rivalry.

So large was the scale of the Japanese rush to East Asia, in fact, that between 1966 and 1977 the value of Japanese FDI in East Asia finally equaled (historically larger) American investments (see Figure 4-1). Like the Americans, Japanese multinationals concentrated most of their investments in a very few countries: Indonesia, already the second largest host for U.S. FDI in the region, now became the principal destination for Japanese investors, accounting for over two-fifths of their total East Asian investment (compare Figure 4-4 with Figure 4-5). Another one-fifth of that investment went to Korea, the second largest regional host to Japanese direct investment; while the remaining two-fifths were dispersed broadly across the rest of East Asia. In these few countries, moreover, the Japanese concentrated their East Asian investments in an even smaller number of industries. And once again, they often followed the general pattern adopted earlier by the Americans, at least in natural-resource industries: mining (for the Japanese) and petroleum (for the Americans) each attracted roughly two-fifths of their respective East Asian investments, with Indonesia the principal host (see Figure 4-4). But unlike the Americans, the Japanese invested as much in East Asian manufacturing (especially textiles, an industry that attracted little U.S. FDI) as they did in natural-resource industries, with both Indonesia and Korea emerging as chief manufacturing hosts.[59] This meant little Japanese invest-

---

[57]Komiya and Itoh, "Japan's International Trade and Trade Policy," p. 198.

[58]Todd, *World Electronics Industry,* pp. 54–66.

[59]Japan, Ministry of International Trade and Industry, Industrial Policy Bureau, *The Eighth Survey of the Overseas Business Activities of Japanese Enterprises [Dai hachi-kai wagakuni kigyou no kaigai jigyou katsudou]* (Tokyo: MITI, 1979), table 4-1-1, p. 85.

Figure 4-5. Japanese FDI in East Asia by country and industry, 1977 vs. 1988

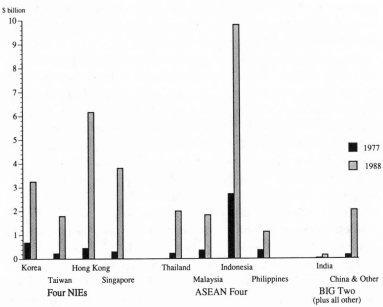

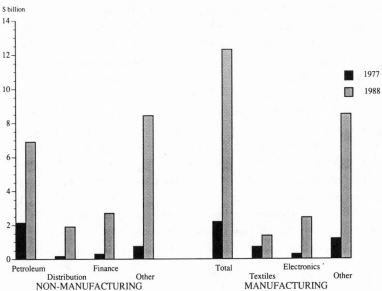

Source: Japan, Ministry of Finance, *Statistics for the Approval/Notification of Overseas Direct Investment [Taigai chokusetsu toshi no kyoka todokede jisseki]* (Tokyo: Ministry of Finance Printing Bureau, selected years).

ment in East Asian wholesaling and finance, two trade-related sectors that attracted a rather large share of U.S. FDI. For the Americans, as we have noted, these service investments augmented an aggressive strategy emphasizing East Asian exports—just as they did for the Japanese.

But eventually, the Japanese pursued such an export strategy only with much reluctance—a change from the enthusiasm they had displayed as recently as 1974. When compared to the Americans during 1977 (the first year for which comparable U.S. and Japanese data are available), for example, the Japanese sold much less outside the local market hosting their East Asian investments. In fact, during 1977, that local host-country market accounted for fully three-fifths of total foreign sales generated by all Japanese multinationals in East Asia (see Figure 4-6). For the Americans, as already noted (in Figure 4-3), that local-sales contribution remained much lower, and it was constant across industries. For the Japanese, however, wider variation could be observed across industries—for example, extractive industries remained far more dependent on the local host-country market than did wholesaling, while manufacturing fell between these extremes. And within manufacturing alone, even Japanese textile manufacturers and electronics producers closely followed the larger patterns,[60] thereby reversing (at least in part) earlier trends, as growing host-country markets now consumed an ever-larger share of their total East Asian production.

Still, for many Japanese investors, East Asia remained a major source of supply for export elsewhere. In fact, during 1977, exports continued to account for nearly two-fifths of the total East Asian sales of all Japanese multinationals (see Figure 4-6). Much of this sum came from distribution, where Japanese trading companies occupied a unique position, one that granted them access to markets back home and in third countries. (This fact is reflected in the rather even share, between Japan and third countries, of export sales recorded by Japanese investments in East Asian distribution.) By comparison, in manufacturing, Japanese multinationals

[60]Ibid.

Figure 4-6. Destination of sales by Japanese subsidiaries in East Asia, 1977 vs. 1988

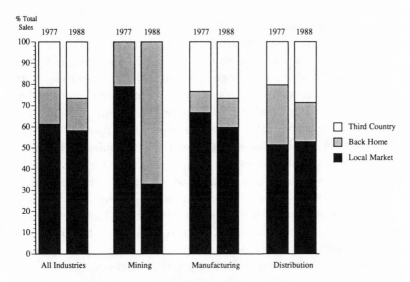

Sources: Japan, Ministry of International Trade and Industry, Industrial Policy Bureau, *The 8th Survey of the Overseas Business Activities of Japanese Enterprises [Dai hachi-kai wagakuni kigyou no kaigai jigyou katsudou]* (Tokyo: MITI, 1979), table 56, p. 57; Japan, Ministry of International Trade and Industry, Industrial Policy Bureau, International Business Affairs Division, *The 19th Survey of the Overseas Business Activities of Japanese Enterprises [Dai jyuukyuu-kai wagakuni kigyou no kaigai jigyou katsudou]* (Tokyo: Ministry of Finance Printing Bureau, 1990), pp. 74–75.

sold nearly one-quarter of their East Asian production in third-country markets (principally other East Asian countries, plus the United States)—more than twice as much as they exported back to Japan. Specifically in textiles, third-country trade reached a high of one-third of total East Asian sales, while exports to Japan generated less than 5 percent of total sales.[61] In marked contrast to the Americans, the Japanese seemed less inclined to employ their East Asian investments as a major source of low-cost supply for markets back home; instead, they more often channeled this supply to

[61] Ibid.

third-country markets, either in the United States or lying elsewhere in East Asia.

That condition changed little over the next decade, even though Japanese multinationals flooded into East Asia, moving well past the Americans in the value of their foreign direct investments (see Figure 4-1). The Japanese had finally caught up with the Americans just a decade earlier, by 1977, when both recorded roughly $6 billion in cumulative East Asian investments. Subsequently, that investment parity disappeared: between 1977 and 1988, even as American investments in East Asia tripled, Japanese FDI in the region grew nearly twice as fast, reaching $32.3 billion. That huge sum entered East Asia in two stages: the first, during the early 1980s, followed the 1979 oil price shock and an acceleration of U.S. protectionism; the second, after 1985, followed a rapid rise in the exchange value of the Japanese yen. Yet that currency appreciation had little impact on exports to Japan, which remained a roughly constant share of total sales (see Figure 4-6). Instead, exports to third countries and (especially) local sales in the host-country market remained the principal attraction for new Japanese investment in East Asia—again, in marked contrast to the nature of U.S. FDI across the region.

Like the Americans, Japanese multinationals still preferred to concentrate their ever-growing investments in a very few East Asian countries. What did change, however, were the relative Japanese shares hosted by specific countries. For example, Indonesia remains the principal East Asian host for Japanese FDI, but between 1977 and 1988, its relative share declined from roughly one-half to less than one-third of all Japanese FDI in East Asia (see Figure 4-5). When combined, another one-third went to Hong Kong and Singapore, which had now moved well ahead of Korea and (in the case of Singapore) the Philippines, to rank second and third (respectively) among East Asian hosts to Japanese investment. Indeed, between 1977 and 1988, Japanese FDI in both Hong Kong and Singapore grew at twice the rate recorded in East Asia as a whole, leaving Hong Kong with one-fifth and Singapore with one-tenth of all Japanese FDI in East Asia. In total, nearly $3 of every $5 invested through 1988 by the Japanese in East Asia went to Indonesia, Hong Kong, and Singapore—the same three countries that, as we noted above, also hosted $3 out of every $5 of all U.S. FDI in East Asia.

In these three countries, moreover, a similar pattern of national specialization emerged by 1988. By then, for example, Indonesia hosted 90 percent of all Japanese FDI in East Asian mining (up from 80 percent in 1977)—which in turn contributed the largest share of all Japanese FDI in Indonesia.[62] Over time, the proportionate decline of Japanese FDI in the mining industry (from two-fifths to one-fifth of all Japanese FDI in the region) has still served effectively to increase Indonesia's preeminence in this industry. Similarly, Hong Kong hosted three-fifths of all Japanese investment in both East Asian finance and distribution, and these two trade-related services also contributed the major portion of all Japanese FDI in Hong Kong. Even the rapid growth between 1977 and 1988 of Japanese service investments has done little to dilute Hong Kong's preeminence in these sectors. Thus, for both the Japanese and the Americans, Indonesia has emerged as the East Asian center for extractive industries, while Hong Kong must be regarded at present as the regional center for trade-related services.

In East Asian manufacturing, however, Japanese multinationals became even more diversified than the Americans, with far more investment spread out across numerous sectors and several countries. Valued at $12 billion in 1988 (see Figure 4-5), Japanese manufacturing investments in East Asia grew impressively to be twice as large as comparable U.S. investments, and to contribute a larger share of total Japanese FDI in East Asia. Moreover, while electronics has surpassed textiles, accounting for the greatest share of all Japanese investments in East Asian manufacturing, that sectoral share (one-fifth during 1988) still remains well below electronics' contribution to comparable U.S. investment (two-fifths during 1988). And while Singapore has grown to rank second as an East Asian host to Japanese manufacturers, that national share (one-sixth) remains well below Singapore's relative contribution to

[62]MITI, *19th Overseas Survey,* table 4, pp. 7–8.

comparable U.S. investment (one-third during 1988). As a result, Singapore now represents less of a regional manufacturing center for the Japanese than for the Americans.

Significantly, the geographic spread of Japanese investments in East Asian manufacturing has actually been increasing—moving in a direction opposite that of the Americans. During 1988, Thailand emerged as the largest recipient of new Japanese investments in East Asian manufacturing, followed far behind by Malaysia. Indeed, during 1988 alone, more Japanese investment entered the manufacturing sector in Thailand than entered the combined manufacturing sectors of all the 4-NIEs. Here, Korea has suffered the greatest relative losses: hosting 22 percent of all Japanese manufacturing investments in East Asia during 1977, Korea's share of that investment was cut nearly in half by 1988. While several factors—the appreciation of the Korean won, growing labor costs, political riots—have undoubtedly played an important role in Korea's decline as a host to Japanese FDI, strict capital controls in Korea also have figured prominently: for in East Asia as a whole during 1988, 54 percent of all Japanese-owned projects remained majority Japanese-owned.[63] Here, like the Americans, the Japanese retain a strong preference for majority ownership.

Just such majority ownership granted both the Americans and the Japanese considerable managerial control over their subsidiaries' decisions concerning both the sources of critical inputs and the marketing of subsequent output. As a result of sourcing decisions, for example, American and Japanese subsidiaries in East Asia consumed during 1988 roughly comparable shares (14 percent for the Americans, 17 percent for the Japanese) of their home country's exports to the region.[64] However, the dollar value of such trade was nearly twice as large for Japanese subsidiaries (see Figure 4-7), reflecting the fact that Japan's total exports to East Asia during 1988 were one-and-a-half times as large as the United

[63] Ibid.

[64] For the Japanese, see MITI, *19th Overseas Survey*, pp. 74–75, 86–87; for the Americans, see Commerce Department, *U.S. FDI: 1988 Survey*, tables 16, 18, 52, 53, n.p.; for trade data, see International Monetary Fund, *Direction of Trade Statistics Yearbook, 1989* (Washington, D.C.: IMF, 1990).

Figure 4-7. Trade by Japanese and U.S. subsidiaries in East Asia, 1988

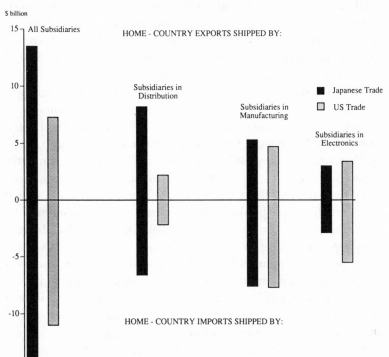

Sources: Japan, Ministry of International Trade and Industry, Industrial Policy Bureau, International Business Affairs Division, *The 19th Survey of the Overseas Business Activities of Japanese Enterprises [Dai jyuukyuu-kai wagakuni kigyou no kaigai jigyou katsudou]* (Tokyo: Ministry of Finance Printing Bureau, 1990), pp. 74–75, 86–87; U.S. Commerce Department, Bureau of Economic Analysis, *U.S. Direct Investment Abroad: Operations of U.S Parent Companies and their Foreign Affiliates, Preliminary 1988 Estimates* (Washington, D.C.: USGPO, July 1990), tables 16, 18, 52, 53, n.p.

States trade.[65] By contrast, the total sales of all Japanese subsidiaries in East Asia ($85.5 billion during 1988) were just one-third larger than comparable U.S. sales ($65.9 billion), leaving Japanese

[65]U.S. exports to East Asia equaled $51.4 billion, while Japanese exports to that region equaled $77.4 billion; see IMF, *Trade Statistics Yearbook, 1989.*

sales more dependent on exports from back home (16 percent of total sales, versus 11 percent).[66] Most of these exports, moreover, were channeled through Japanese subsidiaries engaged principally in overseas distribution—as Japanese multinationals consistently followed the same strategy of foreign investment and related trade that we saw earlier in the United States.

By contrast, U.S. manufacturing subsidiaries consumed most U.S. exports to American multinationals in East Asia. These subsidiaries, in turn, shipped a far greater amount back to the United States than they bought from the United States, and thus contributed to America's burgeoning trade deficit with East Asia. Similarly, Japanese manufacturers in East Asia also shipped more back home than they bought from Japan. But that resulting trade deficit was virtually offset by the trade surplus for Japan generated by Japanese-owned distributors in East Asia. Outside of distribution, this important contrast between Japanese and American trade strategy is most apparent in electronics: While Japanese producers in East Asia did maintain a rough trade balance with Japan, their U.S. competitors did not. Instead, in their response to import competition back home, U.S. electronics companies invested in their own East Asian sources of low-cost imports; and thus, among U.S. subsidiaries in the region, those that produced electronics contributed the greatest share to the U.S. trade deficit.

In response to American competition, Japanese electronics companies invested in their own East Asian sources of low-cost supply, pursuing an investment strategy that would be imitated by other Japanese manufacturers.[67] In contrast to the Americans, however,

[66]See the citations in note 64.

[67]For Japanese strategy in East Asian electronics, see Yamada Bundo, "Internationalization Strategies of Japanese Electronics Companies: Implications for Asian Newly Industrializing Economies" (Paris: OECD Development Centre, Technical Papers No. 28, Oct. 1990); Gee San, "The Status and an Evaluation of the Electronics Industry in Taiwan" (Paris: OECD Development Centre, Technical Papers No. 29, Oct. 1990); Urata Shujiro, "The Rapid Globalization of Japanese Firms in the 1980s: An Analysis of the Activities of Japanese Firms in Asia," a paper prepared for the Research Programme on Globalisation and Regionalisation, Organization for Economic Cooperation and Development, Paris, June 20–21, 1990; Dieter Ernst and David O'Connor, *Technology and Global Competition: The Challenge for Newly Industrialising Economies* (Paris: OECD, 1989); Jung Taik Hyun and Katherine Whitmore, "Japanese Direct Foreign Investment: Patterns and Implications

these Japanese developed a fundamentally different trade strategy: while shipments back to the United States accounted for over three-fifths of the total sales reported by U.S. electronics subsidiaries in East Asia, the Japanese became far more diversified in their marketing.[68] For them, during 1988, for example, electronics shipments back home represented only 25 percent of their total sales, yet that figure was well above the East Asian average for Japanese manufacturers as a whole. For these manufacturers, as for Japanese electronics subsidiaries, another 17 percent of total sales came from exports to other countries in East Asia—where (as we have noted) the Americans also remained quite active by pursuing their own intraregional trade. However, the Americans and Japanese differed sharply in their shipments to each other's home market. For Japanese electronics affiliates in East Asia (indeed, for all Japanese manufacturing subsidiaries in the region) the U.S. market during 1988 contributed 12 percent of total sales—well above the East Asian shipments to Japan recorded by U.S. (electronics) subsidiaries in East Asia.[69] Thus, in the larger U.S.-Japan rivalry, the Japanese again managed to gain far greater access to the U.S. market than the Americans secured in Japan—and subsidiaries in East Asia offered important sources of competitive advantage.

Into the 1990s, that conclusion seems unlikely to change. For the Americans, Japanese investments in East Asia expand an already intense three-front contest[70]—as import competition now emanates from both Japan and East Asia—with products feeding

for Developing Countries" (Washington, D.C.: World Bank, 1989); Nakakita Toru, "The Globalization of Japanese Firms and Its Influence on Japan's Trade with Developing Countries," *The Developing Economies* (Dec. 1988): 306–322.

[68]For the Americans, see *U.S. FDI: 1988 Survey*, tables 6 and 29, n.p.; for the Japanese, see MITI, *19th Survey*, pp. 74–75.

[69]For the Japanese, see MITI, *19th Survey*, pp. 74–75. For the Americans, data here are for 1982; see U.S. Commerce Department, Bureau of Economic Analysis, *U.S. Direct Investment Abroad, 1982* (Washington, D.C.: USGPO, April 1984).

[70]For an analysis of this three-front contest, see Yung Chul Park and Won Am Park, "Changing Japanese Trade Patterns and the East Asian NICs," in Paul Krugman, ed., *The U.S. and Japan: Trade and Investment* (Cambridge: MIT Press for the National Bureau of Economic Research, 1991); in this same volume, also see Peter A. Petri, "Market Structure, Comparative Advantage, and Japanese Trade under the Strong Yen."

expanded Japanese investments in U.S. manufacturing and distribution, all integrated and coordinated by the same Japanese multinational. By contrast, limited American investments in Japan, especially in majority subsidiaries, have limited intracompany trade between U.S. subsidiaries in both East Asia and Japan. Instead, that trade comes back to the United States, but now as a defensive response to Japan's three-front strategy. For the Japanese, then, U.S. direct investment and related trade in East Asia have done little to dull the American challenge—a challenge which, so far, they have effectively blunted back home.

CHAPTER FIVE

Alternative Explanations

W HY DO THE Japanese sell more in the United States than Americans sell in Japan? In this sensitive bilateral relationship, one that is easily polarized, no other question has produced so much vitriolic debate. When we sort through the polemics, four "standard" answers can be discerned, each suggesting its own set of remedies. Certainly, other remedies have also been prescribed; and not every explanation of the U.S-Japan rivalry can be fit so neatly into one of these four categories. Indeed, in the pages of this chapter, I shall propose a fifth—and in my view, the preferred—explanation, which departs significantly from all earlier answers. Before we turn to my own alternative, however, we should review the principal components of the most popular interpretations of the U.S.-Japan rivalry. These components range from various corporate strategies to styles of managerial psychology; and, of course, they include all the official policies of both the U.S. and Japanese governments. Now, putting these components together, we consider the "standard" explanations:

First, critics in both America and Japan often interpret bilateral imbalances in trade and investment as merely secondary evidence of the larger tragedy created by *America's declining competitiveness.* Among the principal villains here, American corporations are typically blamed for squandering their early advantages in technology, marketing, and organization.[1] In addition, the U.S. government

---

[1]See, for example, Robert H. Hayes and Steven C. Wheelwright, *Restoring Our Competitive Edge: Competing through Manufacturing* (New York: John Wiley, 1984),

shares some of the responsibility, since it stands idly by while American corporations surrender their technological lead to foreign rivals actively supported by their own governments.[2] America's relations with Japan, by this measure, are not considered unique; instead, they are seen to fit a general pattern. And so does the approved remedy: by reinvesting in tangible and intangible assets, while also paying sufficient attention to both quality and price, Americans should be able to sell abroad as much as foreigners sell in America. Selling in Japan and matching the Japanese should prove no exceptions to the rule.

Second, the U.S. government can be faulted for allowing a strong dollar to erode America's productive base, and again, for allowing a strong yen to purchase that American base once it has become weakened.[3] This explanation, not unrelated to the first, emphasizes *foreign exchange rates;* and in the United States, at least, it has been widely accepted as sufficient reason for both Japan's success and America's demise. Here, economists routinely argue that the levels and movements of U.S. prices, relative to America's principal competitors, account for changes in both U.S. exports and imports.[4] Again, the problem is not simply bilateral. Nor is the proposed solution: if the United States and its several trading partners allow exchange rates to adjust properly, then U.S. multilateral imbalances will soon disappear. And any vestigial U.S. deficits with Japan simply cease to be important.

Third, and in sharp contrast to the immediately preceding explanation, few of America's critics in Japan feel convinced that the

---

esp. pp. 1–23; William J. Abernathy et al., *Industrial Renaissance: Producing a Competitive Future for America* (New York: Basic Books, 1983).

[2]See, for example, Bruce R. Scott and George C. Lodge, eds., *U.S. Competitiveness in the World Economy* (Boston: Harvard Business School Press, 1984); John Zysman and Laura Tyson, eds., *American Industry in International Competition: Government Policies and Corporate Strategies* (Ithaca: Cornell University Press, 1983).

[3]Felix Rohatyn, "America's Economic Dependence," *Foreign Affairs* 68 (Jan. 1989): 53–65; Norman J. Glickman and Douglas P. Woodward, *The New Competitors: How Foreign Investors Are Changing the U.S. Economy* (New York: Basic Books, 1989), pp. 105–111.

[4]See, for example, Dennis M. Bushe et al., "Prices, Activity, and Machinery Exports: An Analysis Based on New Price Data," *Review of Economics and Statistics* 68 (May 1986): 248–255; Irving B. Kravis and Robert E. Lipsey, "Prices and Market Shares in the International Machinery Trade," *Review of Economics and Statistics* 64 (Feb. 1982): 110–116.

dollar's value can possibly be the real cause of bilateral imbalances.[5] Instead, according to this popular belief, the real problem lies with the psychology of U.S. managers, whose *benign neglect,* fed by both indifference and ignorance, blinds them to rich business opportunities in Japan.[6] If only Americans would try harder to understand how Japan works—and how to work in Japan—then Americans would soon be selling in Japan as much as the Japanese sell in America. One result of this belief has been a plethora of books on how to do business in Japan.[7] Of course, by saying that the psychology of U.S. managers is (or needs to be) somehow *different* in Japan from what it is elsewhere in the world, advocates of this view powerfully reinforce the equally common notion of Japanese uniqueness.

Fourth, Japan's critics in the United States have championed the competing argument that unfair *Japanese trade policies* and inscrutable Japanese business practices share major blame for persistent trade imbalances.[8] Certainly, just to contend that Japanese policies and practices differ drastically from international norms serves

[5]Indeed, the Japanese often express a certain disdain for this notion; see, for example, Japan, Ministry of International Trade and Industry, *White Paper on International Trade: 1988* (Tokyo: MITI, 1988), esp. pp. 10–31.

[6]This belief finds support among both American and Japanese analysts; for an American view, see James Abegglen and George Stalk, Jr., *Kaisha, The Japanese Corporation* (New York: Basic Books, 1985), esp. p. 217; for a Japanese view, see Ozawa Terutomo, "Japanese Policy Toward Foreign Multinationals: Implications for Trade and Competitiveness," in Thomas Pugel, ed., *Fragile Interdependence* (Lexington, Mass.: D.C. Heath, 1986), p. 147.

[7]Among the more recent publications in this genre, see American Chamber of Commerce in Japan, *Trade and Investment in Japan: The Current Environment* (Tokyo: ACCJ, June 1991), esp. pp. 29–40; T. W. Kang, *Gaishi: The Foreign Company in Japan* (New York: Basic Books, 1990); Jackson N. Huddleston, Jr., *Gaijin Kaisha: Running a Foreign Business in Japan* (Armonk, N.Y.: M.E. Sharpe, 1990); Commission of the European Communities, *Guide for European Investment in Japan* (Tokyo: EC, 1990); Look Japan, *Taking on Japan: How 18 Companies Compete in the World's Second Largest Market* (Tokyo: Look Japan, 1988); American Chamber of Commerce in Japan, *Direct Foreign Investment in Japan: The Challenge for Foreign Firms* (Tokyo: ACCJ, September, 1987); Robert C. Christopher, *Second to None: American Companies in Japan* (New York: Crown, 1986); Japan, Ministry of International Trade and Industry, Office for the Promotion of Foreign Investment in Japan, *Investing in Japan* (Tokyo: MITI, 1985).

[8]For a recent expression of this argument, see Edward J. Lincoln, *Japan's Unequal Trade* (Washington, D.C.: Brookings Institution, 1990); for the most forceful statement, see Clyde V. Prestowitz, Jr., *Trading Places: How We Allowed Japan to Take the Lead* (New York: Basic Books, 1988).

once more to reinforce the familiar notion of Japanese uniqueness, as well as to imply the existence of a peculiar cure: by putting foreign pressure on Japan to change its formal government policies and explicit industrial structures, the U.S. government should be able to open the Japanese market wide enough to reverse existing bilateral imbalances.[9] Here, the principal protagonists are national governments; business is seen to play a secondary role.

No matter how popular, however, none of these standard views finds sufficient justification in this book to be accepted as complete. Instead, my observations reveal the need for a *fifth* explanation predicated on the seemingly elementary notion that the Americans and the Japanese are far more alike outside Japan than inside. For outside Japan, American and Japanese multinationals have pursued markedly similar foreign-investment strategies: relying on foreign production and overseas distribution, both sell much more abroad through majority-owned subsidiaries than do exporters located in either country. Meanwhile, inside Japan, business and government have erected markedly different trade restrictions, capital controls, and industrial structures from those in America. Taken together, these persistent asymmetries in what I term "strategic investment policies" best explain why American multinationals inside Japan invest and trade differently than they—and the Japanese—do outside of Japan. Only by *reversing* such asymmetries will the Americans then be able to sell in Japan as much as the Japanese sell in America.

Forced to search outside the limits of popular myth for a better and more complete explanation, we are led well beyond trade, to study the particular role of foreign direct investment in the U.S.-Japan rivalry. That role has too often been overlooked by U.S.

[9]Among Americans strongly advocating this view, see Kent E. Calder, "Japanese Foreign Economic Policy Formation: Explaining the Reactive State," *World Politics* 40 (July, 1988): 518–519; also see his *Crisis and Compensation: Public Policy and Political Stability in Japan, 1949–1986* (Princeton: Princeton University Press, 1989), esp. p. 450. Among the Japanese this view has become a staple conviction; see, Kosaka Masataka, "The International Economic Policy of Japan," in Robert Scalapino, ed., *The Foreign Policy of Modern Japan* (Berkeley: University of California Press, 1977), pp. 211, 214; Komiya Ryutaro, "Direct Foreign Investment in Postwar Japan," in Peter Drysdale, ed., *Direct Foreign Investment in Asia and the Pacific* (Canberra: ANU Press, 1972), p. 152.

critics of Japanese trade policies and private Japanese business practices. We have seen that such policies and practices figure prominently in Japan's investment strategy: restrictive practices affecting intercorporate shareholdings, mergers and acquisitions, and buyer-supplier relations have served to limit foreign sales in Japan. And even before the emergence of any Japanese oligopolists powerful enough to enforce these private restrictions, trade regulations protected domestic industries from unwelcome import competition. Used without capital controls, however, these same import-substitution policies worked to attract foreign direct investment seeking to supply local, as opposed to export, markets. Indeed, as we have noted, U.S. trade barriers have certainly accelerated Japanese direct investment in the United States. By contrast, we have also seen that East Asia outside Japan implemented export-promotion policies to attract both American and Japanese multinationals seeking to supply international markets, either back home or elsewhere in the region. Yet in Japan, neither import substitution nor export promotion has attracted much U.S. direct investment—least of all, investment in majority U.S.-owned subsidiaries. Just such investment has long been the principal source of foreign sales by American multinationals elsewhere in the world, but not in Japan—a fact that seems lost to many U.S. trade analysts.

To explain the absence of foreign sales in Japan, critics there have called into question the tenacity of American multinationals, creating yet another strong myth, according to my alternative explanation. Certainly, U.S. direct investment in Japan today remains well below the relative levels found in other industrialized countries. And certainly little of this investment is presently concentrated in majority U.S.-owned subsidiaries, the principal source of foreign sales by American multinationals outside Japan. Inside Japan, however, those few Americans who have successfully established majority subsidiaries simply had to muster far more determination and perseverance than was required elsewhere in other industrialized countries. Yet even then, in Japan at least, no amount of American tenacity alone has been sufficient to insure majority ownership. Nor has the requisite possession of technological, marketing, and organizational assets, even when these assets have been jealously protected by their multinational owners and eagerly coveted by the Japanese. In addition to such firm-specific assets, various political skills have also been required, both to muster foreign pressure in negotiations with Japanese regulators and oligopolists, and to form among these oligopolists a Japanese constituency supportive of change. In Japan, the initiative for such policy change has come neither from the Japanese state nor from the U.S. government—a fact that calls into question much of the earlier research on the economic role of the state, and on foreign determinants of domestic policy, both in Japan and cross-nationally. In marked contrast to this research, we see here that Japanese oligopolists managed to control both the timing and the substance of changes in their country's strategic investment policy by aggressively mediating those foreign pressures initiated by American multinationals. Nevertheless, by combining their managerial tenacity with a unique set of firm-specific assets and political skills, a few American multinationals have established majority subsidiaries in Japan. In the United States, by contrast, much less tenacity and fewer such skills have been necessary to trade and invest successfully, and just these differences have allowed the Japanese to sell more in America than Americans sell in Japan.

For the Americans as well as the Japanese, most foreign sales come from combinations of overseas production and intracompany trade, both of which dilute the impact of foreign-exchange rates on global competition. American multinationals invest far more aggressively in foreign production than do the newly emergent Japanese; and these U.S. investors gain a hedge against exchange-rate movements not enjoyed by those national exporters who add little local content in overseas markets. For the Americans, in fact, a strong dollar has accelerated foreign production across much of East Asia—except in Japan, where strategic investment policies have further weakened the impact of exchange rates on U.S. direct investment. By comparison, Japanese multinationals actually engage in intracompany trade far more frequently than do the more well-established Americans; and this Japanese trade remains strong despite increasing foreign production and a continuing rise in the value of the yen. Generally speaking, intracompany shipments prove far more responsive to relationships among multinational parents and their foreign subsidiaries—and thus, far less price-sensitive—than do more distant arm's-length transactions among unaffiliated buyers and suppliers. In this way, foreign investment reduces the impact of currency movements on foreign sales by American and Japanese multinationals, a fact that calls seriously into question the role of foreign-exchange rates in the U.S.-Japan rivalry.

Finally, my own alternative explanation of why the Japanese sell more in America than Americans sell in Japan compels a serious reassessment of competitiveness itself; for that popular notion has all too often been misunderstood. Here, the distinction between ownership and location is especially important: the problem with much existing research derives from its failure to view the United States as anything more than a base of production—and not as the home of multinational corporations that successfully manage both tangible and intangible assets across national boundaries. Managing just these assets, in fact, U.S.-*owned* multinationals (their American parents and majority subsidiaries worldwide) have created and sustained competitive advantages in world markets, advantages which simply lie beyond the reach of U.S.-*based* exporters (including both American-owned enterprises and foreign-owned subsidiaries in the United States). Proof of this American competitiveness can be found in nation after nation—except, of course, in Japan. There, both the complex interactions and the enduring legacies of trade restrictions, capital controls, and industrial structures—the three critical components of Japan's strategic investment policy—have played key roles in guaranteeing to Japanese oligopolists certain competitive advantages that remain unavailable to either U.S.-*owned* multinationals or U.S.-*based* exporters.

THE DOLLAR AND U.S. COMPETITIVENESS

In the 1980s, America's declining competitiveness became a *cause célèbre*. From the voluminous literature on this diverse subject, at least one conclusion has been generally accepted: that America's standing as an economic superpower has declined precipitously, especially in comparison with Japan. To arrest or, better, reverse this decline, popular analysts propose two remedies: One school argues that the crux of America's problem remains internal to U.S.-*owned* corporations, to be found there in faulty incentive systems that reward short-term results, and in declining R&D investments for commercial (as distinct from military) applications.[10] From this perspective, an American remedy will require fundamental changes in American corporate management, as well as smaller alterations in the U.S. corporate environment. That corporate environment figures far more prominently in the American remedy proposed by a second school of thought, which blames U.S. government policy for unwittingly encouraging America's fall from grace.[11] From this second perspective, the declining competitiveness of U.S.-*based* enterprises must be reversed by alterations in certain national policies—changes that begin in the short term with a currency devaluation designed to bring down relative prices; changes that may in the long term remake U.S. industrial policy on the model of America's strongest national competitors. Both schools of analysts, it should be noted, draw an implicit distinction between geographic location and equity ownership: in this case, between U.S.-*based* and U.S.-*owned* enterprises.

Re-Thinking U.S. Trade

The critical distinction between location and ownership has been analyzed more explicitly by Robert Lipsey and Irving Kravis in their ongoing research on the trade performance of U.S. multinationals. These analysts argue that a steady decline in the U.S. share of world manufactured exports, well documented from the mid-1950s through the mid-1970s, "could be accounted for by movements in U.S. export prices relative to those of its main competitors."[12] Yet that country-level decline has not been matched by

[10]Hayes and Wheelwright, *Restoring Our Competitive Edge;* Abernathy, *Industrial Renaissance.*

[11]Scott and Lodge, *U.S. Competitiveness in the World Economy;* Zysman and Tyson, *American Industry in International Competition.*

[12]Robert E. Lipsey and Irving B. Kravis, "The Competitiveness and Comparative Advantage of U.S. Multinationals, 1957–1984," *Banca Nazionale del Lavoro Quarterly Review* 161 (June 1987): 163; for supporting evidence, see pp. 149–151, as well as

any corresponding fall in the combined trade of the parents of American multinationals and their majority subsidiaries abroad. To the contrary: since 1966, both the parents and the subsidiaries of American multinationals have consistently exported a stable share of world manufactured exports—a combined share that, in recent years (after 1983), has once again shown signs of growth. Indeed, for majority U.S.-owned subsidiaries, shares of world manufactured exports have actually grown steadily—first offsetting and then surpassing the export shares of their U.S.-based parents. Thus, through foreign direct investment, American multinationals have managed to overcome the competitive disadvantage of higher relative prices that came with being based in the United States.

In the evolution of American multinationals, 1977 stands as a crucial turning point.[13] Before that year, while the share of world manufactured exports shipped by the parents of U.S. multinationals had fallen, that U.S.-parent share still remained larger than the proportion of world manufactures exported by majority U.S.-owned subsidiaries abroad. From 1977 onward, however, the U.S.-parent share stabilized at a level below the ever-growing U.S.-subsidiary share. As a result, the proportion of world exports shipped by American multinationals—including both their U.S. parents and foreign subsidiaries—grew to exceed a rather stable (after 1977) country-level share for the United States. "That contrast [in shares]," Lipsey and Kravis argue, "suggests that it is important to distinguish between the factors that determine the competitiveness of the United States as a production location and those that determine the competitiveness of U.S. firms. The latter might include characteristics such as the firm's management and technology, since [they] would affect the firms' performance in both home and foreign operations."[14] Indeed, as we have seen re-

---

two of their earlier publications: "The Competitiveness and Comparative Advantage of U.S. Multinationals, 1957–1983," NBER Working Paper No. 2051, October 1986; and "The Competitive Position of U.S. Manufacturing Firms," *Banca Nazionale del Lavoro Quarterly Review* 153 (June 1985): 88–106.

[13]Lipsey and Kravis, "Competitiveness of U.S. Multinationals: 1957–1984," p. 151.

[14]Ibid., p. 147.

peatedly throughout this book, such firm-specific assets are often exploited most effectively by American multinationals through foreign direct investment—especially since the United States has become less competitive as a production base for world trade.

Still, this declining competitiveness in world trade did not affect all U.S. exporters equally. As Lipsey and Kravis also demonstrate, the share of world manufactured exports shipped by the parents of U.S. multinationals fell at a rate slower than that suffered by the United States as a whole.[15] And that slower relative decline was not simply the result of wide variation in the types of goods traded by multinational parents and other U.S. exporters; instead, Lipsey and Kravis document that, even within the same industry, U.S. exports by American multinationals declined at a slower rate—or alternately, increased at a faster rate—than did all U.S. exports in that industry. Thus, the parents of American multinationals appear to be more strongly immune to the same higher relative prices that have adversely affected other U.S.-based exporters operating in comparable industries.

That relative immunity derives, at least in part, from the fact that so much trade conducted by those multinationals based in America and elsewhere is shipped intracompany—among and between their parents and subsidiaries—a fact simply ignored by Lipsey and Kravis. For these parents, intracompany trade insures greater control over both upstream supplies and downstream markets than do more arm's-length transactions among unaffiliated buyers and suppliers. Intracompany trade also substantially lowers the high costs that these arm's-length transactions normally impose on cross-border exchanges of the technological, marketing, and organizational assets necessary to compete successfully through foreign production and overseas distribution. Thus, relationships resulting from equity ownership and managerial control, and not just transactions based principally on relative prices, can be expected to determine patterns of intracompany trade. Specifically, we should expect such trade to remain far less sensitive to exchange-rate movements than will more arm's-length transactions.

[15]Between 1966 and 1977, for example, the U.S.-parent share of world exports fell from 11 percent to 9.2 percent, while during that same period, the U.S.-country share fell from 17.5 percent to 13.3 percent; see Lipsey and Kravis, "Competitiveness of Competitive Advantage of U.S. Multinationals," Appendix U-1.

Figure 5-1. U.S. Trade: Intracompany vs. arm's-length shipments, 1982–88

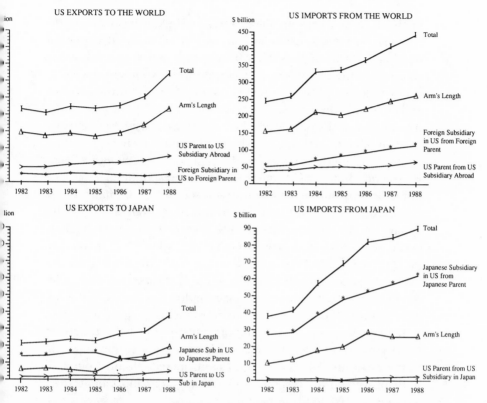

Sources: U.S. Commerce Department, Bureau of Economic Analysis, *U.S. Direct Investment Abroad: Opera-tions of U.S. Parent Companies and their Foreign Affiliates* (Washington, D.C.: USGPO, various years), tables 50 and 57, n.p.; U.S. Commerce Department, Bureau of Economic Analysis, *Foreign Direct Investment in the United States: Operations of U.S. Affiliates of Foreign Companies* (Washington, D.C.: USGPO, various years), table G-4, n.p.; U.S. Commerce Department, International Trade Administration, Office of Trade and Invest-ment Analysis, *U.S. Foreign Trade Highlights: 1989* (Washington, D.C.: USGPO, Sept. 1990), pp. 31, 36.

To test this hypothesis, at least within the bounds of available data,[16] Figure 5-1 examines U.S. trade during the three years preceding and then following 1985, when the Plaza Accord accel-erated a significant decline in the dollar's value. Before that accord,

[16]Available data, for example, do not permit explicit calculations of price elas-ticities, since quantity and price cannot be individually distinguished. Moreover, available data do not permit an examination of the actual product shipped, but instead classify trade by the industry in which subsidiaries derive a plurality of their sales. For a discussion of these problems see, Lipsey and Kravis, "Competitiveness of U.S. Multinationals: 1957–1983," pp. 11–23, as well as Appendix U, pp. 29–56.

in the face of a strong dollar, total U.S. exports to the world languished; in fact, arm's-length trade by U.S.-based exporters unaffiliated with their foreign buyers experienced a modest decline. After the Plaza Accord, however, U.S. exports to the world boomed, led by arm's-length exports by U.S.-based producers unaffiliated with their foreign buyers. In contrast, U.S. exports by American multinationals to their overseas subsidiaries experienced modest growth at best, while U.S. exports by foreign-owned affiliates in America back to their foreign parents actually declined. If we shift now to U.S. imports, the corresponding impact of intracompany and arm's-length trade seems less dramatic, but it consistently moves in the expected direction. Namely, when the dollar was strong, arm's-length trade by U.S. importers experienced the most rapid growth (1983–84), which fell off quickly (during 1985) and then grew at lower rates (after 1985) as the dollar weakened. Meanwhile, U.S. imports shipped back home by the foreign subsidiaries of American multinationals seemed to be unaffected by these exchange-rate movements—which also failed to alter the steady pattern of import growth recorded throughout the 1980s, as foreign multinationals continued supplying their own affiliates in America. Thus, as anticipated, all intracompany trade proved far less responsive to exchange-rate movements than did more arm's-length shipments.

Nowhere was this responsiveness more apparent than in U.S. exports to Japan: while the dollar remained strong, total U.S. exports to Japan experienced lackluster growth and, indeed, even declined. When the dollar plummeted, however, total U.S. exports to Japan immediately jumped, aided by a sharp decline in the yen-price of U.S.-made goods. Once again, those U.S.-based exporters unaffiliated with their Japanese buyers were among the first affected by exchange-rate movements. While the dollar's value increased in 1984 and 1985, for example, the dollar value of these arm's-length exports actually declined; but that value nearly tripled during 1986, following a 40 percent drop in the yen-value of the dollar. By contrast, U.S. exports among affiliated companies were far less responsive to major swings in foreign-exchange rates: prior to the Plaza Accord, when the dollar was strong, for instance, exports by U.S. parents to their subsidiaries in Japan recorded *no* decline; instead, these exports actually increased modestly, as U.S. FDI in Japan increased as well. After the Plaza Accord, moreover, this intracompany trade responded much more slowly to the dollar's decline than did more arm's-length transactions by other U.S. exporters. Slower still was the response of Japanese-owned affiliates exporting from the United States: while the dollar was strong, U.S. exports by these foreign affiliates back to their Japanese parents experienced lackluster growth. But when the dollar became weak, these intracompany exports initially *declined* before modestly recovering, even though the yen-price of such U.S. goods should have looked more attractive.

Most U.S. exports to Japan, however, are actually commodities—mainly farm products and raw materials—all presumably very sensitive to the dollar's precipitous fall. In fact, U.S. exports of these commodities did flood the Japanese market during 1986 and 1987, but only in arm's-length trade between American suppliers unaffiliated with their Japanese buyers (see Figure 5-1). At the same time, Japanese trading companies initially cut their own intracompany purchases of U.S. commodities, thereby partially and temporarily neutralizing the aggregate impact of surging U.S. exports. Here, the Japanese were aided by their strong market position, for Japanese subsidiaries in America shipped most U.S. commodities to Japan before 1987. Subsequently, more arm's-length commodity trade finally matched, and then surpassed, intracompany shipments. Even then, however, a sizable proportion of U.S. commodity exports required more than competitive prices alone to sell in Japan; otherwise, U.S.-owned exporters would have long since dominated this trade. In addition to low prices, U.S. commodity exports needed the preferential access to the Japanese market that Japanese ownership and intracompany trade grants to only a few U.S.-based suppliers.

Preferential access to the Japanese market need not be limited to U.S. exports, of course. In East Asia, for example, Japanese multinationals also established affiliates to supply their parents back home. These Japanese affiliates faced production costs comparable to those attained in East Asia by U.S. subsidiaries (not to mention native exporters); and Japanese subsidiaries confronted the same Japanese import restrictions faced by their U.S. (and East

Asian) competitors. Yet, compared to such foreign competitors, Japanese affiliates proved far more successful at exporting both their East Asian and their U.S. production back to Japan. Again we see how much ownership matters: for lower relative prices and weaker exchange rates do little to overcome strong affiliations between Japanese parents and their overseas affiliates. Indeed, such close affiliations can actually work to blunt the initial shock of a weaker dollar, as the Japanese proved in their purchases of U.S. commodity exports after the rapid appreciation of the yen—demonstrating once again the strategic value of foreign production and intracompany trade, even in the face of major fluctuations in foreign-exchange rates.

Similarly, strong affiliations between Japanese multinationals and their subsidiaries in America have also exercised an overriding influence on U.S. imports (nearly all manufactured goods) from Japan, again insulating much of that trade from rapid exchange-rate movements. During the early 1980s, as the value of the U.S. dollar rose against the Japanese yen, total U.S. imports from Japan grew rapidly (see Figure 5-1). After 1985, however, when the dollar's value began its precipitous decline, the growth rate of U.S. imports slowed considerably. Leading that slowdown, as predicted, were U.S. importers unaffiliated with their Japanese suppliers. Indeed, such arm's-length trade actually fell in dollar value during 1987, and then remained at that lower level during 1988, as the lagged effects of dollar devaluation finally became apparent. By contrast, such devaluation had virtually no effect on already small U.S. imports by American multinationals from their majority subsidiaries—a fact that reflected the continued paucity of such subsidiaries in Japan. Dollar devaluation, moreover, had even less effect on intracompany shipments by Japanese multinationals to their subsidiaries in America—the largest channel for U.S. imports from Japan. What did change was the growth rate of these sizable shipments, which stabilized at a lower level. Once again, as predicted, intracompany trade proved far less responsive to exchange-rate movements than did more arm's-length U.S. imports.

The continuing growth in intracompany trade reflected an important change in the composition of U.S. imports from Japan: to original imports of final products and replacement parts,

Japanese-owned subsidiaries in America first added intermediate components for assembly; then, equipment for assembly; and finally, machinery for full-scale manufacturing of intermediate components and final products (e.g., automobiles), whose volume often declined while unit prices increased. At times, these U.S. imports were shipped to Japanese subsidiaries in America by their multinational parents; at other times, these shipments came from closely affiliated suppliers operating in the same Japanese keiretsu as their multinational buyer. Throughout, close buyer-suppliers relations interacted with product characteristics (e.g., high quality), to make U.S. imports much less responsive to exchange-rate movements.

Beyond Trade, Foreign Sales

Intracompany shipments are not, of course, the only multinational source of foreign sales that remain insulated from rapid exchange-rate movements. In addition, foreign production with relatively high local content also provides a hedge against exchange rate losses—because it closely matches revenues and costs in the same currency.[17] So, when a host-country currency goes down (or up) against the multinational's home-country currency, some of the revenue losses (or gains) are automatically offset by savings (or increases) in expenditures. This reduced exposure to exchange-rate risk is not available to national exporters engaged in arm's-length trading and unaided by diversified production locations. By contrast, multinationals investing in such diversification will prove far more resilient to large swings in exchange rates, as well as to persistent over- or under-valuations of major currencies. Thus, by combining foreign production and intracompany trade, multinationals enjoy competitive advantages that remain unavailable to nationally based enterprises with no foreign investment.

For American multinationals, these competitive advantages have proved especially valuable. While U.S-based exporters have

[17]For further discussion, see DeAnne Julius, *Global Companies and Public Policy: The Growing Challenge of Foreign Direct Investment* (London: Royal Institute of International Affairs, 1990), esp. pp. 90–91.

seen their foreign sales surpassed by American imports, U.S.-owned subsidiaries abroad continue to boast foreign sales far greater than the U.S. sales of foreign-owned affiliates in America (see Figure 5-2). During the early 1980s, at least through 1982, the U.S. trade deficit hovered around $1 billion every two weeks. At the same time, U.S. subsidiaries abroad consistently outsold foreign affiliates in America by more than $1 billion every day. By 1987, when America's trade deficit peaked, reaching an unprecedented $1 billion every two days, U.S. subsidiaries abroad continued to outsell foreign affiliates in America by nearly $1 billion daily. This remained true even though, between 1985 and 1987, and continuing subsequently, the value of the U.S. dollar plummeted, while foreign direct investment in America skyrocketed. Yet, U.S.-owned multinationals continued to dominate their foreign rivals in America, even as the competitiveness of U.S-based exporters lessened.

A similar conclusion has recently been documented by DeAnne Julius, who uses a very different methodology.[18] From the foreign sales of U.S. multinationals, Julius subtracts their foreign purchases, arguing that these are the analytical equivalent of U.S. imports, and therefore reflect the competitiveness of foreign suppliers. Similarly, from the U.S. sales of foreign multinationals, she subtracts their U.S. purchases, arguing that these (like U.S. exports) reflect the competitiveness of American suppliers. To these adjusted foreign and U.S. sales, Julius then adds sales by U.S. exporters and importers, corrected to avoid double-counting trade by either American or foreign multinationals. Her result is an "ownership-based trade balance," which consistently shows a surplus for the United States, even as more traditional trade balances record consistent deficits. Still, such U.S. trade deficits, Julius argues, are more than offset by the foreign sales of U.S.-owned subsidiaries (again, net of American- and foreign-made inputs); and those foreign sales, in turn, greatly exceed net U.S. sales by foreign affiliates operating in the United States. For 1986, Julius estimated that this "ownership-based trade balance" exceeded $56 billion—a figure subsequently corrected and revised downward by

18Ibid., esp. pp. 78–83.

Figure 5-2. U.S. balance of sales with the world, 1988

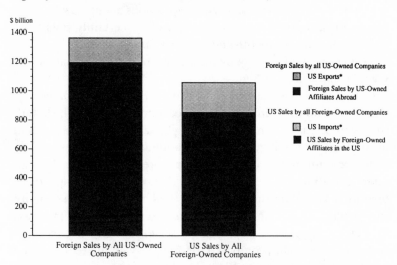

$ billion

Foreign Sales by all US-Owned Companies
- US Exports*
- Foreign Sales by US-Owned Affiliates Abroad

US Sales by all Foreign-Owned Companies
- US Imports*
- US Sales by Foreign-Owned Affiliates in the US

Foreign Sales by All US-Owned Companies

US Sales by All Foreign-Owned Companies

Sources: U.S. Commerce Department, Bureau of Economic Analysis, *U.S. Direct Investment Abroad: Operations of U.S. Parent Companies and their Foreign Affiliates, Preliminary 1988 Estimates* (Washington, D.C.: USGPO, July 1990), tables 6, 16, and 18, n.p.; U.S. Commerce Department, Bureau of Economic Analysis, *Foreign Direct Investment in the United States: Operations of U.S. Affiliates of Foreign Companies, Preliminary 1988 Estimates* (Washington, D.C.: USGPO, Aug. 1990), tables E-5 and G-2, n.p.; U.S. Commerce Department, International Trade Administration, Office of Trade and Investment Analysis, *U.S. Foreign Trade Highlights: 1989* (Washington, D.C.: USGPO, Sept. 1990), pp. 31, 36.
*U.S. exports exclude shipments to U.S.-owned affiliates abroad (to avoid double-counting both as U.S. exports and as foreign sales by U.S. affiliates), and they exclude shipments by foreign-owned affiliates in the United States (to narrow the focus to U.S.-owned exporters). Similarly, U.S. imports exclude shipments to foreign-owned affiliates in the United States (again, to avoid double-counting), and they exclude shipments back home by U.S.-owned affiliates abroad (to narrow the focus to foreign-owned sources of U.S. imports).

The Economist, to a $14 billion surplus.[19] (Note that these 1986 surpluses stand in marked contrast to more traditional measures of America's trade balance, which recorded a $155 billion deficit.)

[19]For the original calculations of Julius, see ibid., table 4.4, p. 81; for revised calculations, see *The Economist,* Dec. 22, 1990–Jan. 4, 1991, p. 44.

This surplus in America's "ownership-based trade balance," in the words of *The Economist*, "raises basic questions about how international transactions should be thought of. It certainly puts fears about American competitiveness in a sharply different light." The same may be said for my own measure of the "U.S. balance of sales," summarized in Figure 5-2.

In fact, this clear distinction between U.S.-*based* enterprises and U.S.-*owned* multinationals should direct our attention to the latter's successful management of both tangible and intangible assets in technology, marketing, and organization. With just these assets, American multinationals generate far more sales overseas through direct investment and related trade than do those foreign rivals operating as traders and investors in the United States (see Figure 5-2). Unless, of course, those traders and investors are Japanese (see Figure 5-3): While on a global scale, foreign sales by U.S.-*owned* multinationals, compared to foreign rivals, may compensate for the relative weakness of U.S.-*based* enterprises, this compensation process does not necessarily operate bilaterally, especially not between the United States and Japan. Worldwide, Julius calculates that Japan also enjoys a sizable surplus (estimated at roughly $42 billion) in its "ownership-based trade balance."[20] That surplus also extends, it seems, to the United States. Yet, Ohmae Kenichi has long argued that net foreign sales resulting from cross-investment have actually grown to equalize asymmetries reflected in bilateral trade imbalances.[21] Using 1984 data, Ohmae declares that the combined production and sales of the 300 largest (majority and minority) U.S.-owned manufacturers in Japan greatly exceeded comparable output by all Japanese affiliates in the United States. That substantial difference, Ohmae goes on to demonstrate, neatly offsets America's 1984 trade deficit with Japan. "In other words," he observes, "the product presence, or market penetration, of both countries into each other's turf is now practically identical."[22] Thus, a rough parity had allegedly been established.

[20]Julius, *Global Companies*, table 4.4, p. 81.
[21]Ohmae Kenichi, *Beyond National Borders: Reflections on Japan and the World* (Homewood, Ill.: Dow Jones-Irwin, 1987), esp. pp. 26–28; and *The Borderless World* (Homewood, Ill.: Dow Jones-Irwin, 1990).
[22]Ohmae, *Beyond National Borders*, p. 28.

Figure 5-3. U.S. balance of sales with Japan, 1987

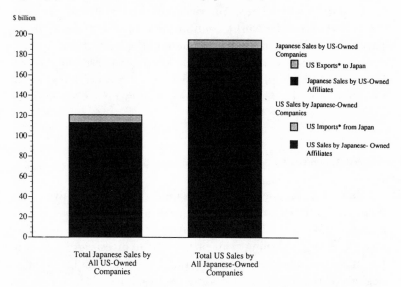

Sources: U.S. Commerce Department, Bureau of Economic Analysis, *U.S. Direct Investment Abroad: Operations of U.S. Parent Companies and their Foreign Affiliates, Revised 1987 Estimates* (Washington, D.C.: USGPO, July 1990), tables 6, 16, and 18, n.p.; U.S. Commerce Department, Bureau of Economic Analysis, *Foreign Direct Investment in the United States: 1987 Benchmark Survey, Final Results* (Washington, D.C.: USGPO, Aug. 1990), tables E-5, G-19, and G-33, n.p.; U.S. Commerce Department, International Trade Administration, Office of Trade and Investment Analysis, *U.S. Foreign Trade Highlights: 1989* (Washington, D.C.: USGPO, Sept. 1990), pp. 31, 36.
*See Figure 5-2 for adjustments made to both U.S. exports and U.S. imports.

Yet, Ohmae's conclusion—questionable even for 1984—has found little additional support during subsequent years. After 1985, as we saw in earlier chapters, the appreciation of the yen led the Japanese to double their foreign direct investment in the United States, achieving in the process twice the growth rate for U.S. FDI in Japan. Between 1984 and 1988, moreover, local sales by Japanese multinationals in America nearly doubled; and so did America's trade deficit with Japan. Over the same period, the local sales of U.S.-owned subsidiaries and affiliates in Japan also doubled, but nevertheless, that growth still failed to offset the combined U.S. sales of Japanese exporters and Japanese investors crossing the Pacific. Thus, American multinationals—so competitive elsewhere in the world, even in the face of a strong dollar—perennially fail to outsell the Japanese in the United States.

To summarize: neither America's competitiveness nor the dollar's value can adequately explain why the Japanese sell more in the United States than the Americans sell in Japan. Some other explanation must be found.

AMERICAN NEGLECT VS. JAPANESE STRATEGY

While the Japanese have retained their competitive edge through foreign investment in America, a broad consensus of opinion in Japan declares that the Americans have forfeited their own advantage by failing at an earlier time to invest significantly in Japan. Summarizing that view, Ozawa Terutomo cites the "benign neglect of the Japanese economy by foreign multinationals" to explain low levels of foreign investment in his country.[23] This explanation is not limited to Japanese scholars, moreover; it has also been endorsed by American analysts working in Japan. James Abegglen, for one, has long decried the "indifference and ignorance of possible foreign investors regarding Japan" in explaining why few such investors have actually established foreign subsidiaries there.[24] For supporting evidence, critics of American management recount only a very few examples of "the successful foreign company in Japan"—the "success story" which one officially sanctioned study has defined as a multinational with sufficient "commitment" and "perseverance" to survive the daily rigors of doing business in Japan.[25] Absent such tenacity, few foreigners have entered Japan successfully as either traders or investors.

Foreign Pressures

Among those who did enter, American multinationals had to fight long and hard to establish majority-owned subsidiaries. For

[23]Ozawa, "Japanese Policy Toward Foreign Multinationals," p. 147.
[24]Abegglen and Stalk, *Kaisha*, p. 217.
[25]Look Japan, *Taking on Japan*, p. ix.

only in Japan, alone among industrialized countries, did such success typically follow upon *years* of difficult, and sometimes bitter, negotiations involving a complex web of trade restrictions, capital controls, and industrial structures—those three critical components of Japan's "strategic investment policy." Such lengthy negotiations usually took place within at least a partial view of other potential investors, who typically reacted negatively to both process and outcome. This negative "signalling" undoubtedly discouraged countless other would-be investors (especially those less well endowed than an IBM), who concluded that investing in Japan insured high up-front costs but offered less-than-certain prospects of future benefits. Yet, their response did follow a rational calculus; seldom was it the simple result of "benign neglect" or of "indifference and ignorance," as others have alleged.

Sheer tenacity, while necessary, was not alone sufficient for multinationals to secure majority ownership in Japan. In addition, they had to skillfully manage the tangible and intangible assets of the technology, marketing, and organization that have been their hallmark around the world. When such assets were jealously protected by their owners and eagerly coveted by the Japanese, the establishment of majority foreign subsidiaries became possible. But when foreign assets were neither successfully protected nor widely coveted, a more likely outcome was technology licensing decoupled from foreign equity. Early on, in fact, the licensing of products and processes represented almost the only way for foreigners to share in the Japanese market, since foreigners could neither export manufactured goods to Japan nor invest directly there. Only after failing to secure the requisite technology (without equity attached) did Japan permit foreign investment; and then, preferably an investment in minority and equal-partnership joint ventures with Japanese oligopolists. Majority foreign ownership came as a last resort, and only after Japan secured numerous concessions from American multinationals—concessions that often granted the Japanese far greater access to foreign technology and overseas markets.

Even well endowed multinationals which doggedly negotiated with the Japanese soon discovered that if, in addition, they hoped to secure majority ownership (and other prerogatives) in Japan, they needed to exert foreign political pressure. Indeed, a broad consensus of Americans and Japanese advocates the use of foreign pressure (*gaiatsu*), both to negotiate limited concessions for individual projects and to secure more general liberalizations. In the absence of such gaiatsu, "often the crucial catalyst for policy decisions," Japan has been "unable to undertake major independent foreign economic policy initiatives," in the words of Kent Calder.[26] "When confronted by explicit foreign political pressure, Japan," Calder points out, "has been more forthcoming with specific, formal policy changes than is generally realized." Most Japanese would agree: Indeed, Kosaka Masataka summarizes a popular Japanese view when he argues that trade and capital liberalization "represented a passive adaptation to outside pressure," one that always remained "defensive."[27] Much of that requisite outside pressure came either directly from the U.S. government or indirectly from international organizations that the United States greatly influenced (such as the Organization for Economic Cooperation and Development and the International Monetary Fund). In fact, official "requests" and "urgings" from these organizations proved essential to policy change in Japan, according to Komiya Ryutaro, writing in the midst of his country's liberalization of trade and capital.[28] And outside Japan, as well, such foreign official pressures have long figured prominently in the wealth of cross-national research that identifies the foreign determinants of domestic policymaking.[29]

[26]Calder, "Japanese Foreign Economic Policy Formation," pp. 518–519, 522.

[27]Kosaka, "The International Economic Policy of Japan," pp. 211, 214. In that analysis, Kosaka goes so far as to assert (on p. 224) that "taking initiatives in shaping and maintaining international order cannot become a basic task for the Japanese. Their task is to catch up with their superiors."

[28]Komiya, "Direct Foreign Investment in Postwar Japan," p. 152. This opinion is not limited to the Japanese, of course. Gary Saxonhouse, for example, also concentrates primarily on U.S. initiatives to explain Japanese policies; see his "The World Economy and Japanese Foreign Economic Policy," in Robert Scalapino, ed., *The Foreign Policy of Modern Japan* (Berkeley: University of California Press, 1977), pp. 281–318.

[29]In the extensive literature on foreign determinants of economic policymaking, the following titles figure prominently: John B. Goodman, *Monetary Sovereignty: The Politics of Central Banking in Europe* (Ithaca: Cornell University Press, 1992); Michael Loriaux, *France after Hegemony: International Change and Financial Reform* (Ithaca: Cornell University Press, 1991); Peter Gourevitch, *Politics in Hard Times: Comparative Responses to International Economic Crises* (Ithaca: Cornell University Press, 1986); Peter J. Katzenstein, *Small States in World Markets: Industrial Policy in Europe* (Ithaca: Cornell University Press, 1985).

Yet, of the multinational "success stories" documented in preceding chapters, a mere handful actually depended heavily on
foreign official pressure to aid their initial entry and subsequent
expansion in Japan. Instead, most multinationals largely relied on
their own political skills, as Hugh Patrick noticed long ago: "The
pressures on Japan to liberalise emanate mainly from American-
based firms."[30] Of course, at times these same firms have deftly
used U.S. and other foreign official pressure to their own advantage. International treaty commitments, for example, did force
Japan to create a small regulatory loophole (for the yen-based
company, such as IBM) during the 1950s, just as bilateral negotiations during the 1980s benefited a few American multinationals
(notably Motorola). These scarce examples, however, offer only
limited testimony to the efficacy of foreign official pressure; and it
mattered little whether such pressure derived from foreign policy or whether it emanated from international financial regimes.
Rather, even in these examples, the necessary foreign pressure—
when it has been successful—has principally come from those
powerful American multinationals that managed to combine *both*
firm-specific assets and effective political strategies in their negotiations with government regulators and local oligopolists. Only by
using such potent combinations have American multinationals
succeeded in expanding local production and intracompany trade
throughout Japan. And based on this success, American multinationals have now emerged as the most important foreign determinants of economic policymaking in Japan.[31]

Domestic Constituencies

Early on, multinationals also have to learn that political skills
will produce only limited impact unless a domestic constituency
comprised mainly of Japanese oligopolists also champions policy
change. Otherwise, foreign (private and official) pressures on the

[30]For Hugh Patrick's "Comments" on Komiya Ryutaro's "Direct Foreign Investment in Postwar Japan," see Drysdale, ed., *Direct Foreign Investment in Asia and the
Pacific*, p. 168.

[31]For an early statement of this proposition, see Dennis J. Encarnation and Mark
Mason, "Neither MITI nor America: The Political Economy of Capital Liberalization in Japan," *International Organization* 44 (Winter 1990): 25–54.

Japanese state remain feeble and ineffective. Yet this need to acti-
vate a domestic constituency in Japan seems to be ignored by most
American and Japanese scholars, who agree instead with Dan
Henderson that "Japan's capital liberalization has been largely
a response to . . . international [meaning OECD and U.S.-Japan
treaty] standards rather than an initiative flowing from felt needs
at home."[32] Most Japanese would completely agree.[33] Moreover,
even when a need for domestic constituencies is suitably acknowledged, scholars do so grudgingly, without ever fully recognizing
the pivotal role in national policymaking being played by Japanese
oligopolists. Michael Yoshino, for example, does accord domestic
forces some importance in the liberalization process, but only after
that process was well underway.[34] Leon Hollerman, by contrast,
concedes that "economic liberalization had its beginnings . . . under a combination of internal and external pressures."[35] Yet, he
refuses to go further, preferring instead to place heavy emphasis
on official U.S. demands. This is misleading, however; for as we
have noted in preceding chapters, Japanese oligopolists themselves generate most of these "internal pressures," by positioning
themselves as aggressive intermediaries, operating between foreign multinationals and the Japanese state. From that middle position, Japanese oligopolists have deftly manipulated foreign demands, acting both to the oligopolists' domestic advantage over
local competitors and the state, and to the oligopolists' foreign
advantage over all those who (in retaliation against Japanese restrictions) would restrict Japanese export markets and overseas
investments.[36] To insure such advantage in the future, Japanese

[32] Dan Fenno Henderson, *Foreign Enterprise in Japan* (Tokyo: Charles E. Tuttle, 1975), p. 237.

[33] See, for example, the citations above for the works of Komiya Ryutaro, Kosaka Masataka, and Ozawa Terutomo.

[34] Michael Yoshino, "Japan as Host to the International Corporation," in Isaiah Frank, ed., *The Japanese Economy in International Perspective* (Baltimore: Johns Hopkins University Press, 1975), pp. 277ff. For further support of this view, see Ozawa, "Japanese Policy Toward Foreign Multinationals," pp. 149ff.

[35] Leon Hollerman, *Japan, Disincorporated: The Economic Liberalization Process,* (Stanford: Hoover Institution Press, 1988), p. xii.

[36] The state's reactions to the domestic intermediation of foreign demands may also explain patterns of financial deregulation; see Frances McCall Rosenbluth, *Financial Politics in Contemporary Japan* (Ithaca: Cornell University Press, 1989),

oligopolists have moved additionally to replace public regulations with private restrictions, as a way of combining their ongoing domestic political influence with their expanding international economic power. In the real Japan, then, local oligopolists emerge as critical domestic determinants of foreign economic policymaking in Japan—just as they do in other industrialized economies.[37]

The Japanese state did not, of course, stand powerless in the face of powerful foreign and domestic pressures. To the contrary: In Japan, a broad and stable consensus has long viewed MITI and related government agencies as preeminent in economic policymaking. Standing in the forefront of this consensual view is Chalmers Johnson, who argues that "most of the ideas for economic growth came from the bureaucracy" of the "developmental state"—and not from the "business community," which otherwise reacted with "responsive dependence," where "economic interests are explicitly subordinated to political objectives."[38] Following Johnson, other American scholars also consider Japan to be a prime example of "state-led capitalism" or "guided free enterprise," in which "statist Japan" has typically "dominated" domestic industry.[39] Certainly, in its early years, the Japanese bureaucracy did encourage combina-

---

pp. 50–95; and her "Foreign Pressure and the Liberalization of Japan's Financial Markets," a paper presented at the 1989 annual meeting of the Association for Asian Studies, Washington, D.C.

[37]For an early statement of this proposition in Japan, see Encarnation and Mason, "Neither MITI nor America," pp. 25–54. More generally, for the role of local oligopolists in determining foreign economic policy, see Helen V. Milner and David B. Yoffie, "Between Free Trade and Protectionism: Strategic Trade Policy and a Theory of Corporate Trade Demands," *International Organization* 43 (Spring 1989): 239–272; Helen V. Milner, *Resisting Protectionism: Global Industries and the Politics of International Trade* (Princeton: Princeton University Press, 1988); Vinod K. Aggarwal et al., "The Dynamics of Negotiated Protectionism," *American Political Science Review* 81 (June 1987): 345–366.

[38]Chalmers Johnson, *MITI and the Japanese Miracle: The Growth of Japanese Industrial Policy, 1925–1975* (Stanford: Stanford University Press, 1982), p. 24.

[39]These several quotations come from the following sources: T. J. Pempel, *Policy and Politics in Japan: Creative Conservation* (Philadelphia: Temple University Press, 1982), esp. chap. 2; Ezra Vogel, "Guided Free Enterprise in Japan," *Harvard Business Review* 56 (May–June 1978): 161–170; Katzenstein, *Small States in World Markets*, pp. 20–23; Stephen D. Krasner, *Defending the National Interest: Raw Materials Investment and U.S. Foreign Policy* (Princeton: Princeton University Press, 1978), p. 58; John Zysman, *Governments, Markets and Growth: Financial Systems and the Politics of Industrial Change* (Ithaca: Cornell University Press, 1983), p. 233.

tions of trade and capital controls designed to both restrict imports and promote exports by favoring local producers at the expense of foreign rivals. Even in the absence of these policies, of course, market imperfections (large economies of scale and scope, steep learning curves, high transaction costs) already operated to narrow global competition to a few oligopolists in automobiles, electronics, and other industries. What Japanese policies assured most of all was that many of the oligopolists in these industries would be Japanese-owned.

These Japanese oligopolists did not, however, remain subservient to the Japanese state; rather, they aggressively pursued opportunities to change government policy in favorable directions. Here, the period of capital liberalization proved to be an especially important turning point for business-government relations in Japan. That liberalization, according to Johnson, "came to Japan only slowly, not through MITI's *initiative* but as a consequence of the weakening of the ministry and the growing realization on the part of industry that it had to 'internationalize' if it was to avoid isolation."[40] Yet, such a compelling analysis simply does not square with the popular views of MITI and of a strong Japanese state— views that Johnson himself helped to create. Nor does his analysis square with the more general view that capital liberalization did in fact take place during the late 1960s and early 1970s. For as James Abegglen asserts: "Within only six years, the apparatus of controls had been dismantled, with Japan as open to capital investment as any other of the OECD member countries."[41] Just such de jure liberalization, Chalmers Johnson labels "a strictly *pro forma* acquiescence in international conventions," one still consisting of "a vast tangle of rules and procedures" engineered by both business and government.[42] In fact, as a whole, Johnson's analysis of capital liberalization actually serves to reinforce what this book has already shown: that Japanese oligopolists managed to control both the timing and substance of gradual changes in their country's strategic investment policy by aggressively mediating among conflicting foreign pressures—pressures that may be traced to Ameri-

---

[40]Johnson, *MITI and the Japanese Miracle*, p. 279 (emphasis added).
[41]Abegglen and Stalk, *Kaisha, The Japanese Corporation*, p. 223.
[42]Johnson, *MITI and the Japanese Miracle*, pp. 278–279.

can multinationals, but not to MITI or, for that matter, to the U.S. government.

While controlling the evolution of Japan's strategic investment policy, Japanese oligopolists often did forge alliances with MITI and other government agencies. Indeed, the "interdependence" of business and government, seeking (in the words of Daniel Okimoto) "consensus on a common set of collective goals" has become a popular new theme among those academic scholars keen to correct earlier images of "statist Japan."[43] According to this alternative characterization of business-government relations, Japanese oligopolists actually entered into a "compact" with a "congenial" Japanese state, to use the words of Richard Samuels, who contends that this relationship was based on a "reciprocal consent" whereby Japanese oligopolists "surrender jurisdiction [to the Japanese state in order] to retain control."[44] That control, however, increasingly came at the expense of the Japanese state—a result wholly unanticipated by these alternative explanations. Indeed, as Japanese oligopolists erected their own barriers to foreign investment and trade at home, they no longer required government restrictions. And as these oligopolists freed themselves from Japanese controls on capital outflows, they began to engineer their own independent responses (e.g., investment in U.S. assembly) to prevalent foreign pressures. Thus, Japanese oligopolists have become the most important force shaping the evolution of their country's strategic investment policy.

Persistent Legacies

Only when Japan finally changed its strategic investment policy did American multinationals actually rush to invest in foreign

[43]Daniel I. Okimoto, *Between MITI and the Market: Japanese Industrial Policy for High Technology* (Stanford: Stanford University Press, 1989), pp. 236–237. A similar theme has also been voiced by Inoguchi Takashi, *The Composition of the Political Economy of Contemporary Japan [Gendai nihon seiji keizai no kouzou]* (Tokyo: Toyo Kaizai, 1983); David Friedman, *The Misunderstood Miracle: Industrial Development and Political Change in Japan* (Ithaca: Cornell University Press, 1988); Ellis S. Krauss and Muramatsu Michio, "The Conservative Policy Line and the Development of Patterned Pluralism," in Daniel I. Okimoto, ed., *The Political Economy of Japan*, vol. I: *The Domestic Context* (Stanford: Stanford University Press, 1990), pp. 72–97.

[44]Richard J. Samuels, *The Business of the Japanese State: Energy Markets in Comparative and Historical Perspective*, (Ithaca: Cornell University Press, 1987), p. 2

production and overseas distribution. Their reaction, in short, did not result from "benign neglect," or from any "ignorance and indifference" to investment opportunities in Japan. Instead, "the major multinationals functioning in Japan today," according to Itoh Motoshige and Kiyono Kazuharu, writing in the late 1980s, "used the partial relaxation on foreign capital inflows under the 'system of free purchase of yen-denominated stock'. . . to make inroads into the Japanese economy."[45] Specifically, in 1988, of the ten largest foreign-owned companies in Japan—including IBM— all had invested in postwar Japan during the late 1950s and early 1960s as yen-based companies.[46] Subsequently, even the more general liberalization of formal capital controls during the 1970s did little to attract American multinationals, as emerging private restrictions combined with persistent public regulations. Not until after the formal abolition of capital controls, in 1980, did American multinationals finally accelerate their investments in Japan; and they continued to invest when the dollar price of Japanese assets skyrocketed, after 1985. Dollar devaluation, in fact, opened new Japanese opportunities for U.S. exports, which drew a quick response, in turn, from American multinationals. For example, to overcome Japan's closed distribution system, American multinationals invested heavily in Japanese wholesaling, where majority subsidiaries captured a far greater proportion of U.S. FDI in Japan than they did in any comparable country. Among industrialized countries overall, Japan finally ranked among the most favored current sites for American multinationals investing abroad.

The legacies of the past, however, continued to haunt the Americans: While most new U.S. FDI entered majority subsidiaries, overall during 1988 these subsidiaries still contributed less than two-fifths of all sales by American multinationals in Japan.[47] Minority U.S.-owned affiliates sold the remaining three-fifths. By

[45]Itoh Motoshige and Kiyono Kazuharu, "Foreign Trade and Direct Investment," in Komiya Ryutaro et al., eds., *Industrial Policy of Japan* (Tokyo: Academic Press, 1988), p. 166.
[46]For data on the largest foreign-owned companies in Japan, see *The Economist*, Aug. 19, 1989, p. 52.
[47]U.S. Commerce Department, Bureau of Economic Analysis, *U.S. Direct Investment Abroad: Operations of U.S. Parent Companies and their Foreign Affiliates, Preliminary 1988 Estimates* (Washington, D.C.: USGPO, July 1990), tables 6 and 29, n.p.

such measures, Japan has less in common with industrialized Germany than with developing India. Indeed, even after the rapid influx of U.S. FDI in Japan, the combined sales of all majority U.S. subsidiaries there remained well below comparable subsidiaries' sales in Canada, the United Kingdom, Germany, and France—each with economies less than one-half Japan's size. This lower incidence of majority subsidiaries in Japan has thus worked to deny American multinationals the same level of market access they have otherwise exploited in other industrialized countries.

Just as Japan's strategic investment policy managed to limit majority U.S. ownership in Japan, so it has limited related U.S. exports to Japan as well. Here, those parties specifically damaged include U.S. exporters of manufactured goods; for as we have noted, most of this trade in other industrialized countries heavily depends on majority U.S. subsidiaries to create final markets and distribution channels for shipments from their American parents. (Certainly most U.S. imports from Japan—nearly all manufactured goods—are shipped intracompany, from Japanese multinationals to their majority subsidiaries in the United States.) This fact suggests that the trade effects of Japan's strategic *investment* policy are probably much greater than most estimates of the narrower concept—strategic *trade* policy—currently reveal.[48] This difference represents a serious discrepancy; it has resulted from a general failure on the part of trade analysts to understand fully enough the close interrelationship between direct investment and international commerce.[49] Moreover, foreign direct investment, operating as a powerful economic force, has thrust global competition far beyond international trade—to a point where foreign production now accounts for more overseas sales than do cross-border transactions. This present condition means that strategic policies regarding investment, so often ignored in the past and

---

[48]For an early effort to quantify the potential gains from strategic trade policies, see Elhanan Helpman and Paul R. Krugman, *Market Structure and Foreign Trade* (Cambridge: MIT Press, 1985), esp. pp. 155–180.

[49]See, for example, Edward M. Graham and Paul R. Krugman, *Foreign Direct Investment in the United States* (Washington, D.C.: Institute for International Economics, 1989); on p. 54 they argue that "FDI in the United States is still a smaller factor than conventional integration through trade." It is not, as the preceding analysis has shown.

even now only partially understood, operate nonetheless in America and Japan to determine the size and scope of both a persistent trade gap and an emergent investment gap. Today, as those two gaps widen, so does the rift in U.S.-Japan relations.

BEYOND RIVALRY

The Japanese sell more in the United States than the Americans sell in Japan, I have argued, not because of America's declining competitiveness or Americans' ignorance of Japan—and not even because of U.S. exchange rates or Japanese trade policies and practices. Rather, persistent differences in the strategic *investment* policies pursued by business and government in the two countries have allowed Japanese multinationals to trade and then invest in the United States with much greater freedom than the Americans have ever enjoyed in Japan. Outside Japan, however, American and Japanese multinationals look a lot alike, as they both combine foreign investment and related trade to dominate world markets. Yet, in Japan, such symmetries in strategy break down, with government policies and private restrictions working together to deny American multinationals the same access enjoyed by the Japanese in the United States.

In Japan, business managers, government policymakers, and academic analysts all argue adamantly that differences in the strategic investment policies of the two countries have narrowed, so that *today's* Japan looks a lot like *yesterday's* America. Indeed, as the United States has tilted away from liberal trade and toward selective protectionism, Japan has leaned in the opposite direction, toward trade and capital liberalization. Yet, despite that liberalization, the Americans continue to sell far less in Japan than the Japanese sell in the United States. One Japanese response to this fact is to deny that it is true, despite all the evidence mustered above; for a popular Japanese myth declares that American multinationals sell just as much in Japan as do Japanese exporters and Japanese investors in the United States.[50] But in truth, the Ameri-

[50]As noted above, this proposition is closely associated with Ohmae Kenichi; see *Beyond National Borders,* esp. pp. 26–28.

cans do not sell as much, and they will not—at least so long as the present investment and trade gaps persist.

Even those Japanese who do not contest these facts go on to suggest that real solutions to the sales imbalance must be sought not in Japan but in America. Their two principal proposals, however, have an all-too-familiar ring to them. First, America must clean up its own act, beginning with the U.S. budget deficit, to reverse its declining competitiveness.[51] In its simplicity this argument fails, as noted above, to distinguish between U.S.-*based* exporters debilitated by problems in America, and U.S.-*owned* multinationals well-endowed with technological, marketing, and organizational assets. Second, according to the Japanese, American multinationals simply must try harder to overcome the handicaps of doing business in Japan. Specifically, they must first study carefully, and then begin to mimic, those few foreign "success stories" that do exist in Japan.[52] (After all, the Japanese remind the Americans, study and mimicry have often been keys to Japan's competitive success.) But this argument, too, fails to distinguish between those American multinationals that have remained at bay (for whatever reason) and those that have ventured into Japan. For among those who have actually invested, most foreign "success stories"—even those publicized by the Japanese themselves—have been marred by clashes with Japanese bureaucracy and dominated by Japanese oligopolists enforcing their country's strategic investment policy. By contrast, few such controversies can be found to characterize Japanese "success stories" in America. By itself, this difference provides cause for bitter recrimination since, in Japan, corporate ownership affects national policy.

In fact, citing traditional Japanese intransigence, U.S. business managers, government policymakers, and academic analysts forcefully argue that differences in the strategic investment policies of the two countries must be narrowed unilaterally—often by making *tomorrow's* America look a lot like *yesterday's* Japan. Some in America, as if to imitate their Japanese counterparts at an earlier time, currently propose that the U.S. government extend foreign investment screening beyond the existing mandate—which blocks

[51]MITI, *White Paper on International Trade: 1988,* esp. pp. 15–16.
[52]Look Japan, *Taking on Japan;* MITI, *Investing in Japan.*

all acquisitions that threaten national security—to include economic performance requirements.[53] Earlier, in Japan, such requirements were often imposed by MITI on American multinationals, in order to secure local content, minimum exports, and technology transfer. In the United States today, some of these requirements—most notably, local content—have actually made their way into U.S. legislation but not yet into U.S. law.[54] A few critics in America have even gone so far as to recommend a U.S. equivalent of MITI, an agency to implement these new mandates or, at the very least, an expansion of the interagency Committee on Foreign Investment in the United States (which now screens potential threats to national security).[55] At present, however, there is little in the arcane literature on foreign investment screening—to which I am a contributor[56]—that suggests that government agencies imposing performance requirements have succeeded in bringing to host countries more economic gain than does a competitive marketplace. Worse still, screening agencies may introduce additional economic costs, which they surely did in yesterday's Japan. Finally, then, only one U.S. policy proposal—reciprocity—looks to Europe, and not Japan, for appropriate analogues.[57] Here, foreign multinationals could be denied access to the U.S. market when their home market does *not* grant U.S. firms equal access. But as the recent history of E.C.-U.S. negotiations suggests, the United States is not immune to the charge that its policy (say, in banking) is more restrictive than that of some partner in trade and investment.

Such restrictions, moreover, will inevitably attract strong politi-

[53]See, for example, Norman J. Glickman and Douglas P. Woodward, *The New Competitors: How Foreign Investors Are Changing the U.S. Economy* (New York: Basic Books, 1989), pp. 272–275; Felix Rohatyn, "America's Economic Dependence," *Foreign Affairs* 68 (Winter 1989): 53–65; Malcolm S. Forbes, "Before Japan Buys Too Much of the U.S.A.," *Forbes* (January 25, 1988): 17.

[54]Local content has also been endorsed in Glickman and Woodward, *The New Competitors*, pp. 275–283; also see Prestowitz, *Trading Places*, pp. 314–329.

[55]Glickman and Woodward, *The New Competitors*, pp. 272–275.

[56]Dennis J. Encarnation and Louis T. Wells, Jr., "Evaluating Foreign Investment," in Theodore H. Moran, ed., *Investing in Development: New Roles for Private Capital?* (Washington, D.C.: Overseas Development Council, 1986); idem, "Sovereignty en Garde: Negotiating Foreign Investments," *International Organization* 39 (Winter 1985): 47–78

[57]Prestowitz, *Trading Places*, pp. 314–329.

cal opposition, especially from those U.S. governors who (as we saw earlier) have actively solicited Japanese investment to rejuvenate sagging state economies. To these opponents, add local businesses that benefit directly from this investment, plus the U.S. employees of Japanese subsidiaries. Champion of their cause is Robert Reich, who argues that "if we hope to revitalize the competitive performance of the United States economy, we must invest in people, not in nationally defined corporations. We must open our borders to investors from around the world rather than favoring companies that simply fly the U.S. flag."[58] According to U.S. labor unions, and especially to Reich, any globalization of U.S. companies may actually harm America: "It is a mistake to associate these foreign investments by American-owned companies with any result that improves the competitiveness of the United States." Here, I strongly disagree; and I point to the simple fact that so much U.S. trade depends directly on intracompany transactions between the U.S. parents and the majority subsidiaries of American multinationals. Thus, in Japan, a lower incidence of majority U.S. subsidiaries has effectively denied to American multinationals a degree of market access equal to that enjoyed in other industrialized countries—and equal to that enjoyed in the United States by Japanese exporters and investors. These important differences in market access exist precisely because Japan has not followed Reich's advice for America, to act unilaterally. Instead, the Japanese have accentuated bilateral differences by making corporate ownership central to their stratetgic investment policy.

Rather than unilaterally altering national strategy, or looking to the distant past for guidance, Edward Graham and Paul Krugman have recently proposed that the United States and Japan (along with the other leading industrialized countries) attend more closely to the present; and in particular, to the recent bilateral accord between the United States and Canada.[59] For these two friendly countries, trade and investment disputes can now be settled, as a result of the U.S.–Canada Free Trade Agreement, by special pro-

[58]Quotations from Robert B. Reich, "Who Is Us?" *Harvard Business Review* 68 (Jan.–Feb. 1990), pp. 54, 56, 63; also see his "Who Is They," ibid. 69 (Mar.–Apr. 1991), pp. 77–88.
[59]Graham and Krugman, *Foreign Direct Investment in the U.S.*, esp. pp. 125–131.

visions which extend well beyond the GATT. Specifically, disputes that cannot be resolved through bilateral negotiations can be submitted—when both governments agree—to binding arbitration by a separate panel, where private and public claimants can offer testimony. Using this procedure as their point of reference, Graham and Krugman suggest a further step: those trade and investment disputes that cannot be settled through bilateral government negotiations would then be subject to *mandatory* binding arbitration, which again would entertain both public and private claimants. Even more important, Graham and Krugman propose to extend such arbitration beyond North America, to include Japan and other leading industrialized countries. Certainly, geography and history do make U.S.–Canadian relations unique—a fact that inevitably threatens the multilateral transferability of any bilateral agreement they conclude. But if we focus only on the particular dimensions in question—investment and trade—the United States actually has almost as much in common with Japan as it does with Canada.[60] So much so, in fact, that the introduction of *mandatory* binding arbitration may have an equally revolutionary impact on U.S.-Japan relations—as revolutionary an effect as seems likely in the emerging North American free trade zone.

Clearly, unlike most of its predecessors, the Graham-Krugman proposal is quite exceptional, and it merits much closer scrutiny. Their recommendation ranks among the very few substantive policy suggestions that explicitly acknowledge two fundamental changes which have taken place in the international political economy, changes already discussed in this book. To summarize: First, foreign direct investment has now driven global competition well beyond the limits of international trade, until offshore production presently accounts for far greater overseas sales than do cross-border transactions. And second, FDI has also moved national competition beyond the earlier stage of bilateral rivalries, to encompass multilateral contests among the far-flung (yet closely linked) subsidiaries of foreign multinationals. On balance then,

[60]During 1989, for example, Japan and Canada were the top two markets for U.S. exports, and the top two suppliers of U.S. imports. Moreover, both figure among the top three foreign direct investors in the United States (behind the United Kingdom), and among the top five foreign hosts to U.S. FDI abroad.

when applied to the larger U.S.-Japan rivalry, the Graham-Krugman proposal promises to create new opportunities. It offers American multinationals a rare chance to sidestep the power of Japanese oligopolists, who historically have served as the critical intermediaries between foreign (private and official) pressure and the Japanese state. Similarly, for Japanese oligopolists, this same proposal offers a special chance to diffuse the tension arising from persistent bilateral imbalances in trade and investment, as well as a parallel tension created by an ever-growing Japanese contribution to U.S. imbalances with the rest of East Asia. Experienced together, these tensions have, I fear, already begun to erode mutual agreement between America and Japan, "the most important bilateral relationship in the world bar none" (in the words of Mike Mansfield, former U.S. ambassador to Japan). And in combination, these tensions have worked to fashion an increasing number of dangerous myths and misconceptions, many of which I have sought to dispel in the preceding pages.

At present, that "most important bilateral relationship" is, as we have seen, in the midst of its second major transformation since the Pacific War. During the first such transformation, over the span of three decades, Japan and America swapped their bilateral positions as net importers and exporters.[61] But now during the second transformation—in less time than the single decade of the 1980s—the old U.S.-Japan rivalry has been altered by an even more significant and far-reaching change, created by the potency of foreign investment and especially its demonstrated power to surpass foreign trade in value and importance. Certainly, similar changes have already occurred elsewhere in the world, when foreign production and intracompany shipments grew to displace simpler cross-border transactions among industrialized countries. And elsewhere, these changes proved less difficult to make, since fewer obstacles impeded them. Yet without claiming to be novel, this second postwar transformation must still be regarded as truly remarkable, for it has altered the U.S.-Japan rivalry beyond easy recognition. What previously appeared as a bilateral relationship

---

[61]This exchange of bilateral positions is represented in the title of Clyde Prestowitz's book, *Trading Places*.

has now become complexly multilateral, as the United States and Japan join the many nations of East Asia in seeking their mutual prosperity. In this difficult process, a historical trading relationship has been doubly transformed: first, into a rivalry pitting nation against nation; and now into a modern economic contest waged currently on many fronts, with foreign investments by multinational corporations.

Index

Abegglen, James, 4n, 113n, 185n, 202, 208n
Africa, 152
American Chamber of Commerce in Japan (ACCJ), 65–66, 96n, 185n
American Motors, 132. *See also* Automobile industry
Argentina, 39n, 50, 61
"ASEAN Four." *See* Indonesia; Malaysia; Philippines; Thailand
AT&T, 125–127. *See also* Electronics industry; Telecommunications industry
Automobile industry, 17, 33; in East Asia, 148n, 171; in Japan, 37, 43–45, 72–81, 84, 94–95, 208; in the U.S., 28, 99–102, 116–117, 129–137, 197. *See also* individual companies

Banking. *See* Finance industry
Bank of Japan, 49n, 111, 118. *See also* Finance industry
Banyu, 85–86. *See also* Merck
"Big Two." *See* China; India
Boeing, 28. *See also* Multinationals
Brazil, 39–40, 50n, 61, 78
Brunei, 168

C. Itoh, 12, 76, 170. *See also* Multinationals; Trading companies
Calder, Kent E., 7n, 186n, 204
Canada: Americans in, 40, 81, 90, 96, 113n, 126n, 167, 211; multinationals from, 113n, 119, 126n, 137, 147n
Cargil, 10. *See also* Trading companies
Chemical industry: in East Asia, 153–155, 162–163, 171; in Japan, 56n, 63, 79, 83–84. *See also* individual companies
Chile, 39n, 50n, 61
China (mainland), 148; Americans in, 43, 152–156, 162; Japanese in, 167, 173. *See also* Taiwan
Chrysler Motors, 12; entry into Japan, 72–76; and Japanese in the U.S., 135–136;

offshore sourcing by, 80–82, 94–95, 129. *See also* Automobile industry; Mitsubishi
Coca Cola Company, 54n, 160
Columbia, 39n, 50n
Committee on Foreign Investment, 214. *See also* United States
Computer industry, 53–55, 60, 125–127. *See also* Electronics industry; individual companies

Dai-Ichi Bank, 76. *See also* Finance industry; Multinationals
Department of Commerce, 9, 62, 65, 107, 139. *See also* United States
Department of State, 55–56. *See also* United States
Distribution: in East Asia, 153–155, 162, 173, 175, 179; in Japan, 52, 79, 81, 84–86, 94; in the U.S., 115–116, 120, 122, 139, 141. *See also* Multinationals; individual companies; individual industries
DuPont, 56n. *See also* Chemical industry

East Asia. *See* individual countries
Electronics industry, 17, 33; in East Asia, 153–155, 158, 162–173, 177–181, 208; in Japan, 37, 69–70, 77–80, 84, 88; in the U.S., 28, 99–102, 113, 117, 121–125, 134, 145. *See also* Machinery industry; Semiconductor industry; Telecommunications industry; individual companies
Europe: Americans in, 15–20, 43, 69, 98, 102, 140–146, 214–215; Japanese in, 16–20; multinationals from, 59, 65, 102, 112–116, 119–121, 137. *See also* individual countries
Export-Import Bank of Japan, 118. *See also* Japan; Finance industry
Exxon, 59, 156. *See also* Multinationals; Petroleum industry

Fairchild, 60, 70n, 126, 165. *See also* Electronics industry; Semiconductor industry

219